Re-enchanting the World

CONTEMPORARY AMERICAN INDIAN STUDIES

J. Anthony Paredes, Series Editor

Re-enchanting the World

Maya Protestantism in the Guatemalan Highlands

C. Mathews Samson

THE UNIVERSITY OF ALABAMA PRESS
Tuscaloosa

Copyright © 2007
The University of Alabama Press
Tuscaloosa, Alabama 35487-0380
All rights reserved
Manufactured in the United States of America

Typeface: Bembo

∞

The paper on which this book is printed meets the minimum requirements of
American National Standard for Information Sciences-Permanence of Paper for
Printed Library Materials, ANSI Z39.48-1984.

Library of Congress Cataloging-in-Publication Data

Samson, C. Mathews., 1960–
   Re-enchanting the world : Maya protestantism in the Guatemalan highlands /
C. Mathews Samson.
         p.   cm. — (Contemporary American Indian studies)
   Includes bibliographical references and index.
   ISBN-13: 978-0-8173-1566-5 (cloth : alk. paper)
   ISBN-10: 0-8173-1566-7
   ISBN-13: 978-0-8173-5427-5 (pbk. : alk. paper)
   ISBN-10: 0-8173-5427-1
   1. Mam Indians—Religion. 2. Mam Indians—Social conditions. 3. Cakchikel
Indians—Religion. 4. Cakchikel Indians—Social conditions. 5. Indian Presbyterians—
Guatemala. 6. Presbyterian Church—Guatemala. 7. Guatemala—Religious life and
customs. 8. Guatemala—Social life and customs. I. Title.
   F1465.2.M3S35 2007
   299'.7842—dc22

                                                            2006037513

For Nancy—
Compañera and friend
who daily reminds me that the world can be a better place

Contents

Illustrations

Preface

I was privileged to be in Guatemala City and the *plaza central* during those days of celebration leading to the signing of the final peace accord at the end of 1996. Although I never fully experienced living through *la violencia* firsthand, I did experience some of the tension there for brief periods in 1985 and on visits after the social and political openings of the early 1990s. When our family moved to Guatemala for the major part of my field work during 1997 and 1998, one could often feel a sense of hopefulness, an expectation for peace and dialogue in the wake of so much violence and pain. The difficulties on the way ahead were obvious, and I was working in the midst of a Protestant denomination that was itself rife with conflict, ostensibly theological but with many of the overtones of the ethnic conflict that underlies so much of Guatemala's history and the present situation. Many of the Maya were more circumspect about the possibilities for *la paz* than I was. Past history had made them wary, and on more than one occasion I was reminded simply, directly, and in a matter-of-fact tone that "things can change."

More than a decade has passed since the signing of the final peace accord, and the circumspection of those who had lived through "the situation" seems more than warranted. Concern for personal and familial security in the midst of what has been called a "culture of violence" remains a daily issue for much of the country's population, irrespective of class or ethnicity. No doubt that culture of violence transcends Guatemala in this post-9/11 world, where too many have to struggle too hard to make ends meet, and where violence is too often employed as a means of resolving conflict. We do reap what we sow. In the modest way of most academic contributions, I hope that my work will contribute to the furtherance of peace and reconciliation in Guatemala—and beyond.

Acknowledgments

Primary funding for my research was provided by the Research Enablement Program, a grant program for scholarship supported by The Pew Charitable Trusts, Philadelphia, Pennsylvania, and administered by the Overseas Ministries Study Center, New Haven, Connecticut. A research grant from the University at Albany Benevolent Association allowed me to spend January 1997 in language study in Antigua, Guatemala.

My first word of thanks is to those Mam and Kaqchikel Maya who gave of their time and insights in Guatemala. Many simply were part of welcoming congregations when I did observations in their community. My life is richer because of their presence in it, and I often wonder what I can give back. My hope is that faithfully telling parts of their stories is a beginning, despite the radically different places in which we live and work.

A number of people in my youth and childhood helped shape the kind of vision of the world that I have today as my brother, sister, and I lived through desegregation in the rural South. Their names here remind me again about the importance of being true to oneself and not forgetting where one has come from. Ted Roeling, then minister of Clinton Presbyterian Church, Clinton, Louisiana, set the standards for a view of ministry that transcended *los cuatro paredes* of the church. George Charlet taught me about commitment to the community and helped arrange my first trip to Guatemala through the Louisiana Jaycees (especially the Angola State Penitentiary chapter) in 1974. Among my teachers, Lindley Orr took a number of us to Mexico for the first time, and he and Diane Williams set examples worth reflecting upon when I want to remind myself what teaching is all about. C. J. and Barbara Langton were a source of support and insight when C. J. served the First Baptist Church in Clinton. They taught me much about the meaning of hospitality.

During my first pass through Louisiana State University, rural sociologist Quentin Jenkins befriended me, provided me with insight into community studies in Latin America and in the United States, and strongly influenced me in the qualitative direction indicative of the kind of anthropology I do. Before I discovered anthropology, the community of Austin Presbyterian Seminary supported my initial efforts to learn Spanish and my first extensive experience living in Mesoamerica during an internship with Heifer Project International in Puebla, Mexico, during 1985 and 1986. Dan Garza and Bob Shelton kept me oriented in different directions during those years.

I discovered anthropology during three and a half years spent back in Baton Rouge following my seminary graduation. The congregation of University Presbyterian Church was incredibly tolerant as I learned about ministry and discovered anthropology at the same time. I did my best to fill the heads of the youth with visions of other cultures, and I have now lived long enough that the "kids" are now giving me back more than I ever gave them. Hal Horan offered me the opportunity and the gift of trust.

The two years I spent doing course work for my master's degree in the Geography and Anthropology Department at LSU were the most stimulating intellectual years of my life. Maybe it was the newness of it all, but for two years I learned something new every day. Miles Richardson introduced me to anthropology, and his passion for anthropology and his manner of embracing the human condition in all of its lonesomeness sustain me. I found myself the other day telling a class that here is an anthropologist who talks about love! Then I wondered if I was only talking to myself. Professor Jill Brody was part of anthropology as I came to know it, and she continues to be a colleague, friend, and emotional support through difficult times. Sharing part of her trip to Antigua and the Fourth International Congress of Mayanistas was a nice parting shot from the field. Kathleen, Emily, Rocky, Laura, and Donna all added to the experience. Michelle Moran-Taylor came along after I left, and she keeps me connected during our annual conversations at professional meetings.

Although I have tried to preserve the anonymity of most of the Guatemalans who provided the substance contained in these pages, I do thank Ruperto Romero Meza of La Victoria (and the Full Gospel Church of God), who worked with me in my attempts at learning a little of the Mam language and also provided considerable insight into Mam culture in the Ostuncalco area. His father grows the most beautiful radishes in the world, and I was saddened to hear of his mother's death in early 2002. Rosendo Vásquez, from Cuilco and the Instituto Francisco Marroquín, gave me my first introduction to the language. I have a long way to go. In Quetzaltenango, Moisés Colop and the congregation of the Emanuel Presbyterian Church of Maya Quiché Presbytery welcomed my family into their congregation during our time in Guatemala. From the Hermandad of Maya Presbyteries, Antonio Otzoy and Andrés López have given me both time and friendship. Antonio continues to stimulate many of us by trying to make sense of Presbyterianism and Maya spirituality. I thank Vitalino Similox for various interviews and for welcoming me to the Conference of Evangelical Churches of Guatemala on several occasions. The Evangelical Center for Pastoral Studies in Central America provided space for writing from time to time and a model for dialogue across religious boundaries. The documentation center has been helpful to any number of researchers working on evangelicalism and religion in Guatemala. The National Evangelical Presbyterian Church welcomed me to synod meetings on two occasions, and I am grateful for the hospitality shared during those intense meetings. The Center for Regional Investigations of Mesoamerica (Centro de Investigaciones Regionales de Mesoamérica, CIRMA) gave me a research affiliation while I was in the field, and the resources at CIRMA are indispensable for anthropologists and others working in Guatemala.

Hospitality also came from a number of missionaries during the months in the field. In Xela, Robert and Linda Moore of the Presbyterian Church (U.S.A.) provided good food, insightful conversation, and friendship, as did Joan and Paul Wright of the United Church of Canada.

Dennis and Maribel Smith (and Lucas and Benjamín) have welcomed me into the Hotel Smith-Pérez since 1994. I have enjoyed watching the boys grow and sharing Dennis and Mari's commitment to the Guatemalan context born out of their diverse backgrounds. Dennis is an ever-insightful friend and scholar; his perspective on religion in Guatemala is always provocative. Moreover, it is the result of long experience in the church ecumenical and with communications issues in Latin America. He has lived through the good and the bad in Guatemala, and we are all better for his experiences.

Ken and, later, Kennis Kim have also given me food, shelter, and companionship over several years. They loaned me a vehicle for the better part of six weeks when ours was stolen during the time of my field work. I will miss them as they move to Toronto. Trips to Guatemala won't be as fun without seeing Noë and the triplets, Gabriel, Sophie, and Clara.

Graduate school in Albany was more of a learning experience than any of us expected—beginning with that first winter when the snow kept falling and we thought the warmth would never return. During those years I was supported emotionally and intellectually by Cathy Stanford, Bradley Tatar, Jinsook Choi, Steve Selka, Erika Muse, Betsy Campisi, Nancy Forand, Alberto Esquit (as well as Agustina Teleguario and their daughter, Ixkotz'ij), and Lisa Montiel (along with Miranda and Natasha). Each contributed in different ways to help me stay the course, and I am pleased that Steve and Kristen are finally tying the knot. Teresa Carranza helped me on several occasions with my Spanish, and she was always gracious when I invaded her home for meetings.

Two congregations that I have had the privilege of serving in different capacities have supported my academic endeavors. The people of University

Presbyterian Church in Tuscaloosa, Alabama (some of whom are now scattered in different places), helped give me the confidence to enter a doctoral program, and the congregation of First Presbyterian Church in Albany (to which I was never officially called) provided needed work for several years and heartfelt interest. Shirley and Rudy Nelson and Joanne and Dick Gascoyne have been special companions in too many ways to name. During her tenure as office administrator, Beverly Osborne helped me periodically with various tasks related to what eventually became this book. Tim O'Toole helped with some of the pictures, and James Wessman has been a friend in the breach between university and church.

Beyond Albany, I am grateful to David and Leigh Leslie for their support across both miles and years. From the academic world, John Watanabe, Ginny Garrard-Burnett, and Ed Cleary have been particularly kind and generous colleagues as I developed my anthropological voice in regard to the issues addressed in this work. I now add Tim Steigenga, Chris Chiappari, and Karla Koll to this growing list of dialogue partners.

I again thank Robert Carmack for his patience and scholarly expectations. His concern for applying comparative and ethnohistorical methods to research in Mesoamerica is rarely far from my mind, even when I go in other directions. He has consistently provided opportunities for professional involvement along the way, and his effort to support opportunities for advanced education and other kinds of intellectual interchange for Guatemalans engaged in studying their own context is a model for all of us.

Louise Burkhart has been a critic and friend, and I am grateful for her confidence in my ability to produce something of value. The work is much better thanks to her generous and detailed editing and insightful questions. There are still things missing, and Louise's standards of scholarship give me something to aspire to.

Among other academic involvements, the Department of Anthropology of the University of Oklahoma was a stimulating and congenial place to work as a visiting lecturer for two years, and I am grateful to Pat Gilman for setting the tone in the department, and to Sean O'Neill for asking me often if I had begun work on my book. Students at both the undergraduate and graduate levels made my time enjoyable.

I am also grateful to the University of Alabama Press for its interest in this project and the purposefulness with which the staff has pushed it along. Two reviewers commented on the manuscript, and their insights helped make it stronger. As always, I am responsible for the final product.

Last-minute help with the bibliography and other tasks came from Melissa Mills and Amber Siegler, undergraduates at the University of Oklahoma. Anthropology doctoral candidate Abby Wightman, already a scholar in her own right, read through the entire manuscript and made a number of corrections and helpful suggestions. I probably would not have met the deadline without her help.

In a new place, the Department of Anthropology at Davidson College has been a congenial and stimulating environment over the past year. I appreciate Bill Ringle's expertise with mapping programs that made the map showing Guatemala's indigenous language communities more legible. Ariel Bugosh helped prepare the index with funds provided by the office of the Vice President for Academic Affairs.

Finally, I thank my family. From the beginning, my parents, Sandra and Clay Samson, encouraged us to stand up for what was right and to be independent. By keeping us in public schools, they gave me the opportunity to think about cultural difference and social justice even before I knew what those were. Daddy and my sister remain a part of who I am, and they are missed, especially as my own daughters are setting out on their own paths. Laurie, this is the book I finally wrote—hopefully only the first. Jay Pratt, Mother's brother, has always been there in that avuncular way anthropologists have noted in so many places. Rick Samson, brother and geographer, shared the early years of raising 4-H pigs, Boy Scouts, and taking the field for the Eagles. Later he taught me much about field work and how, at least occasionally, to look at things in the dispassionate way necessary for good scholarship. His partner, Amy Vidrine Samson, and my nephew and niece, Clayton and Jacqueline, remind me that life is supposed to be fun during our all-too-brief time together in the summers. Eleanor Canon not only adopted Louisiana as her home state but also has become the adopted aunt and sister to both families of Samsons. As usual, she read the beginning of this work even though I could never send her anything else.

Jessica and Hannah have endured much as I have tried to balance ministry and graduate school during the entirety of their lives. I hope that somehow they can see why I do this—and that they know that I would not be who I am without them. They are our future—along with all the other children named in these pages. Nancy, my wife, does know why I do it. Whether it was what she expected is another issue.

Abbreviations

ALMG	Academia de Lenguas Mayas de Guatemala (Academy of Mayan Languages of Guatemala)
ANN	Alianza Nueva Nación (New Nation Alliance)
ASC	Asamblea de la Sociedad Civil (Civil Society Assembly)
CAM	Central American Mission
CECMA	Centro de Estudios de la Cultura Maya (Center for the Study of Maya Culture)
CEDEPCA	Centro Evangélico de Estudios Pastorales de América Central (Evangelical Center for Pastoral Studies in Central America)
CEDIM	Centro de Documentación e Investigación Maya (Maya Documentation and Research Center)
CEG	Conferencia Episcopal de Guatemala (Guatemalan Episcopal Conference)
CEH	Comisión para el Esclarecimiento Histórico (Historical Clarification Commission)
CIEDEG	Conferencia de Iglesias Evangélicas de Guatemala (Guatemalan Conference of Evangelical Churches)
CNR	Comisión Nacional de Reconciliación (National Reconciliation Commission)
COMG	Consejo de Organizaciones Mayas de Guatemala (Council of Maya Organizations of Guatemala)
CONAVIGUA	Coordinadora Nacional de Viudas de Guatemala (National Coordinating Group of Guatemalan Widows)
CONCAD	Consejo Cristiano de Agencias de Desarrollo (Christian Council of Development Agencies)
COPMAGUA	Coordinadora de Organizaciones del Pueblo Maya de Guatemala (League of Organizations of the Maya People of Guatemala)

CSC	Coordinador de Sectores Civiles (Civil Sector Coordinating Group)
CUC	Comité de Unidad Campesina (Committee of Campesino Unity)
EGP	Ejército Guerrillero de los Pobres (Guerrilla Army of the Poor)
FDNG	Frente Democrático Nueva Guatemala (New Guatemala Democratic Front)
FEPAZ	Foro Ecuménico por la Paz y la Reconciliación (Ecumenical Forum for Peace and Reconciliation)
FRG	Frente Republicano Guatemalteco (Guatemalan Republican Front)
GAM	Grupo de Apoyo Mutuo (Mutual Support Group)
HPM	Hermandad de Presbiterios Mayas (Brotherhood of Maya Presbyteries)
IENPG	Iglesia Evangélica Nacional Presbiteriana de Guatemala (National Evangelical Presbyterian Church of Guatemala)
MINUGUA	Misión de las Naciones Unidas de Verificación de los Derechos Humanos en Guatemala (United Nations Mission for the Verification of Human Rights in Guatemala)
ORPA	Organización del Pueblo en Armas (Organization of the People in Arms)
PAC	*patrullas de autodefensa civil* (civilian self-defense patrol)
SEPAL	Servicio Evangelizadora para America Latina (Evangelizing Service for Latin America)
URNG	Unidad Revolucionaria Nacional Guatemalteca (Guatemalan National Revolutionary Unity)

Re-enchanting the World

Prologue

Encountering Religious Change in Guatemala

What does it mean to be both Maya and Protestant in Guatemala? This is the question I took with me when I began to study the interplay between evangelical identity and Maya culture in 1995 after leaving a Presbyterian congregation I had served as minister for four and a half years.

Although I had been interested in Latin American religion, particularly liberation theology, since my days as a sometimes student activist on Central American issues during the 1980s, in retrospect, the framing for the question had begun to take shape a couple of years earlier. Following an academic meeting in Guatemala's colonial capital, Antigua, I found myself in the Plaza de la Constitución (Constitutional Plaza) in Guatemala City on the Sunday before Ash Wednesday. The expected afternoon crowds were there, even in those difficult days when the civil war that had wracked the country for some twenty-three years was winding down. Ice cream trucks lined the street dissecting the plaza; women in indigenous dress (*traje*) offered beautifully woven *tejidos* (textiles) to those interested in traditional Guatemalan handicrafts; children covered each other with flour by cracking multicolored hollow eggshells over the heads of unsuspecting victims. Occasionally, a rapidly shifting crowd on one side of the plaza indicated the possibility that some verbal disagreement had given way to fisticuffs. Here and there a small, rather plainly dressed group of people, assisted by a portable speaker system, intoned religious *coritos* (choruses) for the benefit of any who would listen. Other young men passed out religious tracts or verbally reminded passersby of the consequences of unbelief.

What seemed most out of place in the tapestry of human activity was a bandstand erected perhaps fifty yards directly in front of the presidential palace; the banner hung above the bandstand made the focus of this gathering unmistakable, a single red word on the white background—"JESUS." While other activity continued in various segments of the plaza, perhaps a couple thousand people stood listening to the proclamations from the bandstand. Statements were made first by women in knee-length dresses, now from men in suits and ties (some with sunglasses to shade their eyes from the afternoon sun). Later came offerings of music from a choir or musicians playing the instruments carefully placed to one side of the bandstand. In the audience, the faithful lifted their arms heavenward or raised a Bible firmly in their hand, swept

Figure 1. Constitutional Plaza, Guatemala City, February 1993

away in the emotion of a word, or song proclaiming "Jesus es el señor de Guatemala" (Jesus is Lord of Guatemala). Behind the bandstand, a Pepsi banner hanging between the front pillars of the palace announced an art exhibit. Somewhat bemused, I wondered, is it Pepsi, the transnational corporation, or Jesus, who is Lord?[1]

Less than one hundred yards away from the dissonant activities of the plaza, I entered the relatively dark and quiet Metropolitan Cathedral. To the left of the high altar a few candles were burning in front of an image in a smaller side altar positioned parallel to the main sanctuary. A line of people waited patiently for the opportunity to converse with the Black Christ perpetually being crucified on a silverish, worked, vine-covered cross. His feet and knees were shiny from the touches and kisses of the faithful who enter the altar area, cross themselves, move directly to the feet of the Lord, speak words of supplication or thanks, kiss the feet, and touch the knees before exiting by way of the little box that tells part of the story: "Limosna para el santo cristo de Esquipulas" (Alms for the Holy Christ of Esquipulas). As well as Jesus, El Señor, being adored in the park, the Black Christ retained his admirers in the heart of the city.

The contrast between the two scenes on that Sunday afternoon represented a burgeoning religious pluralism in Mesoamerica, and throughout Latin America, that was becoming more evident as Protestantism seemed to burst on the scene in a region that had been overwhelmingly Roman Catholic for

Figure 2. Hands raised in praise, evangelical rally

nearly five centuries. Of course, Catholicism itself is pluralistic, and the veneration of the Lord of Esquipulas is only symbolic of the permutations of Catholicism's history in Guatemala, beginning with the conflict between invading forces led by the conquistador Pedro de Alvarado, a lieutenant of Hernán Cortés, and the Maya defenders led by the K'iche' Maya culture hero, Tekum, in 1524.[2] Catholic practices common to village life and Mestizo or Ladino populations, typically marked by the veneration of saints and versions of sixteenth-century folk Catholicism imported from Spain, simultaneously interplay and conflict with the cosmovision and practice embodied in the indigenous Catholicism of the Amerindian peoples throughout the Americas.[3]

In turn, these permutations of Catholicism contrast with the more recent evangelical practices growing out of Protestant missionary activities dating primarily to the middle and late nineteenth century and often reflecting a North American or European culture ethos that is closely tied to the modernizing agenda of liberalism in post-independence Latin America. Although studies of evangelical religion in Latin America and in Mesoamerica had burgeoned by the late 1980s and early 1990s,[4] I was startled to see the central place of the main plaza in a capital city "taken over" by styles of dress and worship that would have appeared more at home in some nondenominational church building in a major city in the United States. Of course, Guatemala has its own history, and by 1993 a second evangelical in ten years was occupying the president's office, and some were predicting that the evangelical population might be 50 percent by the year 2000. Moreover, as in the cathedral, many of the faithful gathered in the plaza reflected a more humble social origin than those onstage. And there in the heart of the city, framed by the architectural symbols of the power of the government and the institutional church, a number of the devotees in both contexts were identifiable by their dress alone as members of the Maya indigenous population, the vast majority of whom continue to reside in rural communities spread out over the Guatemalan landscape, especially the western highlands.

I
Re-enchanting the World
Identity and Religious Change

God was here before Columbus came.
                    —Vitalino Similox, Executive Secretary, CIEDEG

History is constituted in the space that encompasses both social participation and self-authoring. . . . [Subjectivities and identities] are durable not
because individual persons have essential or primal identities but because
the multiple contexts in which dialogical, intimate identities make sense
and give meaning are re-created in contentious local practice (which is in
part shaped and reshaped by enduring struggles).
                    —Dorothy Holland and Jean Lave, *History in Person*

This work adds a comparative ethnographic portrait of denominational Protestantism in Guatemala to the study of the complex Mesoamerican religious
mosaic. It demonstrates how a religion, initially imposed on the peoples of
Mesoamerica by missionaries benefiting from the largesse of the liberal governments of the late nineteenth century, has been integrated into the cultural
traditions of the region, albeit in rather diffuse and often divisive forms. In addressing what it means to be both Maya and Protestant, this study emphasizes
the interplay between ethnic and religious identity in the religious practices
of historical Protestants who are also Maya, specifically, Mam and Kaqchikel
Maya Presbyterians related to the Iglesia Evangélica Nacional Presbiteriana
de Guatemala (IENPG, National Evangelical Presbyterian Church of Guatemala). Representing two of the four largest Maya communities in Guatemala,
the Mam and Kaqchikel presbyteries are organized as ethnic groupings of
churches in geographic areas with shared Maya cultural traditions. Despite their
shared Maya identity and the fact that the groups belong to the same denomination, they manifest differing responses to the expression of religious and ethnic identity in a time of political violence and repression (1960–present).[1] On
the surface, the Mam represent a more traditional evangelical Christian presence as opposed to the activist and politicized practice of the Kaqchikel. In

neither case, however, do Maya evangelicals reject their cultural identity when participating in an evangelical religious community.

Because the research deals with historical Protestants who stand in the direct lineage of the Protestant Reformation, the story is necessarily a partial one, reflecting the manner in which Mam and Kaqchikel Protestants have reconstituted meaning in their respective contexts since 1960. That year marks both the beginning of Guatemala's civil war and a time when evangelicals constituted a mere three percent of Guatemala's population. At the beginning of the new millennium, evangelicals represented some 25.4 percent of the population after a period of spectacular growth that began to level off around 1993 (Grossman 2002). The growth began to take off in the 1960s, particularly among Pentecostal groups, gained speed when a number of nongovernmental organizations and religious groups were invited into the country following the earthquake of 4 February 1976 (which killed some twenty-five thousand people), and continued apace during the worst part of the violence during the war between 1978 and 1983.

Given that brief trajectory, there is a strong temptation to explain evangelical growth as a response to victimization or misfortune in some "crisis-solace" or deprivation framework. Some of that framing is certainly viable in the context of the social dislocation and cultural change that Guatemala experienced in the last half of the twentieth century. Nevertheless, my concern is with the practices and meaning of evangelical religion rather than the causes of its growth. The interpretation here seeks to situate Maya Protestantism within a nexus including personal understandings of conversion, the ethnography of religion and evangelical practice in Guatemala, the demands of the Maya Movement for the recognition of cultural rights, the nature of the contemporary nation-state in a post-conflict society, and the transnational dimension important to analyses of religion in the light of contemporary concerns with understanding the impact of globalization. While this approach necessarily requires giving attention to evangelical organizations and leaders associated with evangelical communities under consideration, the value of the ethnographic perspective lies in the vantage point it provides for linking local-level analysis with larger scales of analysis.

My work makes two contributions to the discussion of the relationship between religion and culture in Guatemala from an anthropological perspective. First, as a comparative study it provides the outlines of a localized perspective on the heterogeneity of Maya culture and religious practice, even within the same denomination that is spread out over the landscape in a number of particular places. At the same time, it contributes to a more nuanced reading of evangelical practices among the Maya of Guatemala. Ethnographic description and interpretation push us to ask over and over again and in different contexts how the Maya re-create aspects of their culture and worldview in the context of a religion that can no longer be seen simply as a colonialist imposition from the outside. As Protestantism becomes grounded within Maya communities, it unmasks the processual nature of religious experience and frequently becomes a source for new models of community and new expressions of cultural identity. As Lawrence Taylor notes in his ethnography of Irish Catholics, "Rather than begging the question of a universal definition of religion, an ethnographic inquiry is well positioned to explore the particular and specific ways in which 'religion' comes to acquire any number of possible shapes—differing in form as well as in content" (1995, xi).

Beyond these contributions, this work can also be considered as a current historiography of aspects of evangelical practice among the Maya in a context where local practice and imposed religions have been in a dynamic relationship for nearly five centuries. Aspects of this dynamism take shape in a volatile political and social landscape where both religion and ethnicity have provided impetus for indigenous mobilization over the past two decades. Although the literature on social movements sometimes downplays the role of religion, a work edited by Edward Cleary and Timothy Steigenga provides case studies illustrating their view that "indigenous mobilization cannot be understood without a careful consideration of religious factors. While specific political openings and social and economic processes facilitated the indigenous resurgence, religious institutions, beliefs, and practices provided many of the resources, motivations, identities, and networks that nurtured the movement. In turn, indigenous religious practitioners have reshaped the religious field in Latin America" (2004, 2).[2]

In the cases documented here, the interface between religion and ethnicity in the lives of Maya evangelicals has been a space for mobilization around issues such as development, human rights, and cultural activism. The Kaqchikel Presbytery, largely because of its human rights activities and its contacts with the international religious community, is better known and more visible. Among the Mam, issues of local involvement in politics and social concerns have remained largely within a more circumscribed space. Nevertheless, to say that religion has not been influential would understate the case. Mam leadership has promoted a *teológica integral* (integral theology) that emphasizes holistic approaches to development concerns such as agriculture and health care within the larger community. Moreover, following the 1999 national election, I interviewed Mam *alcaldes* (mayors) in three *municipios* (townships) who either had been or continued to be active in the congregations of the Mam Presbytery. This demonstrates the potential for evangelicalism to be used as a source for mobilization in local as well as more expansive fields of interaction. The cases reveal the sphere of evangelical religion as another arena from which Maya voices emerge to take their place alongside those voices that have historically been dominant in terms of social and political power in Guatemala.

The Guatemalan Case

The salience of the Guatemalan case for understanding religious and social change in Mesoamerica stems from its unique position as the country in the region with the largest percentage of evangelicals, and possibly the largest percentage of indigenous population from a single language family, the Maya. The Maya speak some twenty-two related languages (fig. 4) and share aspects of a cultural tradition stretching back some three thousand to thirty-five hundred years.[3] While the actual number of Maya in the country is debated, the 2002 census of the Instituto Nacional de Estadística (INE, National Institute of Statistics) indicated that the Maya make up 39.3 percent of the population of 11,237,196. Maya scholars, however, claim that the census undercounts the Maya majority, providing estimates of the Maya percentage of the population that reach as high as 60 percent (Tzian 1994). Even with the lower numbers, the absolute Maya population is over 4.6 million.

Two factors should be noted here. First, even if one accepts the census figures at face value, the absolute number of Maya in those figures has more than doubled since 1964, and the trend is upward. This is a graphic continuation of the trend in Maya population increase since the end of the drastic decline that began with Spanish invasion and left the Maya population at about 275,000 by the end of the eighteenth century (cited in R. Adams and Bastos 2003, 63). Second, even using the lower census figures, if one adopts the reasoning of George Lovell and Christopher Lutz in their 1996 article, "'A Dark Obverse': Maya Survival in Guatemala," the number of Guatemalan Maya surely rises to more than five million and possibly as many as six million when those who have migrated to other countries because of the violence or for economic reasons are taken into account. This nonresident population also increases the total population of the country into the range of thirteen million. While some might argue that immigrants soon lose their language ability (and therefore can no longer be considered Maya), the back-and-forth movement of the migrant population is significant in maintaining community ties, and the implications of transnational migration are only now being studied in their full complexity. For comparison purposes, the Maya population in the whole of Mesoamerica numbers some seven to eight million. Although speaking a Mayan language is not the only way that Maya self-identify, some thirty languages are spoken throughout the larger Maya culture region, which occupies an area in southern Mesoamerica extending beyond Guatemala into south-

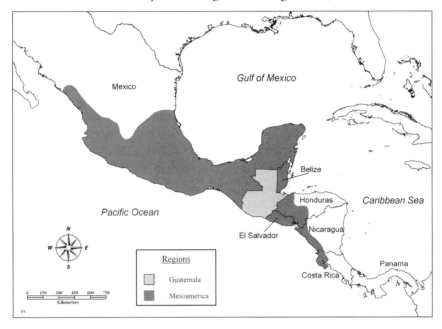

Figure 3. Guatemala in Mesoamerica (map by Dr. James Samson)

eastern Mexico, including the Yucatán peninsula and the states of Tabasco and Chiapas, as well as into Belize and western Honduras.

I dwell on these issues here because one aspect of being both Maya and evangelical in Guatemala today is related to the position of the Maya in the Guatemalan nation. Population statistics are highly important in the continuing debate surrounding the character of the nation in a place where a Ladino minority has wielded social and political power throughout much of the time period since replacing the Spanish colonial elite following independence in 1821. As will be seen, both the civil war (1960–96) and the larger history of the Guatemalan state's assimilationist policies toward the Maya population have at times raised the specter of ethnocide of the Maya people. The discourse growing out of Guatemala's Maya Movement (also called the pan-Maya Movement in order to take into account diversity among the Maya peoples both within and beyond Guatemala), as well as other groups organizing for the creation of a new civil society built on a recognition that Guatemala is a pluricultural state, will be examined more closely in later chapters. At this juncture it is enough to note the difficulties inherent in such an agenda when, during the 2003 national elections, only one of the twenty-two candidates vying for president or vice president among the eleven parties running in the election was identified

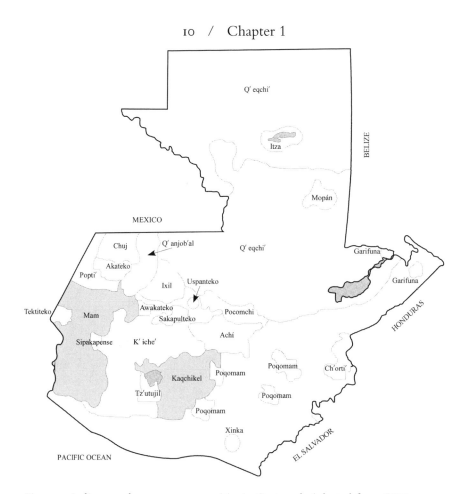

Figure 4. Indigenous-language communities in Guatemala (adapted from CEH 1999, from BEST 520-0374, USAID-Guatemala)

as Maya—Pablo Ceto, the vice presidential candidate of the political party of the former guerrilla movement, the Unidad Revolucionaria Nacional Guatemalteca (URNG, Guatemalan National Revolutionary Unity).[4]

Maya Protestantism and Pluralism in Mesoamerica

On a conceptual level, Maya Protestantism represents an aspect of a globalized "re-enchantment of the world" in the context of a resurgence of religious practices that challenge what has often been referred to as a "disenchantment of the world." Usually associated with Max Weber (1964), the latter phrase connotes the sense of a loss of mystery as human life becomes more rationalized through the application of a scientific worldview and technological innovation. As Brian Morris puts it, this "implied a process whereby explicit, intellectually calculable rules and procedures are systematized and specified, and increasingly substituted for sentiment and tradition" (1987, 68). In the end, rationalization would result not only in more systematized versions of religion but also in "the growth of ethical rationalism, and the progressive decline of ritual and 'magical' elements in religion" (69). Variations of theories of modernization and secularization, which as late as the 1960s and 1970s predicted the demise of religion as a consequence of the Enlightenment worldview of rationalized knowledge and "progress" in human society (Berger 1967; Gauchet 1997), had by the end of the twentieth century begun to be called into question along with the failure of modernity (Berger 1998, 1999; cf. Benavides 1998; Barbero 2001).[5]

Likewise, in the arena of ethnic identity, instead of inertia toward a homogenized global or national culture, the latter decades of the past century saw an increase in the number and intensity of indigenous peoples organizing for recognition as distinct nations with concomitant rights to manage their own affairs in some autonomous fashion (Wilmsen and McAllister 1996; Maybury-Lewis 2002). In a sense, the twin old stories of the end of religion and the assimilation of indigenous peoples who lose their language and culture and become "modern" (or worse, "civilized") were superseded by new stories of the religious marketplace and drives for cultural autonomy and a respect for pluralism among nations of peoples. Despite the reductionist tone, the economistic imagery of the religious marketplace reminds us that magic, science, *and* religion coexist in the postmodern world. Likewise, even as religion has seemingly made a reappearance on the world stage, movements for ethnic renewal and cultural rights are making their own challenges to the nation-state with its pretensions to hegemonic power within its borders. Within these movements, religion, understood as the practices and ways of knowing linked to the particular cosmologies or worldviews of different indigenous groups, has played a part in calling into question the assimilationist narratives of the nation-state.

Of course, it can be argued that Latin America, with Roman Catholic churches lining the plazas of megacities and small villages from the Río Bravo to Tierra del Fuego, as well as the enduring presence of so-called ancient indigenous cultures, would be one of the last places on earth to be disenchanted. Yet the vagaries of the colonial economy, modernization efforts by state polities throughout the post-independence period, and integration of the region, typically on unequal footing, into the global capitalist world-system have challenged the idea of any "essence" of Latin American culture founded either in colonial religiosity or any type of persistent core indigenous identity. Both religious pluralism and the push for space for indigenous national projects grow out of and respond to this history. In Mesoamerica, some of the noteworthy signs of this push at the end of the twentieth century were the movement in response to the quincentenary of Columbus's arrival in the Americas, especially the Segunda Encuentro Continental de la Campaña de los Quiñientos Años de Resistencia (Second Continental Encounter of the Campaign of the Five Hundred Years of Resistance) held in Quetzaltenango; the awarding of the Nobel Peace Prize to Rigoberta Menchú in 1992; and the Zapatista uprising in Chiapas on 1 January 1994, the day the North American Free Trade Agreement (NAFTA) was to enter into force. All of these reflected the gathering strength of Maya voices within the region as well as the different footing upon which the struggle for indigenous rights would be articulated in the future.

In his work on social organizing in the decade leading to the end of the war in Guatemala, Roddy Brett argues that "The *Encuentro* was a key historical moment in the development of indigenous politics in Guatemala and in the transformation of the popular movement to [a movement] of ethnic content. It brought together *populares* and *mayanistas* in a context in which other indigenous and popular movements from all of Latin America were present, and it consolidated the relation between Guatemalan social movements and the transnational indigenous rights movement" (2006, 97). I am using the *encuentro* in a symbolic sense here, following Brett's argument that part of what transpired was "the adoption, by part of the indigenous movement in general, of a broadened concept of rights that took into account human rights and indigenous rights and came nearer to economic, social and cultural rights" (97). From the standpoint of the Maya Movement, the impact of the *encuentro* is less clear, as the movement's own logic is more focused on the cultural rights of the Maya and the right to self-determination.[6] Many movement leaders remain less engaged with the foci of the popular movement's agenda, or they felt excluded from it at the time of the event (Hale 1994; Warren 1998, chapters 1 and 2).

Re-enchantment, then, tracks with both religion and ethnicity in reflecting the way meaning is mobilized in common projects of the group. With that in mind, we can do far worse than Stanley Tambiah's affirmation that "the distinctive feature of religion as a generic concept lies not in the domain of belief and its 'rational accounting' of the workings of the universe, but in a special awareness of the transcendent, and the acts of symbolic communication that attempt to realize that awareness and live by its promptings" (1990, 6). Although interpretive and symbolic approaches to religion are often criticized for not taking seriously enough the relations of power and economy within which symbolic systems are embedded (Asad 1993; Morris 2006, 1, 104–5), others have seen symbols (and ideology) as motivating factors for all kinds of practice and collective mobilization in the face of tendencies toward the homogenization of culture and economy in the context of globalization. The "symbolic communication" in Tambiah's conceptualization of religion reaches out toward something larger than the self, not just God or the gods, but perhaps even to a cosmovision or worldview embodied in the practices of everyday life. Such transcendence compels people who share a particular kind of awareness to act in the world based on their personal commitments.[7] These understandings of the transcendent, whether based in a sense of the ineffable or embodied in those others who share a sense of identity and worldview, form a basis for collective action.[8]

This perspective connects with the processual approach to the ethnography of religion. Such an approach takes into account both personal experience and history while making room for the "history in person" stance elaborated by Dorothy Holland and Jean Lave in the second epigraph to this chapter. This is an interactive stance in which personal narrative and practice embrace history and social location. With that in mind, I work with a conceptualization of culture, arising partially out of critical theory, as "multiple discourses, occasionally coming together in large systematic configuration, but more often coexisting within dynamic fields of interaction and conflict" (Dirks, Eley, and Ortner 1994, 4).[9] The emphasis in such a definition is interactive, with "contentious local practice" engaging power as well as meaning, action as well as narrative, whether in the form of the story of a person's life or the discourse produced by people and movements to announce their presence and stake their claims to the future.[10] Attending to religious practice in Guatemala highlights religious pluralism at the local level even as that pluralism is worked out in communities participating in the transnational movement of people and resources (material and symbolic) central to recent studies of contemporary religious practice in Latin America and elsewhere (Rudolph and Piscatori 1997; Garrard-Burnett 1998b; Corten and Marshall-Fratani 2001).

As a further point of linkage between discourse and practice, even in transnational space, Manuel Vásquez and Marie Marquardt (2003) add the concept of "glocalization" to the analysis of religion in the Americas and the role religion can play in building bridges between "the overarching logics of translocal organization and the discourses and practices of specific congregations" (56). Interestingly, among Japanese corporations the term is defined as a practice (*dochakuka*) that allows them to "tailor their products to meet changing local markets." The image is one of the marketer responding directly to the local context, a process that necessarily entails some give-and-take on both sides when it is seen in the light of "the Fordist-Keynesian economies of scale." The argument is that within the framework of glocalization, "globalization does not necessarily entail homogenization, the erasure of authochtonous cultures, languages, and religions. . . . Rather, glocalization sets up power-laden tensions between heterogeneity and homogeneity and between tradition and modernity, which global institutions and dispersed consumers must negotiate" (57).

The image of negotiation between poles of tradition and modernity is a powerful one from the vantage point of community life in Mesoamerica. It relates as well to the notion of hybridity, which has been used to refine the notion of syncretism that has been used to discuss the fusing or mixing of Mesoamerican religious traditions, especially between Christianity and indigenous practices. For Vásquez and Marquardt, hybridity is a step beyond the coming together of two "pure" cultures or identities and the creation of something new. They find in the term "a useful conceptual device to understand multiple, fluid, and often contradictory religious identities and practices that have proliferated with globalization" (58). While the process of hybridization has the potential for "both domination and resistance in varying degrees" (62), the concept provides another standpoint where the intersection of religion and ethnic identity may come together in the changing religious landscape of Guatemala. The emphasis is on pluralism and hybrid cultural forms, not only among various peoples within the nation-state but also in the light of the multiple identities held by people at a given time in various aspects of their lives.

An ethnographic method rooted in social practice(s) underlies my approach to religion and identity among Maya evangelicals. My approach also builds on historical and ethnographic studies that have looked at the phenomena of religious change in Guatemala more generally as well as at the specific case of Protestantism.[11] At the same time, it builds on other layers of context within which Maya evangelical practices are situated.

A first consideration is the aftermath of the transformation of Guatemala's historical ethnic conflict into a thirty-six-year civil war. More than a decade after the 29 December 1996 signing of the final peace accord brought a definitive end to the conflict, the task of constructing a society that can hold together the tensions between ethnic identity and the continuing disparities in access to the political and economic institutions within Guatemala remains formidable. In the political realm, most representative was the failure, by a sizable majority of the votes cast, of the 16 May 1999 referendum on a series of constitutional reforms designed to codify aspects of the supplemental agreements negotiated in the years leading up to the definitive end of the war. These agreements dealt with a number of underlying structural contradictions within Guatemalan society, including the rights of the indigenous population, socio-economic issues and agrarian concerns, democracy and the strengthening of civil society, and the role of the military in a civil society. The failure of the referendum put a damper on the process of constructing what many hoped would be a new, post-conflict Guatemala. The defeat of the referendum (*consulta popular*) had many causes, including the form of the proposals that were put to the voters. Others have given attention to the high rates of absenteeism (some 80 percent), which led some to conclude that absenteeism itself had won the election. Despite varying interpretations, the failure of the referendum highlighted some of the difficulties of reconciliation and the construction of a viable democracy in a post-conflict society with some of the highest rates of inequality of wealth in the Americas.[12]

Violence is another prominent concern for the population in a situation where impunity for crimes committed both during and after the war has remained the rule rather than the exception. This was reflected in rising crime rates and lynchings that claimed the lives of at least 215 people between the signing of the final peace accord and 2001 (Fernández García 2004, 14). More recently, the specter of social cleansing arose amid an upsurge in gang and drug activity that was frequently linked to occult forces within the military and police. As well, more than a thousand women, mostly in urban areas, were killed, often in seemingly arbitrary murders, during the period from 2001 through the middle of 2004 (Amnesty International 2005). Everyday experiences of violence and insecurity, in both the personal and economic sense, along with a fragmented political system in which no party in the presidency has been returned to power since the return to formal democracy in 1985, indicate that the way into the future is not at all clear.

A second layer of context involves the history of Protestantism in a region where, since the time of the Spanish invasion, religious expression has revolved around poles of traditional Maya religion and Catholicism with a multifaceted relationship between the two. In Mesoamerica, Protestant missionary activities came with the modernization and acculturation projects of the liberal governments of the mid- to late 1800s. Modernization (and progress), often through literacy and the appropriation of new technological prowess in the fields of transportation and communications, was the guiding motif upon which positivist social thought turned. Protestantism was viewed as a movement that could bring enlightenment and be pitted against the massive wealth and political power of the Roman Catholic Church in a new context. The general attitude undergirding the liberal approach to the acculturation and assimilation of the indigenous peoples can be seen in a comment attributed to no less a representative of an indigenous presence on the national scene than the Mexican president Benito Juárez. Although he was raised by a Mestizo family, Juárez was a Zapotec Indian himself, and his comment embodies the persistent tension between Protestant (and liberal) modernization and native *costumbre* (custom or tradition): "I wish that Protestantism would become

Mexican by conquering the Indians; they need a religion which will compel them to read and not spend their savings on candles for the saints" (Baez Camargo and Grubb 1935, 89).

This opening to foreign religious influence has frequently led to charges by the activists (and sometimes the Roman Catholic Church) that there is a conspiracy afoot designed to increase North American political and economic influence in Latin America. Evangelicals would be the harbingers of this influence, destroying local cultures in their wake (Martin 1990, 98–105; Stoll 1990, 34–35). From the Roman Catholic side, the charges sometimes amount to little more than the creation of images of an "invasión de las sectas" (invasion of the sects). The discourse reflects concern over the loss of adherents, and pastoral approaches do take this into account on many levels. While the evidence is extremely mixed on such charges, there can be little doubt that the opening to Protestantism in the second half of the nineteenth century, as well as the attitudes of missionaries from historical Protestant denominations, reflected what Virginia Garrard-Burnett (1990) has referred to as "spiritual manifest destiny." The phrase at once evokes both the ethnocentric cultural baggage of the missionaries and the process of substituting political colonialism with economic colonialism emanating from the north that took place in the latter half of nineteenth-century Latin America. It is difficult to move from there to any manifest pattern of conspiracy or involvement in right-wing political activities designed to prevent social change on the part of the evangelicals.

Even in one of the more notorious cases during the early 1980s, Garrard-Burnett reports that in response to Pat Robertson's promise to send a billion dollars to the strong-armed counterinsurgency government of the born-again general Efraín Ríos Montt, "Donations of funds, equipment, and services from U.S. evangelical groups . . . totaled only around twenty million dollars" (1998a, 157). Particularly in the context of an impoverished nation in the full flush of war, such amounts are not insignificant. Yet a more complete accounting requires a consideration of the geopolitics at the time, including the rise of religious influence in North American politics and the ongoing transnational flow of religious goods and services of all kinds that has been highlighted in research on religion in global perspective. Moreover what happens to transplanted goods and services when consumed in a context different from where they originate is frequently not determined by the sender (Vásquez and Marquardt 2003, 197–222).

Recent attention given to the pluralism represented by various Protestantisms in Guatemala and to Protestantism's potential contribution to democratic tendencies in Latin America provides a link with the earlier history of the movement in Latin America (Twicken 1994; Míguez Bonino 1997; Garrard-Burnett 1998a; Gross 2003; Freston 2006). In Guatemala, evangelical pluralism is particularly marked today in that historic Protestantism, associated with churches growing out of the Reformation, has not been numerically dominant in the region for several decades. It is now well known that Pentecostalism has grown tremendously in number and influence since the 1960s (Shaull 1992; B. Gutiérrez 1995; Freston 1998; Cleary and Stewart-Gambino 1997). Although some have questioned whether Pentecostals are Protestants in the strict sense, some 65–80 percent of evangelicals in all Latin American countries are now believed to be Pentecostal. The emphasis on pluralism is a recognition that Latin American Protestantism is not a monolithic phenomenon (Bastian 1993). Nevertheless, the diversity has its roots in particular historical processes within Mesoamerica, and the varieties of Protestantisms remain at least superficially the product of missionary activities from North America and Europe. This clash between what was brought by missionaries and how it is reproduced and changed in a new context is only one aspect of the interplay between religion and ethnicity in Latin America. More significant is the constant reconfiguration of what Jean Pierre Bastian (1998) calls a "religious neocommunitarianism" at the local level. Maintaining a sense of the plurality of the phenomenon guards against overgeneralization and frames more localized analyses of evangelical practice in different contexts within Latin America.

Pluralism, however, extends beyond Protestantism. And Protestantism in its various guises cannot be understood apart from a more complete consideration of Guatemala's shifting religious panorama. At least four kinds of Catholicism have currency in Guatemala—indigenous, orthodox, charismatic, and activist (some might even include a folk Catholic category for those places where the indigenous component is not as strong). The more than three hundred evangelical groups said to exist in the country can be loosely categorized as evangelical (Bible-believing non-Pentecostal), Pentecostal (focused on experiences of the Holy Spirit in the person's life, including through divine healing), and neo-Pentecostal (usually based in the elite sectors of society and proclaiming some version of dominion or health-and-wealth theology that justifies their place in the upper crust of society). Even the latter group has experienced internal diversification, and this discussion so far has not mentioned those who are now practicing versions of Maya spirituality in an effort to distance themselves as far as possible from colonialist Christianity.[13]

Shifting Identities in Local Perspective

The latter concern, albeit less explicit in my work, involves ongoing debates within anthropology concerning the nature of the discipline and its relationship to colonialism emanating from the West. No study dealing with issues of Christianity and cultural identity within an oppressive state apparatus can avoid addressing this issue. The intent here is to focus on constructive under-standings when dealing with processes of religious change in Mesoamerica and the implications of such change for the relationship between the formation of ethnic identity and the nation-state. From the religious side, it is important simply to acknowledge the process of change and the extant tension in many communities between various forms of religious expression.

In regard to village life in Guatemala, conflict is often highlighted between evangelicalism and *costumbre* embodied in the *cofradías* or cargo system.[14] The image is one of evangelicals who withdraw from various kinds of communal participation such as fiestas for the patron saints and other kinds of community cooperation where donations are required. Their retreat is usually into forms of religious expression involving changes in social mores, especially the avoidance of drinking in the context of ritual activities. There is also tension between different worship practices and a stress on conversion in contexts where communal identity is tied to place and the presence of the community ancestors in establishing a way of life. Essentially, *costumbre* can be considered a practice growing out of a worldview. In her work in San André Semetabaj, Kay Warren affirms that community members "celebrate continuity with the ancestors by following 'their ideas and words' and by replicating the way in which they practiced *costumbre*: 'We should act like our grandparents acted, be-having well, believing in God. . . . If we remember God, he will watch over us. Our ancestors lived a long time because they behaved well before God in loving their fellow man. Thus God rewarded them with good plantings and harvests'" (1989, 49). Based on his work in Santiago Atitlán, Robert Carlsen notes, "A basic distinction between performance and identity as a defining aspect of religiosity constitutes a fundamental difference between the Old Ways and both Guatemalan Catholicism and Protestantism" (1997, 171 n. 6).

Moreover, both evangelicalism and reform versions of Roman Catholicism, such as Catholic Action and liberationist tendencies emanating in the post–Vatican II period, have created tension with age-grade hierarchies and the practice of *costumbre* in Maya communities in Guatemala.[15] A number of stud-ies have dealt with such intra-community tensions, highlighting religious con-version's potentially disruptive nature at the community level.[16] The title of Douglas Brintnall's *Revolt against the Dead* vividly demonstrates how the cate-chist movement and the evangelicals discussed in the work came into conflict with the ancestors in the Huehuetenango community of Aguacatán begin-ning in the early 1950s. Both groups challenged the community's social orga-nization and the way it kept the Maya population subordinate to Ladinos. The influx of the new religious practices had a rapid impact in the midst of other social changes such as the contrast between wage labor on coffee plantations controlled by Ladinos and new wealth among segments of the Maya population generated by garlic production that began to take off in the 1930s. Brintnall says that as early as 1964 "the internal struggle over the hierarchies was over, and the social organization of Traditionalism was dead" (1979, 148).

The affinity between conversion and economic factors is also central to Sheldon Annis's study in the Kaqchikel-speaking town of San Antonio Aguascalientes. His work there centered around what Annis called "*milpa* logic" (cornfield logic), which emphasized ties to the land and a willingness "to invest surplus product in symbolic acts that celebrate and reinforce communalism," and "anti-*milpa* logic," which looked to "a different set of rewards that can confer prestige, familial well-being, or spiritual gratification on a personal, nonvillage basis" (1987, 75). People operating in the latter framework are either those who find themselves with no surplus wealth to invest back into the community (what Annis refers to as a "cultural tax") or those who want to economically expand their horizons. Conversion, in both an economic and a spiritual sense, was supposed to result in a move from "el suelo al cielo." The phrase comes from one of the women with whom Annis worked and has a complex meaning: "from dirt floor to the sky; from rags to riches; from earth to Heaven" (87). In Annis's words, "Economic gain is both the path and the reward. Investment in economically unproductive social institutions is not only a waste; it is a sin" (87). This lack of focus on the community as such meant that Protestants were more likely to engage in nonfarm entrepreneurial activities or in cash-cropping aided by inputs of technology designed to increase yields. When he looked at women and weaving in San Antonio, Annis found that Roman Catholics tend to value their textiles for what they say about the texture of community and the meaning embodied in the designs, that is, "textiles *are* wealth" (133), while Protestants view textiles more for the wealth they can generate.

As in Aguacatán, conversion in San Antonio Aguascalientes was fomented in part by community disruption emanating from events such as the 1976 earthquake and the violence, which abetted Pentecostal rhetoric and frequently made evangelicalism a haven during the repression of the Ríos Montt regime (1982–83). Annis does not focus on direct intra-village conflict between the evangelicals and Catholics or *costumbristas* but rather on shifts in worldview regarding the place of self within the community. The old ways of being in the world are supplanted by progress from "el suelo al cielo." Both Brintnall and Annis trace some of the breakdown in community structure to the time of the reforms instituted during the Guatemalan Revolution of 1944–54. Governmental changes during the period challenged the civil-religious hierarchy embodied in the *cofradías* (themselves nineteenth-century creations according to some accounts), while peasant leagues and other groups brought different ways of conceiving the relationship between land and community (Annis 1997, 78).

Although there can be no doubt that evangelicalism has grown in the breach created by various kinds of social disruption over the past fifty years in Guatemala or that it has contributed greatly to divisiveness within a number of communities in the region, my intent here is to demonstrate how some evangelicals in two particular contexts are practicing their religious convictions and making sense of their own changing circumstances. In the competing fields of discourse surrounding colonialism and postcolonialism, it simply will not do to continue to view second- or third-generation Mesoamerican evangelicals as victims of imposition from the West or of some North American conspiracy. Evangelicalism is now woven into the fabric of quite possibly the majority of Guatemala's Maya communities. It exists alongside an ethnic identity embodied in language and other aspects of Maya culture and cosmology, within the very being of people who consider themselves both Maya and evangelical. This is one of the realities that any anthropology moving in the direction of dialogue and collaboration with people in divergent circumstances, even with people on different sides of community conflict, needs to take into account.[17]

Shifting Communities in Transnational Perspective

A final layer of context that needs to be addressed briefly is the very nature of community itself in Mesoamerica and the anthropological approach to community in this century of globalization. In her recent work based in Chiapas, June Nash eloquently expresses the need for continued focus on the local community in anthropological work in Mesoamerica. After a summary of critiques of some of the problems with community studies (closed communities were not closed, too functionalist, etc.), she notes how "the critique often failed to assess how community studies captured the informants' construction of harmony that served as armor against external power, and how this defense affected their behavior" (Nash 2001, 40). She continues:

> As indigenous people attempt to define the ethnic basis for autonomy at a regional level, they are establishing the authenticity of their claims by reference to the collective basis in communities with a majority of people speaking an indigenous language and sharing collective traditions. Community studies will attain a new significance as evidential support for their claims to distinctive ethnic identity. With cumulative knowledge of the broader landscape in which the communities are located,

anthropologists can take advantage of the ethnographies to situate the separate histories of each locality in the global context of change that is engulfing the region. (40–41)

My reading of Maya evangelicalism requires a definition of community that embraces, even while throwing it into relief, the emphasis on localism embodied in shared culture, language, and place of residence that is one of the hallmarks of Mesoamerican studies (Carmack, Gasco, and Gossen 1996, 6–7; Carlsen 1997, 39–40).[18] The framing of identity among the Maya in Guatemala continues to center on communities of origin and the language spoken when identifying oneself outside the communities of residence. Simultaneously, the migration of people from their home communities in search of more adequate economic resources and better opportunities for their families has become a significant area of research for the study of religion in the Americas. Issues of transnationalization and the de-territorialization of identity and cultural practices have come to the fore as waves of migration have proceeded from rural to urban areas and from Guatemala to "el norte" in recent decades (Petersen, Vásquez, and Williams 2001; Vásquez and Marquardt 2003).

In a similar vein, evangelicalism by its nature represents a reconfiguration of the notion of community in the direction of another horizon of interest. This horizon links adherents to the evangelical faith in a new community of *hermanos y hermanas* (brothers and sisters) who have their eyes focused on a more universal frame of reference involving spiritual goods and resources that originate in other contexts and simultaneously integrate people spiritually into a community transcending boundaries of ethnicity, language, and geography, embracing all those with similar beliefs. This is a shift that in Mesoamerica implies a move away from Catholicism and *costumbre,* and practices that have been labeled "paganism" and "idolatry," and in the direction of belief in a monotheistic God. The distinction is often put directly in a phrase that graphically illustrates the shift in orientation, "Antes que me convertí al evangélio, cuando era católico" (Before I converted to the gospel, when I was a Catholic). The emphasis is on a break with the past community and integration into a new way of living.[19]

There is also continuity, however, as personal identity and community relations are endowed with new meaning. Perhaps Virginia Garrard-Burnett claims too much in the Guatemalan case when she says that a "'Maya' Catholic Church" and more traditional Maya religion "both may owe a debt, like it or not, to the Protestant move to provide a usable template for pluralism, theological fluidity, and contextualized growth" (1998a, 169). Still, the statement acknowledges the reality of religious pluralism in Guatemala, and it provides another piece to the agenda for the continuing study of religious change in

Mesoamerica. The ethnographic approach to the study of this pluralism promises to document not only the panorama of that diversity but also the role of individuals and groups who practice their religion in the midst of such pluralism. This begins at the local level and includes concerns such as personal conversion or generational conflicts between the age-graded authority structures in indigenous communities and younger leaders who often received training in the context of Catholic Action or evangelical churches.[20]

Beyond the local, scholarly discussion is increasingly giving attention to the changing role of civic groups within (and across) the boundaries of nation-states. Movements such as Maya evangelicalism might also be seen as aspects of "transnational civil society," described by Susanne Hoeber Rudolph as "invok-[ing] resistant and polemical connotations, a space for self-conscious, organized actors to assert themselves for and against state policies, actions and processes" (1997, 10–11). Rudolph's comments about religion in transnational perspective are also relevant to cultural projects of ethnic renewal: "Religious networks and communities in domestic and transnational civil society render state claims to monopoly sovereignty problematic. This challenge is less familiar than the challenge from global markets in ideas as well as goods and services. . . . Thousands of interveners in transnational space have the authority and power to provide an alternative to state activity, not replace it" (1997, 12). Documentation of such alternatives is the space for applying an ethnographic and humanistic approach to religion and ethnicity. The transcendent symbols of religion and shared culture of the ethnic group are elaborated in the lives and struggles of people and movements.

A Plan of Action

In addressing these issues, this work moves through various levels of context that serve to place the study of Maya evangelicalism and the study of religion in Guatemala in a more comprehensive social and political frame than is usually the case in studies of evangelicalism. Chapter 2 further refines the theoretical lens for the study by defining issues such as pluralism and ethnic renewal in the light of humanistic approaches to anthropological studies. I then briefly discuss the settings and methods for my research. As will be seen, the engagement transcends an extended field season in 1997 and 1998. By highlighting such involvement, there is yet another connection with the processual approach to ascertaining meaning in religion and ethnic renewal projects. Long-term commitments to particular projects and people provide a specific grounding for research in a social context like Guatemala, and this grounding, in turn, provides a perspective on shifting practices over time.

In chapter 3, I provide the broader context for my research in terms of the violence (*la violencia*) suffered in Guatemala during the internal conflict that began in 1960 and did not end until 1996. This chapter also links that segment of Guatemalan history to the peace process that slowly began to take shape in the late 1980s and early 1990s and to the Maya Movement for ethnic renewal, which burst on the scene in the same period. While some will want more (and different kinds of) ethnohistory in that particular chapter, it is the war that creates the immediate context for the kinds of evangelical practices among the Mam and Kaqchikel that are the subjects of chapters 5 and 6. Evangelical growth exploded and began to level off during the long duration of the conflict, and the post-conflict situation is a time to assess some of the changes in the Guatemalan religious landscape.

Chapter 4 is a bridge chapter in that it summarizes some of the general history of Protestantism in its relationship to the Guatemalan state and links contemporary Protestant organizations and their social and political involvement to the civil-society organizing that has been a moving and powerful force in Guatemala since the late 1980s (Bastos and Camus 1996; Warren 1998). Two Maya organizations are discussed in the second half of this chapter: the Conferencia de Iglesias Evangélicas de Guatemala (CIEDEG, Guatemalan Conference of Evangelical Churches) and the Hermandad de Presbiterios Mayas (HPM, Brotherhood of Maya Presbyteries). During the time of my field work, the executive secretary of each group was a Kaqchikel Presbyterian minister. By giving attention to such Maya organizations with roots in the evangelical community, I expand on the studies of contemporary social movements in Guatemala in which these kinds of religious organizations are nearly invisible. While pan-Mayanism has been the subject of a number of analyses (C. Smith 1991; LeBaron 1993; Otzoy 1996; Fischer and Brown 1996; Warren 1998), much less attention has been given to the role of religion within that movement or to indigenous Protestantism within the context of national culture. In that vein, this chapter highlights the role of social organizations with an evangelical base and acts as a bridge to the more localized expressions of evangelical practice for the groups discussed in chapters 5 and 6. This is a crucial part of the historiography of evangelical practices in Guatemala.

This chapter's first epigraph, from Vitalino Similox, a Kaqchikel Presbyterian minister who figures in several places in this work, was spoken in a group interview when I joined the late David Scotchmer, former Presbyterian missionary, anthropologist, and then professor of missiology at the University of Dubuque Theological Seminary, on an immersion trip to Guatemala in January 1994, while I was pastoring a Presbyterian congregation in Tuscaloosa, Alabama. As I learned when I arrived in Guatemala, the situation for civil organizing was beginning to open up after the bitter repression of the 1980s and Jorge Serrano Elias's attempted *auto-golpe* (self-coup) of the previous

Figure 5. David Scotchmer and Rigoberta Menchú

year. Rigoberta Menchú had been awarded the Nobel Peace Prize in 1992, the quincentenary year of Columbus's "discovery" of America, and former human rights ombudsman Ramiro de León Carpio had been selected to serve out the remainder of Serrano Elias's presidential term. During our visit we learned that the Comunidades de Población en Resistencia (Communities of Population in Resistance) were about to make their presence more forthrightly known throughout the country after ten years of fleeing from the army, and I even bought my wife a T-shirt sold by the Coordinadora Nacional de Viudas de Guatemala (CONAVIGUA, National Coordinating Group of Guatemalan Widows), urging an end to forced military recruitment of young men in local villages. On the plane on the way down, I had opened the *New York Times* I bought in the airport and found the first article about the Zapatista rebellion that had broken out across the border in Chiapas as a protest against the initiation of NAFTA. In our rounds of interviews over the next few days we ended up in the CIEDEG offices, where Similox made this comment.

Any attempt to understand the nature of religious expression in postcolonial Mesoamerica needs to contend with the contrast embodied in Similox's statement.[21] Resistance to impositions from the outside and innovation in combining aspects of thought and practice are as characteristic of religion in the region as are continuity with the past in the corporate community and cultural

homogeneity represented by the advent of globalization. My work highlights lived space and various kinds of discourse produced in the midst of national-level political and ethnic conflict in Guatemala. Even so, the situation of Mam and Kaqchikel evangelicals reflects Vásquez and Marquardt's commentary that "globalization reconfigures the goals and actions of religious institutions and the everyday practices of the faithful to create new boundaries that are every bit as real, although more permeable and more often transgressed" (2003, 229). How this articulates with Guatemalan history and a concern for religion—in both Maya and evangelical practices—is the story to be told in the rest of this work.

2

A Humanistic Approach to a Post-Conflict Society

We have very little sense of what a long-established, religiously pluralistic indigenous community would look like. . . . While attention has been focused on the reasons for religious change and the ensuing decay of communal institutions in Mesoamerica, perhaps the most significant contemporary development lies in the new civic arrangements being forged in religiously heterodox communities.

—John D. Monaghan, *Ethnology*

In broad strokes, this summary statement by John Monaghan (2000) in his overview of religion in Mesoamerica provides a context for the work that follows. By looking ethnographically and comparatively at Maya evangelicals in two places within the same denomination, I hope to provide some of the background for understanding pluralism and heterodoxy in both community and nation within Guatemala. For Latin America as a whole it is important to consider the relatively short frame of reference we have for religiously heterodox nations as well as communities. Situated between the past and the future, we might also do well to consider how second-, third-, and fourth-generation Maya evangelicals will be sustained by the traditions of their ancestors some twenty-five or fifty years from now.

The purpose of this chapter is to articulate a more specific grounding for the work that follows by looking briefly at three issues that were touched upon in the previous chapter. After addressing the meaning of pluralism in more specific terms, I turn to a brief consideration of ethnic renewal as a more technical conceptualization for looking at the interplay between identity and religion among Maya evangelicals. That discussion will refer to the concept of revitalization, which some have used in describing religious movements in various contexts since Anthony Wallace (1956) wrote his famous article on the subject. Both *renewal* and *revitalization* are useful terms, although the former reflects the more processual approach to religion and the study of identity and community outlined in chapter 1. Finally, I situate my analysis in the context of humanistic concerns within anthropology that promise a more engaged practice of ethnography based on a "critical humanism," one that holds

in tension the subjective aspects of religious practice as people turn their beliefs into action in very specific contexts. After addressing these issues, I turn to a description of the setting within Guatemala and to the methods I employed as this project evolved during the course of my own engagement with religion in that country.

Pluralism, Renewal, and a Humanistic Approach to Ethnography

As is the case with terms such as *modernity* and *secularization,* the meaning of the term *pluralism* is much debated these days. Although I have so far used it consistently to highlight the diversity of religious practice within the field of ethnicity (including within the wider Maya community), it should be clear that, in the context of nation building in a post-conflict society, the term has a more specific meaning and not a little ethical import. Diana Eck, director of the Pluralism Project, which is geared toward understanding religious change in the United States, argues that "[t]he language of pluralism is the language not just of difference but of engagement, involvement, and participation. It is the language of traffic, dialogue and debate" (2001, 69). This is a helpful beginning point for thinking about diversity and the often-expressed hopes for a "multiethnic, pluricultural, and multilingual" Guatemala that will include the four peoples who make up the nation—Maya, Ladino, Xinca, and Garifuna—as full partners in the national project. Such framings tend to make one reflect upon diversity and difference, but Eck is quick to point out that "*pluralism* is not just another word for diversity. It goes beyond mere plurality or diversity to active engagement with that plurality" (70). Finally, Eck also notes that pluralism is a move beyond both tolerance and relativity (70–71), and this is where the concerns of the Maya (and other ethnic groups) in Guatemala, Mexico, and throughout Mesoamerica for autonomy and space for active participation in their respective societies come into play.

Jesús García Ruiz argues that the state can be defined as "an organic modality of the social relation that makes territory, population, and juridical system coincide" (1997, 32). In analyzing the implications of the Accord on the Identity and Rights of the Indigenous Peoples (signed in 1995) in the push for the final peace accord, he argues, "The State . . . must be the guarantor of respect for the rights of dominated groups so that they can integrate into the nation as citizens and not as subjects controlled directly or indirectly by social groups that think they are 'superior' and who claim rights over others in the name of this superiority" (43). This might be considered a basic framework for the acknowledgment of ethnic pluralism from the side of the state. This per-

spective holds up the possibility of the recognition of collective as well as individual rights, a significant point of contention in the struggles of ethnic nations within the territory of the nation-state. Benjamin Colby and Pierre van den Berghe put the issue in more general terms in one of the first studies to address the issue of pluralism in Guatemala. Based on their work among the Ixil, they reflected on the way in which the character "of a given plural society is determined at one level by the *structure of intergroup relations,* and at another level by the *overlap and interplay between institutional structures*" (1969, 20).[1]

Following Joane Nagel and her work in the American Indian context in North America (1996), I tend to refer to ethnic renewal movements as a rubric for discussing movements seeking to define or strengthen their identity in relation to other groups. While similar in some respects to the work of Anthony Wallace (1956) on revitalization movements, this rubric captures the active and processual nature of the struggle for identity that, however rooted in some primordial sense of the group, remains in part a constructed identity in the wake of outside impositions. The concept of revitalization continues to be used in a number of settings (Kehoe 2006; Harkin 2004), and the idea of creating "a more satisfying culture" (Wallace 1956, 265) in the wake of the upheavals (natural and human) in Guatemala during the last half of the twentieth century surely resonates. In calling attention to the concept of ethnic renewal, I am informed in part by Kay Warren's comments on the use of the term specifically in regard to pan-Mayanism. Warren notes that at issue for Wallace "was the politics of a resynthesis, the authors of which have been compelled to reach across cultural divides to imagine a radical transformation of indigenous culture" (1998, 208). Later, in critiquing the model, she notes both its functional quality and "the assumption that cultures find a steady state between times of crisis rather than the more dynamic, heterogenous views of culture now advocated by anthropologists" (208–209). Finally, she notes that the psychoanalytic cast to the model is not a help to "a fuller exploration of historicized self-consciousness and agency" (209).

The recognition of agency and history in the creation of culture is an aspect of the interplay between constructivism and structure in processes of ethnic renewal. Nagel is helpful in her reference to "cultural construction techniques" that "aid in the construction of community and . . . serve as mechanisms of collective mobilization" (1998, 253). Her perspective is that renewal is at once individual and collective, as these are "intertwined aspects of general ethnic renewal. Individual ethnic renewal involves mainly matters of personal identity and the groups with whom one identifies and associates. Collective ethnic renewal involves mainly matters of community and culture and history associated with those groups" (1996, 11). This focus on agency and process is as appropriate and necessary for the study of ethnicity in contemporary Guatemala

as it is for the understanding of religion as process. Both Roman Catholicism and the more recent Protestantisms, while originally cultural impositions, have taken root and are being indigenized even as they have changed aspects of traditional culture in Guatemala.[2]

An understanding of the indigenization of Christian thought and practice in the Maya communities of Guatemala cannot be divorced from the role played by either pan-Maya activists or Maya Protestants themselves in the construction of a new civil society in the wake of a war in which most of the victims were Maya. Holding all these levels of analysis in tension, two strains of humanistic anthropology inform the interpretive approach I use in this work. The first strain of humanistic anthropology has affinities with what Bruce Knauft (1996) has called a "critical humanism," one that simultaneously embodies a critique of inequality while affirming the cultural relativism that is central to anthropology as a discipline. Tension between these two poles is truly dialectical, but ethnography needs to be grounded on both ends of the continuum. This perspective provides an approach to the study of contemporary colonialism, ethnicity, and religious expression on the one hand and the nature of the nation-state on the other without losing sight of the centrality of local or micro-level ethnography for the description and analysis of cultural difference. The wedding of experience and agency in the construction of meaning and the symbols involved in such construction ultimately leads to the possibility of a narrative and dialogical anthropology that begins from an ethnographic location in a particular place or situated in a context that shapes but does not determine action. This implies a concern with the social as well as with ethnohistory (Carmack 1971; Krech 1991), for although they are not determinative of action, historical processes provide the framework out of which action takes place.

At a more basic level, the humanistic stance raises the issue of intersubjectivity, the way in which the beliefs and practices of self and other come together and in concert turn the present into the future. This view foregrounds issues of agency and social constructivist views of culture wherein human beings create the world in which they live and simultaneously endow the world with meaning. While it has affinities with class-oriented approaches to culture and agency such as practice theory (Ortner 1989, 1994) as well as with phenomenological approaches (Berger 1967; Berger and Luckmann 1966), this perspective is shaped by an interactive view of the relationship of individuals and groups to culture (Richardson and Dunton 1989). In the words of Miles Richardson, the effort of anthropologists to understand religion "strives to recognize the role of beliefs in constituting the lived-in world of practitioners and so attempts to disclose belief claims as pronouncements, often eloquent, sometimes cruel, but always significant, about human yearning" (1996, 614). In a place like Guatemala, engaged scholarship loses sight of the local and mundane to its own peril.

Setting and Methods

My primary field research consisted of rather traditional anthropological field work involving participant observation and interviews in the Mam and Kaqchikel presbyteries of the IENPG between September 1997 and August 1998. Following six weeks of Mam language study, I began formal observation in the Mam Presbytery. This work consisted primarily of open-ended interviews with presbytery and congregational leaders and attendance at various presbytery activities for approximately six months. I then turned my attention to participant observation with the Kaqchikel Presbytery. In both contexts the research was conducted primarily in Spanish. Direct participant observation in the Mam Presbytery assumed a larger role than in the Kaqchikel Presbytery, where there was more emphasis on interviews and the review of public documents related to events in that region over the five previous years.

The Mam and Kaqchikel presbyteries are headquartered in the departments of Quetzaltenango and Chimaltenango, respectively. Most of the congregations of the two presbyteries are in the two departments as well. Ten of the seventeen presbyteries in the denomination of sixty thousand adherents pertain to one of five groups of Maya people—K'iche', Mam, Kaqchikel, Q'eqchi', and Q'anjobal—with whom the denomination has established work since its beginning in 1882.[3] Currently, the Mam Maya population consists of over 600,000 people living in a large segment of the northwestern part of the country extending into Mexico, where some 30,000 Mam live near the southernmost boundary of the state of Chiapas and where some refugees fled in the 1980s during the height of the civil war. The Kaqchikel Maya are the third-largest Maya group, with over 825,000 people centered in the department of Chimaltenango in the part of the highlands closest to Guatemala City.[4]

Although I focus on identity and ethnographic methods, the larger project gave attention to political events in Guatemala and the manner in which the Kaqchikel Presbytery responded to those in a more activist fashion than is typical among Guatemalan evangelicals. During my extended field stay, I lived with my family in Guatemala's second-largest city, Quetzaltenango, and conducted research in a fashion that resulted in more of a regional study of how historical Protestantism and ethnicity relate to the national context than a study of a single ethnic or religious community. Quetzaltenango is situated on the eastern periphery of the Mam area and provides access to the southern Mam region while providing contact with other organizations involved in Maya cultural and political education. More in-depth work has been con-

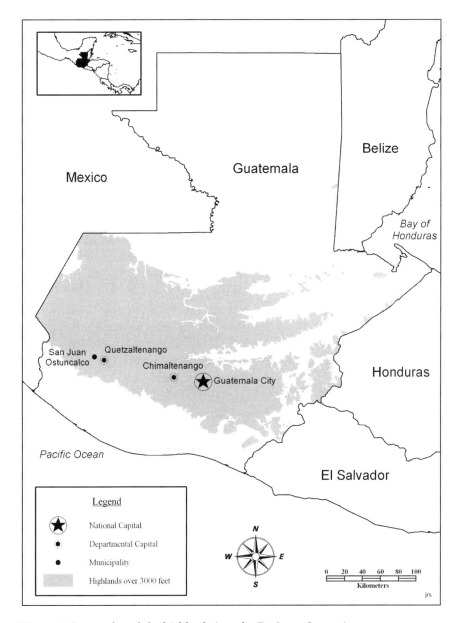

Figure 6. Guatemala and the highlands (map by Dr. James Samson)

ducted in the Mam area because there is a solid base of academic work on evangelicals in this region (Scotchmer 1986, 1989, 1991, 1993) as well as some effort to look at Maya religion itself in the area (Peck 1970; Greenberg 1984). For the larger Mam region, the work of John Watanabe (1990, 1992, 1995, 1996, 1999) provides a solid base for the investigation of Mam culture in general as well as contemporary religious expression in Mesoamerica (see also W. Smith 1977; Hawkins 1984). The region also affords an opportunity for learning how Maya Protestants understand their participation in religious and social processes in situations more geographically removed from the pressures of the capital city.

Description of the activities and organizational structure of the Mam Presbytery provided a framework for less-extensive work with the Kaqchikel Presbytery, which is headquartered in the city of Chimaltenango, in the department of the same name. The Kaqchikel are better known outside Guatemala than the Mam because they are leaders in the intellectual wing of the Maya Movement and because a number of Kaqchikel have published texts detailing desired changes in the relation of the Guatemalan government to the Maya population in addition to their own research. Historically, the Kaqchikel have played a prominent role in opposition to the governing powers after first supporting the Spanish invaders in their conflict with the K'iche', who resisted their initial incursion into the Quetzaltenango area in 1524 (Carmack 1981; R. Hill 1992). Finally, a number of Kaqchikel have made their voices heard in the midst of the religious pluralism that is the focus of this research. These individuals include two prominent Presbyterian ministers (Otzoy 1996, 1997; Similox Salazar 1992, 1997; cf. Colop 1997) as well as a former Catholic priest who returned to traditional Maya religious practices (Wuqub' Iq' 1997). Their work provides a textual basis for comparison and contrast that is not always immediately available in anthropological studies of indigenous religious expression.

Even with these resources, the complexities of working in Guatemala were best revealed during a trip I made to Guatemala in May 1996, first to travel with some students under the auspices of the Centro Evangélico de Estudios Pastorales de América Central (CEDEPCA, Evangelical Center for Pastoral Studies in Central America), then for a month-long period of reconnaissance in order to begin establishing a framework for my research. During that time I participated as an observer in the annual five-day meeting of the synod of the IENPG and experienced firsthand some of the tensions and conflicts that permeate religious and political issues in the Guatemalan context. Three days before the meeting, the moderator for that year was abducted and held for ransom in what was generally taken to be an act perpetrated by dissidents who had left the IENPG during a bitter split within the denomination in 1992.

Figure 7. March to Constitutional Plaza for signing of the Firm and Lasting Peace, 1996

The moderator was released several days later and made a dramatic appearance toward the end of the meeting when he was reunited with his family. This event seemed at the time to embody some of the ongoing conflicts within Guatemala at large as well as some of the tensions over religion that play a divisive role in local communities. For the IENPG these conflicts sometimes manifest themselves in terms of ethnic conflict, and this relatively small religious group can serve as a lens for better understanding some of the issues of ethnicity and religious identity as they are worked out in a complex and violent manner in postcolonial Guatemala. Subsequent interpretations of the event reveal the difficulties of this rather straightforward interpretation, as not only the dissidents but also family members and others have been rumored to have actually carried out the kidnapping. In December 1996, I returned to Guatemala for the better part of a month with assistance from a Benevolent Grant from the University at Albany to begin study of the Mam language, and I was present with my eldest daughter in the central plaza of Guatemala City on the day the final peace accord was signed (fig. 7).

Throughout my field work in Guatemala, my research was supplemented by the existence of ecclesiastical documents (both Roman Catholic and Protestant), by publications and pamphlets from some of the more than three hundred Maya organizations in Guatemala, by the Conferencia Episcopal de Guatemala (CEG, Guatemalan Episcopal Conference), and by reports by numerous nongovernmental organizations working in Guatemala, particularly the Misión de las Naciones Unidas de Verificación de los Derechos Humanos en Guatemala (MINUGUA, United Nations Mission for the Verification of Human Rights in Guatemala). These texts, along with academic publications by both indigenous and Mestizo Guatemalans, provided a wealth of material for the research project. They furnished a strong basis for making comparisons across the two presbyteries and linking events in the local situations to religious and political events at the national level.

Following my return from extended field work, I went back to Guatemala on several occasions for a total of nearly three months. On one of these occasions I participated as a presenter in the Second Congress on the Popol Wuj, held in Quetzaltenango. This gave me firsthand experience in dialogue with Maya who were reflecting on some of their own experiences in a more academic fashion as well as a perspective on how such public events are often used as organizing tools within the context of contemporary Maya activism. On two other occasions I spent over a month conducting interviews as a research consultant for a Pew Charitable Trust–funded project on Evangelical Christianity and Political Democracy in Asia, Africa, and Latin America (Freston 2006). My participation in this three-year project, which focused on the role of evangelicals in processes of democratization on three continents, provided additional information regarding pluralism in the religious arena in Guatemala and the nature of the communities I had been working with during both projects. Pluralism has already been discussed in this chapter, yet the relationship of evangelical religion to democracy and pluralism in the political sphere is inadequately studied in terms of case studies of religious actors and their participation in or eschewing of political involvement.[5]

The primary texts I used in my analysis are ethnographic field notes taken in some thirty observational contexts, including worship services, a mass baptism and a mass wedding ceremony held outside normal worship settings, formal meetings of the presbyteries, workshops sponsored by the two groups, and an experience of teaching a course on Latin American theologies in the Mam Seminary.[6] Information obtained in these experiences provided the basis for comparing contemporary practice across the two presbyteries with other of the numerous evangelical groups in Guatemala and with work that has already been published on the Protestant presence in Mesoamerica. The symbols, themes, and interpretations are elaborated in relation to information obtained in some twenty detailed interviews with leaders from the two groups and another dozen interviews situating the primary research within current events including the Maya Movement and the shaky peace process under way in Guatemala.

My interviews were semistructured (i.e., directed) in nature, and they resulted in a narrative structure as people recounted their religious experiences and then articulated their vision for the future in the light of their current beliefs and practice. I paid particular attention to the manner in which the correlation between symbolic expression and the interview data reveals how Presbyterian practice is only one component of religious pluralism coexisting with Maya ethnic identity in Guatemala. This pluralism includes aspects of Maya spirituality that are frequently integrated into the various Protestantisms practiced by Maya evangelicals. Rather than focusing on specific reasons for conversion, the emphasis is on the self-understanding of Maya evangelicals and how that self-understanding is brought to bear on the larger social and political context in which Guatemalans practice religion today.

With its narrative focus on the meaning of their religion to Maya Protestants, my research seeks to give voice to Maya people working out their own destiny in the present moment, particularly in regard to the manner in which the indigenization of Christianity is now directed by indigenous peoples themselves. In summary, for the Kaqchikel, theology and political involvement are linked in religious practice that seeks to directly confront social issues affecting the place of Maya people within Guatemalan society. The Mam, in contrast, promote an "integral theology" wherein social action (a clinic, women's development projects, agricultural capacitation, primary school education at three sites) grows out of a theological agenda and responds more directly to the local situation than to cultural or political agendas at the national level. Even with these emphases, worship activities and places of worship figure heavily as orienting symbols in the Mam context, and the baptism discussed in chapter 5 may well be an appropriate symbolic frame for the presbytery's activities. The way in which the concerns are articulated constitutes a "re-enchanting" of the world in the face of modernization and interpretations of evangelicalism in Mesoamerica that have often focused on economic motivations for conversion and the divisiveness of evangelicalism in local communities. In this vein, re-enchantment and renewal provide a useful framework for interpreting ethnic identity in concert with religious aspects of human activity.

3
The National Context
War, Peace Accords, and the Maya Movement

Our struggle both shapes and purifies the future. Our history is a living history, which has throbbed, resisted, and survived many centuries of sacrifice. Now it rises again with new vigor. The seeds, dormant for such a long time, break out today with confident expectation.

> —Rigoberta Menchú, Nobel Prize acceptance speech

The Crucible of *La violencia*

Maya nationalism in Guatemala cannot be understood apart from *la violencia,* the violence that engulfed Guatemala from the late 1970s through the mid-1980s. The cruelty of the state during this period was a primary catalyst for the current magnitude of Maya ethnic sentiment and the volubility with which it has captured national and international attention. Arturo Arias indicates that an early wave of Maya political activism dating to the 1970s precipitated the repression by the Guatemalan government. Indicating that the native community itself was divided in its approach, Arias claims that "[e]thnic identity had been transformed in the search for political force" (1990, 251). In this transformation, older symbolic practices and codes were discarded without new ones taking their place. Yet Arias contends that "just as identity was being talked about more openly, it was experiencing its deepest crisis" (251). It was in the context of dashed hopes for inclusion in the national project of the Guatemalan state that a new and more profound type of resistance began to engage Guatemala and the international community. This costly resistance often found expression in revolutionary activity, but it also manifested itself in other kinds of organizing. During the early 1980s in the United States, the popular film *El Norte* (1983) and Rigoberta Menchú's personal statement in *I, Rigoberta Menchú* (1984) were two of the few sources that called attention to Guatemala while most political and activist involvement was centered on the conflicts in Nicaragua and El Salvador. By the end of the decade, Robert Carmack's edited volume *Harvest of Violence* (1988) and Beatriz Manz's *Refugees of a Hidden War* (1988) had helped bring the situation to the attention of academics and those concerned with geopolitics in the region.[1]

The immediate historical roots of the civil war date from the overthrow of the democratically elected president Jacobo Arbenz in a 1954 coup largely planned and supported by the United States' Central Intelligence Agency (Schlesinger and Kinzer 1999). From then until the democratic election of Vinicio Cerezo Arévalo in 1985, Guatemala's political and social history was dominated by a series of military dictatorships or by civilian presidents who served at the military's pleasure (Woodward 1999). Beginning in 1960 a series of primarily Ladino guerrilla uprisings, led initially by disaffected military officers, challenged the government's hegemony, although by 1975 repression and counterinsurgency had destroyed most of the guerrilla forces (Woodward 1999; LaFeber 1993). Jim Handy (1984, 244) gives 1972 as the date of the appearance of the Ejército Guerrillero de los Pobres (EGP, Guerrilla Army of the Poor) in the Quiché region of the western highlands, and by 1978 the nation was clearly in the midst of a civil war in which the government resorted to violent repression and eventually a scorched-earth policy to silence dissident voices (LaFeber 1993; Woodward 1999).

During the worst of *la violencia,* the period from 1978 to 1985, estimates indicate that some 50,000 to 70,000 people were killed (Carmack 1992a, 295). Another commonly cited figure states that 440 villages were destroyed between 1980 and 1984 (Alecio 1995, 33; Jonas 2000, 24). The *Fourth Report on the Situation of Human Rights in Guatemala* gives the figure of 100,000 deaths and 45,000 disappearances between 1960 and 1991. It goes on to say that "in 1992 there were approximately 45,000 widows and 150,000 orphans because of acts of violence attributable to security forces and to actions of irregular or 'guerrilla' armed groups" (OAS 1993, 45). Another million people were reported to be internal refugees within Guatemala and 85,000 to 90,000 refugees in Mexico, approximately half "under the protection of the United Nations High Commissioner for Refugees" (63). Finally, some 500,000 Maya were living in exile in various countries, including the United States (Carmack 1992a, v).[2]

No scholarly assessment would dispute that the vast majority of the violence was perpetrated by the government through the military or security forces. By the time of the completion of the reports of the two truth commissions formed after the signing of the final peace accord at the end of 1996, estimates of the total number of deaths and disappearances in the conflict had risen to over 200,000 (CEH 1999, 17).[3] On the other hand, the participation of the indigenous population in the revolutionary movement is the subject of much debate and interpretation. Numerous writers suggest that regardless of its involvement in revolutionary activity, the government's seeming attitude in many places was that to be Maya made one a subversive (see R. Adams 1992, 287). David Stoll's work in the Ixil Triangle of the department of Quiché

(Stoll 1992, 1993) suggests that when the Maya realized the lengths to which the government would go to rid the area of suspected subversives, many opted for accommodation with civil patrols and other government security apparatuses rather than siding with guerrillas, who could not protect them from the repression.[4] Stoll also sees this as one of the reasons why evangelical religion, frequently perceived by the government as apolitical, took hold in the region.[5] The situation was complicated even more by the existence of the Comunidades de Población en Resistencia (Communities of Population in Resistance), Maya who for more than ten years remained in three areas of the country in order to avoid being accosted by the military (Falla 1992, 1994; Sinclair 1995; Delli Sante 1996, 288–289). Kay Warren summarizes the combination of forces that drove the Maya variously into exile or into the guerrilla ranks: "Both their desire for wider political participation and their distinctiveness in language and community were seen as political threats by rightist political groups and the military. The ironic fact that the foot soldiers for this counterinsurgency effort were overwhelmingly Mayan was not lost on rural populations" (1993, 26–27). In the larger frame of Latin American political culture, a significant aspect of Guatemala's version of the national security state was the way in which the Maya both resisted the oppression and were victimized by the coercion of the military.

Two particularly important conclusions arise from this scenario. First, it is doubtful that either the political opening growing out of the 1985 return to a democratic political system or the subsequent peace process in Guatemala would have been possible without both the guerrilla presence and, afterward, the human rights movement operating in both the national and international arena (Davis 1992; Carmack 1994). The combination of international pressure in a number of forums referring to Guatemala as having one of the worst human rights records in the hemisphere and the military defeat (though not the complete destruction) of the guerrilla forces brought the government to the negotiating table with the Guatemalan National Revolutionary Unity (URNG).

Second, from the Maya nationalist point of view, the most prominent Maya intellectual articulating a vision of Maya ethnic identity, Demetrio Cojtí Cuxil, is adamant that neither the government nor the guerrillas have been concerned about the indigenous peoples of Guatemala. For Cojtí, the government has clearly been engaged in a process of ethnocide through a combination of political and military programs. Politically, this assimilation takes place not only as a result of government policy geared toward ladinoization but also through the undercounting of the indigenous population in the national census (Cojtí Cuxil 1991; Tzian 1994; cf. R. Adams 1998). Most evident from outside Guatemala has been the repression. The Comisión para el Esclarecimiento Histórico

(CEH, Commission for Historical Clarification) used the formal definition of genocide to label the activity of the military in four particular areas during the war (CEH 1999, 42). At the same time, his view is that the leftist rebels were not particularly concerned with the nationalist issues of the Maya population. In Cojtí's words:

> The Marxist-Leninism that was the frame of reference of the National Revolutionary Union of Guatemala (URNG), because of its own internal logic, never interested itself in the colonial situation of the Maya People. To the contrary, it minimized that situation, postponed it, and even fought against it. The internal logic of this doctrine demands that the revolution, in order to install socialism, interests itself in the class situation and position of individuals, and, therefore, in developing the class struggle in order to eliminate the bourgeoisie. It does not interest itself in the ethnic condition of people or in developing some national liberation struggle to gain independence for oppressed Peoples and nationalities. (1997, 34)[6]

Cojtí attributes some of this blindness on the part of the leftists to their status as urban middle-class Ladinos. With such status comes the concomitant prejudices resulting in "the firm conviction that the monoethnic social project preached by a large part of the Ladino intelligentsia and operationalized by State organisms is the solution to *the Indian problem* and to the problem of cultural diversity" (1997, 35; also Cojtí Cuxil 1994, 15). Aspects of this perspective continue to have validity in the light of the 2003 presidential elections, in which the hierarchically structured URNG, running on a ticket headed by former guerrilla leader Rodrigo Asturias (aka Gaspar Ilom) and vice presidential candidate Pablo Ceta, garnered only slightly more than 2 percent of the vote.[7]

This becomes doubly significant in view of the fact that the vast majority of the victims of the civil war in Guatemala have been Maya (Davis 1992). These concerns were raised even in the midst of the peace talks, which were given new impetus with the signing of the Comprehensive Agreement on Human Rights on 29 March 1994 (UN General Assembly 1995). Estuardo Zapeta, then of the Centro de Estudios de la Cultura Maya (CECMA, Center for the Study of Maya Culture), wrote: "The two groups participating in the dialogue, the government and the URNG, are typically ladino . . . urban, and above all, exclusionary. Guatemala, on the other hand, is primarily rural, multicultural and the majority (65%) is Maya. Consequently, the 'dialogue for peace' is seen as a 'monologue' between two minorities who basically maintain the same colonial discourse" (1994, 26).

Although some will quibble with Zapeta's population estimate, the larger is-. sue of the position of the Maya in the Guatemalan nation-state should not be obscured. When Zapeta wrote, the government and URNG were stalled in the midst of negotiating a side agreement to the peace accords having to do with identity and rights of the indigenous peoples of the country. The agreement was eventually signed on 31 March 1995. Although the Coordinadora de Organizaciones del Pueblo Maya de Guatemala (COPMAGUA, League of Organizations of the Maya People of Guatemala) regarded the signing as "a minimal but significant first step to strengthen the hope of the Maya people to end the marginalization, oppression, discrimination, dominance, exploitation and colonialism we suffer" (URNG-Government dialogue 1995), Zapeta's concern that Maya rights and identity were negotiable is well founded. Zapeta also notes that both the government and the URNG had responded negatively when Maya representatives asked to be included in the discussions. His discussion provides a clear point of departure for considering the intellectual and cultural underpinnings of Maya nationalism: "It appears that in Guatemala, after 500 years, history repeats itself; two minorities are making decisions for the Maya majority" (Zapeta 1994).[8]

The Shape of Maya Activism

In his 1994 survey of Maya activism in Guatemala, Richard Adams notes three types of political organizations active in Guatemala. Following the work of Santiago Bastos and Manuela Camus (cf. 1995), he designates the first two as "indigenous popular organizations" and "Mayan institutions." A third category, of his own, is that of "community level movements" (1994, 162). These organizations reflect differing degrees of willingness to make common cause with non-indigenous peoples when involved in political organizing. The distinction between the first two groups is essentially culturally based in that "[t]he fact that [indigenous popular organizations] are 'popular' means that membership, issues, and arguments may include elements not regarded as salient by all Maya." Organizations included in this category are as diverse as the Comité de Unidad Campesina (CUC, Committee of Campesino Unity), the Grupo de Apoyo Mutuo (GAM, Mutual Support Group), CONAVIGUA, and Majawil Q'ij, which is said to have its roots in the coordination of activities around the quincentenary of Columbus's "discovery" of the Americas. One could say that the defining characteristic of these organizations is a focus on political issues; in Adams's words, "the issues at stake have been generated at least in part by policies followed by the Guatemalan government and are, therefore, issues of concern in state-Indian relations" (1994, 163).

Maya institutions, on the other hand, are distinguished by "their total concern with the promotion of Mayan culture and society" (Adams 1994, 165). The primary institution noted here is the Academia de Lenguas Mayas de Guatemala (ALMG, Academy of Mayan Languages of Guatemala), recognized by Guatemala's congress in 1990 and "the first State recognized and funded institution with direct responsibility for Mayan languages" (England 1995, 129).[9] Other organizations that have Maya culture as their essential focus include the publishing house Cholsamaj, the Centro de Documentación e Investigación Maya (CEDIM, Maya Documentation and Research Center), and the Consejo de Organizaciones Mayas de Guatemala (COMG, Council of Maya Organizations of Guatemala), a coordinating group composed of a number of Maya organizations. The major emphasis of these organizations is their concern with various aspects of Maya language and culture as essential to all of their activities and their political involvement. They begin their involvement in political and social activities from the basis of their ethnicity (C. Smith 1991).[10]

What Richard Adams labels "community level movements" have received relatively little attention in the literature. Consistent with the importance of local communities in Mesoamerica, these movements are structured around communal needs, often in response to the violence of the civil war. A well-known case mentioned by Adams (1994, 167) is that of an uprising to remove the army from the village of Santiago Atitlán in response to the massacre of fourteen villagers by the army in 1990 (Loucky and Carlsen 1991; Carlsen 1997, 151–69). These movements might receive support from the prior types of organizations, but their focus is on immediate concerns such as violence, land rights, or bilingual education (R. Adams 1994, 168). There is a potentially organic exchange between the community movements and the other institutions being discussed. The community acceptance of the institutions means that "those principally urban-based institutions are, in turn, discovering the immense potential available at [the community] level" (169). In addition to Adams's examples, other groups would include *municipio*-level committees that actually organize to bring resources and ideas from the national level. Some of these are organized for specific purposes, such as the establishment of a communal cemetery or the procurement of electricity in an area outlying the *municipio* center. Many activists and politicians began their political involvement through participation in such local-level committees.

Adams's summary of the interrelations among the three types of movements is helpful not only in reemphasizing the focus of each group but also in delineating the political space occupied by each group. Popular organizations are more class oriented, even Marxist, in their objectives, while "[m]ost Mayan institution leaders . . . are extremely careful to focus on cultural issues, on the preservation, protection, and regeneration of Mayan society as viewed through its ancestrally based ethnic rights and traditions" (1994, 170). Even so, other authors have acknowledged the tension between various Maya organizations (C. Smith 1991; Otzoy 1996; C. Jones 1996; Warren 1998), and Gálvez and Esquit's conclusion seems warranted in the light of the difficult political climate in Guatemala: "Efforts to stimulate convergence between Mayan and non-Mayans as well as discussion of the possibilities of reaching new agreement, constitute the most hopeful option for overcoming the 'all or nothing at all' position of certain Mayans, as well as reducing the intransigence and the lack of comprehension of *ladinos*" (1997, 90–91).

Nationalism and the Guatemalan State

Colonialism is an appropriate beginning point for the consideration of nationalism in Latin America and in Guatemala in particular. Without wading too far into the definitional morass surrounding the nation and nationalism, it is not insignificant that both Ernest Gellner's (1983) rationalistic approach to the formation of nations and Benedict Anderson's (1991) interpretive and constructivist approach to "imagined political communities" situate the advent of nations within the time period of the Enlightenment and "modern" industrial society. Stretching the definitions slightly, we can delineate this as the period from roughly the middle of the eighteenth century to the middle of the nineteenth.[11] This wave of nationalism continued through the first quarter of the twentieth century in the aftermath of World War I. Anderson reports that by 1922 "the legitimate international norm was the nation-state, so that in the League [of Nations] even the surviving imperial powers came dressed in national costume rather than imperial uniform" (113). The most recent waves of nationalism, involving colonized states in the Third World and Eastern Europe, were rooted in processes of decolonialization and became particularly significant from World War II onward, intensifying in the late 1950s (113–16).

Within this context, Anderson sees the new states formed in the Americas between 1776 and 1838 as embodying the first group of "political entities" considering themselves "self-consciously" as nations (46). Part of the uniqueness in this phenomenon is that the self-conscious aspect of this development transcended strict cultural boundaries such as language. Anderson continues, "whether we think of Brazil, the USA, or the former colonies of Spain, language was not an element that differentiated them from their respective imperial metropoles. All . . . were creole states, formed and led by people who shared a common language and common descent with those against whom they fought" (47). The creation of the nation in Latin America grew out of the very need for differentiation from colonial centers on the part of creole elites. According to Rodolfo Stavenhagen: "It is no wonder, then, that post-colonial Latin American elites adopted a nationalist ideology as the guiding orientation in their search for legitimation. Once the new republican political units had been established, true nations would have to be constituted as an act of state and government. In Latin America, as in so many other post-colonial societies, the state and its intellectual and political elites created the nation; the sociological nation itself did not struggle to create its own state, as happened—and is happening again—in Europe" (1994, 33).[12]

This brief historical perspective provides another contextual layer for the consideration of Maya nationalism in Guatemala. If the new nations formed in the wake of independence from Spain and other Western European empires were formed in opposition to imperialism, contemporary concerns for indigenous national identity in Guatemala and elsewhere, rooted as they are in ethnicity and cultural manifestations of ethnicity in a primordial sense, harken back to pre-Enlightenment and pre-industrial forms of political and social communities. Ethnic nationalist movements challenge what Stavenhagen refers to as "the model of the unitary state, which was adopted after the wars of independence and developed during the republican period, and the ethnic and cultural diversity of the societies of Latin America" (1994, 330). Postcolonial nationalism and national consciousness in Latin America form a bridge from the past into the present. But it is a sometimes fragile bridge in view of the challenges to the state hegemony that these nations attempted to construct within their boundaries, in part because they were not pluralistic constructions of nationalism.

The processes of state hegemony and national formation in Guatemala were particularly complex because of the failed attempts at establishing a Central American Federation immediately after independence (Perez-Brignoli 1989; Woodward 1999). Steven Palmer notes that Guatemala never actively participated in the fight against Spain but rather passively received independence based on events in Mexico (1990, 38).[13] And Palmer's perspective on the formation of true nationalist sentiment in Guatemala can be seen more clearly when he asks, "Why is it only in the 1870's and 1880's that, in the eyes of the liberal oligarchy, everything suddenly becomes national, or is conceived in terms of its relationship to a newly imagined (but imagined as ancient) national community?" (1990, 78). This is, of course, the period of the accession to power of the liberal dictator Justo Rufino Barrios and the establishment of the liberal project in Guatemala with all of its political and social consequences. It is not a mere symbolic coincidence that the one-quetzal note, the basic unit of Guatemalan currency, bears Barrios's portrait.

Carol Smith's hypothesis regarding Guatemalan nationalism suggests that significant changes in the relationship between class and ethnic groups within Guatemalan national space during the liberal process of national consolidation were the precursors to the most recent Guatemalan violence, violence often cast in terms of a conflict between two ethnic groups, Maya and Ladino. Both liberal ideology and the economic relations related to coffee production contributed to this redefinition of class and ethnicity. Demographic factors included the unique (for Central America) concentration of indigenous peoples in the western highlands. Although the conservative dictator Rafael Carrera (1844–48, 1851–65) came to power after leading a revolt against the liberal government of President Mariano Gálvez (1831–38), Smith finds that "the most striking aspect of the documents that describe Carrera and his regime is their failure to make clear distinctions between Indians and people who are now known as ladinos" (1990, 81). Coupled with a situation in which rural communities were given a fair degree of political autonomy, the result was a social division "between the white Creole elite and the nonwhite masses" (82). These are class divisions in which the indigenous population maintains some of its traditions, but not at the expense of being able to participate in national (or pre-national) economic production.

A prevalent theme in liberal thought from the early period was the imitation of European models of national institutions in Guatemala. According to Smith, this involved Guatemalans in a project of enlightening and whitening, one implication of which was that "Indians had to be actively integrated into the Guatemalan nation as equal citizens rather than as special wards of the church and state" (1990, 76). This implied the breakdown of the colonial notion of the two republics, Indian and Spanish (*república de los indios* and *república de los españoles*). Smith's description of the resulting attitudes toward the indigenous population on the part of the Creoles is significant for understanding subsequent ethnic relations in Guatemala, and quite similar views are articulated by proponents of Maya nationalism today: "Indians began to associate cultural assimilation programs with much more dangerous attacks on their political rights, while Guatemala's white elite, who embodied the Guatemalan state at that point, came to see Indian cultural backwardness as the source of the political rebellions brought on by the final and most 'progressive' part of the Liberal program" (78).

Beginning in 1871, the second liberal period in Guatemala resulted in the consolidation of capitalist modes of production as well as nationalist self-consciousness. At this juncture the (supposed) class unity existing between Mayas and Ladinos in the conservative period was broken. Large-estate coffee production, arising out of shifting land tenure associated with foreign investment in league with the creole elite, resulted in the need for a seasonal labor force during the harvest. Coercion was the method of choice for acquiring this labor (see Bunzel 1959, 8–11; McCreery 1994). One result was that Ladinos, by this time defined as anyone "not culturally Indian" (C. Smith 1990,

86), became state agents involved in the recruitment of the native population for the white plantation owners in accordance with legal requirements demanding such labor.

Although set in historical context, Smith's argument suggests that when definitions of ethnicity are overlaid on a persistent racial and cultural hierarchy, they can shift in response to political, social, and economic factors. At least in Guatemala, these shifting ethnic definitions resulted in changing class status as well. Most indigenous communities in the western highlands were never completely dispossessed of their community lands, but the Maya were relegated to the lowest social status as Ladinos were moved into the highlands specifically to recruit labor on behalf of the state (Smith 1990, 85–89).[14] While differences between the two groups seemed to collapse in Guatemala's eastern mountains, "by the early twentieth century, the term *ladino* had disappeared in the rest of Central America (to be replaced by mestizo) and ladino had come to mean something new in Guatemala: oppressor in the western highlands . . . and homeless (and therefore permanent) worker in the cities and lowlands" (86).

Even at this point, Smith argues, the Maya "resisted the status of full proletarian" (88). The implication is that the indigenous population maintained a degree of cultural and subsistence autonomy that both exacerbated ethnic division and created resistance to their full integration into the Guatemalan national space. The 1944 Revolution changed some of this (Gleijeses 1991; Handy 1994), but the seeds of Guatemala's "democratic spring" need to be understood as originating in the urban context and as a reflection of the concerns of the period when the assimilationist policies of *indigenismo* were prominent in much of Latin America (Stavenhagen 1994, 336–37). Despite the emphasis on "ancient" peoples such as "the Aztec" or "the Maya" in art and other cultural forms, the ideal was still the appropriation of the symbols of indigenous identity and the acculturation of the native peoples into the nation-state.

Although distinctions can be made in the character of class relationships within different regions of the nation, it was in the densely populated highlands that the power relations became symbolized in the Indian-Ladino dichotomy. One of Smith's conclusions is that "the coffee economy reorganized the regional and class patterning of ethnicity in Guatemala, disguising the interests that Indians and many ladinos might still have held in common, and created the internal divisions within Guatemala that still wrack the present" (1990, 89). Ultimately, however, Smith adheres to a view that would take into account some of the regional differences in class relations in the consideration of national unity in Guatemala. For her, the ethnic division is not the principal division in Central America. The "intrinsic division" is instead one between locals of whatever ethnicity and nonlocals "whose power and identity rest upon ties outside of the national territory" (91). Referring again to the time of Rafael Carrera, she sees historical evidence that cultural plurality need not hinder either economic development or nation building.

While provocative, Smith's argument is at odds with other interpretations of the development of nationalism and national consciousness in Guatemala. It is overdetermined by a focus on class as opposed to ethnicity, especially in the Carrera period and in the period of the early development of coffee as representative of capitalism in the Guatemalan economy (see Gudmundson and Lindo-Fuentes 1995, 120–25). While coffee growing did result in significant changes in modes of production, the relationship between capitalist social forces and ethnic relations in the last half of the nineteenth century in Guatemala remains complex (cf. Cambranes 1985).

In his study of the K'iche' town of Momostenango (1990, 1995) Robert Carmack argues that it is precisely the attention given to the indigenous *as indigenous* that created the support for the Carrera regime and the linkages Smith notes between indigenous communities and the conservatives. Communal autonomy is the interpretive key here. Beginning with Barrios, the liberals more directly return to the implementation of a system of assimilation designed to subordinate the indigenous population as wage laborers in a burgeoning capitalist economy. Even here, however, the argument is that rebellion fueled accommodation between the liberal state and the indigenous communities after uprisings in the early part of the twentieth century. Carmack links this with status-based forms of political organization at the municipal level from precolonial and colonial times. In this interpretation, a significant portion of the indigenous population of the western highlands retains enough land or other economic resources so as to never become fully incorporated as proletarians in a capitalist economy (1995, 386–89).

Historian Douglass Sullivan-González even links the figure of Carrera to a Mesoamerican cosmology:

Carrera's power with the Indians . . . emanated not only from a colonial-style relationship, as Carmack has argued, but also from one based in the preconquest traditions. For the indigenous peoples Carrera was a divine figure who had redeemed them from their conquerors. The divinelike accolades heaped upon Carrera during the insurrection and subsequent battles emerge out of a long man-god tradition described by Serge Gruzinski. Carrera's hold upon the people reached a mythic quality in the indigenous highlands. Like many who swore that Zapata would return one day on his white steed, numerous reports coming out of the indigenous highlands indicate that a good portion of the people awaited the caudillo's return even after he had been dead for several years. Reports even circulated that one liberal military leader invoked the dead caudi-llo's name in order to attract the indigenous peoples into his military ranks in the 1870 liberal rebellion. (1998, 129)

Another case comes from Momostenango, where Julián Rubio, the creole leader of a major rebellion during 1886 and 1887, used the alias Ramón Carrera (Carmack 1995, 142).

Maya Nationalism

The foregoing provides a provocative context for the consideration of Maya na-tionalism. The Maya perspective itself links the ideological power of ethnicity with actual relationships of power in ways that are consistent with Smith's per-spective but which also privilege the symbolic construction of identity rela-tions in trying to understand current Guatemalan reality. While this symbolic construction is based on social reality, the difference in interpretations demon-strates some of the reasons for an ongoing division within the indigenous com-munity between strict nationalists and those who favor linkages with "popu-lar" organizations. Still, what is different in the present case is that the Maya themselves are articulating a vision of cultural plurality. Stavenhagen's view of the past is clearly not true in this case: "As elsewhere in the world, it was the ruling class and the intelligentsia who imagined and invented the modern Latin American nations, trying to shape them in their own image. The indige-nous peoples were excluded from the 'national projects' that emerged in the nineteenth century. They have remained in the background since then, shad-owy figures which, like Greek choruses, step into the historical limelight dur-ing revolutions, rebellions and uprisings, only to recede again into a forgotten world" (1994, 333–34).

Carol Smith also wrote one of the first articles focusing attention on Maya activism as a nationalist movement. Highlighting its roots in Maya culture, she argued that "Maya nationalists are attempting to create and sustain a Maya cul-ture that will remain vital and alive even as small peasant communities suc-cumb to the pressures of war and modernity. A full generation ago there were more Maya traders, artisans, and workers than corn farmers. Today there are more Maya living in cities, plantations, and refugee camps than in the self-enclosed communities of the past" (1991, 33). This demographic shift is worth noting in situating contemporary Maya activism in a more historical perspec-tive.[15] On one level, the intellectual, or symbolic, frame for Maya nationalism is ladino colonialism. Cojtí's perspective is rather straightforward. He sees the time period from Pedro de Alvarado's invasion until the Revolution of 1944 as a period of subordinate relations between the dominant Mestizo population and the "Indian nationalities." The internal colonialism suffered in the contemporary period, even at times in the context of the human rights movement, is one of pressure for "assimilation or ethnic fusion" (1994, 15). Neither of these options, at its best, can be effective, because each builds upon the economic, political, and cultural subordination of the indigenous people in the present.

The assimilationist or acculturationist project requires that "the Indian nation be absorbed by and within the Ladino nation" (Cojtí Cuxil 1994, 18). Cojtí faults this project for focusing only on external factors such as language or dress, since even if Maya were to give up such cultural markers, they would not necessarily be accepted by Ladinos. When other factors such as economics are considered, prevailing neoliberal strategies attempt to replace the historically disadvantageous position of the indigenous population in the Guatemalan and world labor markets by integrating them into the modern economy as consumers and producers of real goods and services. Acculturation, then, is perceived as an attempt to replace the barbarity of Maya culture with the civility of the Ladino, who only lifts up Maya culture when the need is to emphasize the age or uniqueness of Guatemala before the international community.[16] Cojtí's response to this distinction between civilization and barbarity is scathing: "The recent tortures of citizens for political reasons are not a good representation of civilized conduct on the part of the mestizo public administration" (1994, 19).

Ultimately, Cojtí's critique of the state's syncretistic project is that it legitimates the "cultural genocide" of the Maya. This is intimately related to his view of the internal colonial nature of the Ladino-dominated state in Guatemala as one in which the ethnocide of the Maya is both sanctioned and carried out by means of violence and repression. This is sanctioned by a legal system that does not recognize the Maya as a nation while it symbolically privileges *mestizaje* (the fusion of the Maya with the European) in the construction of Guatemalan national culture. Rather than generating a fusion of Maya and Hispanic into a single biological and cultural (i.e., national) entity, the project of *mestizaje* results in "a predominance of Hispanic culture and a degrading of the Maya" (Cojtí Cuxil 1994, 23).

Maya nationalist discourse transcends the perspective of its critics, who sometimes argue that it is merely the latest in a string of rather sophisticated theories of victimization (cf. Warren 1998). While this discourse is rooted in a recognition of the marginality of the Maya within Guatemalan political and social space, and of the repression of the Maya people at the hands of the state, it is also a constructivist project seeking to engage the state with a defined social and political agenda growing out of that state's creation of ethnic divisions through the discussion of abstractions like "the Indian problem."

As a political project, Maya nationalism is a pluralistic alternative to the current construction of Guatemala as a state dominated by the culture of one ethnic group, that of the Mestizo or Ladino. It does not seek to discount that culture, but it insists that Maya culture be recognized on equal terms within the context of the nation. While drawing upon terms of political discourse such as "democracy," terms of social discourse such as "participation," and terms of moral discourse such as "social justice" and "human rights," it bases its agenda on a cultural or ethnic perspective while incorporating insights from other disciplines into its analysis and proposals. It is a view of the nation as an imagined and constructed "community" (B. Anderson 1991), corresponding to a pan-Maya nationalist vision founded on a union of the various Maya linguistic and cultural communities within Guatemala. Other references even seem to envision a movement spanning national boundaries and uniting all of the various Maya nationalities in Guatemala, Mexico, Honduras, and Belize (Cojtí Cuxil 1994, 11; Montejo 1999, 187–89).

In the movement at large, Maya nationalist discourse and processes of ethnic renewal are partially rooted in interpretations of international law focusing on individual and group rights (including the rights of nations) and concern for such cultural rights as *ley consuetudinaria* (customary law), which recognizes indigenous ways of dealing with communal legal problems (Dary F. 1997; Ordóñez Cifuentes 1997), as well as with definitions of ethnic identity and modes of spirituality.

Relating Religion to Ethnicity and the State

The discussion so far has given more attention to ethnicity and the Guatemalan state than to religion within the context of Maya ethnic renewal. This is a fair picture of the manner in which religion seems to play a supporting role in Maya activism and Maya nationalism. It is not an unimportant role, but one that complements the role of language, historical cultural continuity, and the emphasis on place as distinguishing markers of ethnic identity. This accords with the view of Alan LeBaron, who, in one of the early examinations of the pan-Maya movement in Guatemala, concludes that "[r]eligion as a Maya cultural marker has not become a significant rallying point" (1993, 278). The argument can even be made that language is often the primary cultural marker of ethnicity in segments of the movement. In the words of the coeditors of the seminal volume *Maya Cultural Activism in Guatemala:* "As a banner for ethnic pride, the Mayan languages are appropriate because, unlike many other cultural elements, they have remained largely intact throughout the centuries of foreign incursions and upheaval in Guatemala" (Fischer and Brown 1996, 14).

Religion is largely absent from the discussion, although Carol Hendrick-

son notes that the Academy of Mayan Languages of Guatemala promotes revitalization in terms of indigenous religious practice (*costumbre*) among other
elements of culture, such as indigenous dress (*traje*) (Hendrickson 1996, 159).
Regarding Protestantism in particular, the two entries in the book's index direct the reader either to economic reasons for conversion (Brown 1996, 167)
or to activities of linguists of the Summer Institute of Linguistics as representatives of evangelical churches in opposition to the unified Maya alphabet promoted by the academy. While Brown recognizes some of the division within
the Maya community between the movement leadership and other Maya, Nora
England argues that the issue in this conflict is one of control over who deter-
mines the alphabet (1996, 184). Perhaps as much by what is not said, these brief
references promote the standard line that evangelical religion is a disempowering and culturally destructive force within Maya communities. Although this
is certainly true on some levels, it does little to help in understanding the implications of the tremendous growth of evangelical religion since the 1960s
in Guatemala among the Maya as well as the Ladino population. More recent
works do pay more attention to the issue, sometimes even noting the tensions
within the pan-Maya movement itself. Particularly insightful is Edward Fischer
in his *Cultural Logics and Global Economics:* "In many ways, religion presents
the greatest threat to Maya unity, highlighting ideological differences with the
weight of religious fervor. Protestant evangelization, in particular, has been the
subject of much criticism from pan-Maya leaders for destroying local bases of
culture and encouraging ladinoization. Yet, in Tecpán and Patzún at least, religious affiliation is not necessarily incompatible with any particular ethnic affiliation. Indeed, ethnicity is the most pervasive vector of self-identity and
plays a more prominent role in shaping individual agency" (2001, 189).

Although in the early 1990s some predictions saw Guatemala as majority
Protestant by the turn of the millennium, a study by Grossman (2002), based
on research carried out in late 2000 and early 2001 in conjunction with the
Servicio Evangelizadora para America Latina (SEPAL, Evangelizing Service
for Latin America), found that evangelicals made up only 25.4 percent of the
population.[17] Assuming that the percentage holds among the Maya population (and growth rates have tended to be higher among indigenous and rural
populations in Mesoamerica), one simply cannot write off roughly a quarter
of that population as victims of foreign impositions.[18] A more interesting perspective, in line with my own research, is to address how indigenous populations use religion for their own purposes in either a political or spiritual sense.
The ethnographic approach to religion, grounded in a humanistic perspective,
is broad enough to take into account the complexities of various kinds of relationships between religion and ethnicity in Guatemala and throughout Mesoamerica. My thinking here applies to methodological concerns regarding the

place of ethnography in anthropology and to more nuanced scholarly evalua-
tions of Protestantisms throughout Latin America that have appeared since the
early 1990s (Bastian 1992, 1993; Deiros 1991; Garrard-Burnett 1992; Garrard-
Burnett and Stoll 1993; Miller 1994; Hallum 1996; Cleary and Stewart-Gambino 1997; Míguez Bonino 1997; B. Smith 1998; Sanchíz Ochoa 1998; C. Gros
1999; Le Bot 1999; Levine 2000; Drogus 2000; Dow and Sandstrom 2001; Chiappari 2002).[19]

Religion, then, in its many guises in Guatemala—Maya, indigenous Catholic,
orthodox Catholic, activist Catholic, historical Protestant, Pentecostal, and neo-
Pentecostal—articulates in varied and complex ways with ethnicity and the
state as well as within local community contexts. In terms of Maya ethnic renewal, this is seen in the 1995 Accord on the Identity and Rights of the Indigenous Peoples. The Acuerdo Indígena insists that national unity can only be
constructed on the basis of the acknowledgment of the identity of indigenous
peoples, and that part of this identity resides in "a cosmovision that is based
on the harmonious relation between all the elements of the universe, in which
the human being is only one element more, the earth is the mother that gives
life, and maize is the sacred sign, the way of its culture. This cosmovision has
been transmitted from generation to generation through material production
and writing and through oral tradition, in which women have played a determinative role" (Cabrera and Cifuentes 1997, 81). Even in the light of the critique of the peace process as exclusionary of Maya presence, this is a significant
statement exemplifying some of the underlying aspects and concerns of Maya
spirituality when it is manifest in the public arena (cf. Wuqub' Iq' 1997).[20]

The Maya community's confrontation with religious diversity shows the
complexity of the religious dimension in contemporary Guatemala. At the
Segundo Conferencia sobre el Popol Wuj, held in Quetzaltenango in May
1999, participants from numerous Maya communities struggled with putting
together a *memorial* (summary of the events) of the weeklong conference fea-
turing academic presentations (both Maya and North American) and numerous
workshops led by Maya themselves concerning issues such as youth, the role of
women in society, and fundamentalist churches. During the discussion, moves
were made by a group of Maya priests and others to insert language encouraging a *decristianización* (de-Christianization) of Maya religion because Christianity has so *satanizado* (satanized or demonized) Maya religious practices. Finally, a woman in *traje* was recognized to speak. Speaking against this notion,
she bluntly said, "Pertenezco a una iglesia Maya" (I belong to a Maya church).
For that moment, her words carried the day; *decristianizar* did not appear in the
memorial. Yet the conference had begun in the courtyard of a Roman Catholic
retreat center when participants bowed in the four cardinal directions and
kissed Mother Earth at the behest of a Maya priest.[21]

From my perspective, religion plays a largely auxiliary role in the Maya movement in contemporary Guatemala. This is not to say religion is unimportant, but it is often used for purposes of identity formation in the context of larger social and political agendas having to do with indigenous rights and access to political and social space in the midst of movements for social change. Religious pluralism is manifest in ways that reflect ideals of ethnic pluralism. While perhaps determinative of neither the social relations within the nation-state nor particular agendas of the state, religion has an ideological force that makes its consideration important in the cultural explanations of contemporary Guatemala.

Maya nationalism in Guatemala brings together and extends perspectives on ethnicity and religion elsewhere in Mesoamerica, perspectives that either have given primary attention to the construction of indigenous identity in opposition to colonial powers (Friedlander 1975; Hawkins 1984) or have focused on the construction of ethnicity in the local context with religion as the core component of ethnic identity (Sandstrom 1991, 1992). In Guatemala, the renewal of Maya identity takes place within the space of the Guatemalan state and with a focus squarely on the cultural as opposed to the religious essence. Richard Adams situates the construction of "the Maya" in historical context when he states that "the Mayas of Guatemala triumphed in the invention of a new ethnic group: the Maya, which did not exist in 1950, but which many Maya clearly acknowledge exists now. . . . Often ethnicities need to redefine themselves, although in recent history not many cases of ethnic expansion have been observed" (1995, 410). Looking at the "ethnic reorganization and redefinition" taking place in contemporary Guatemala, he notes that it is "part of an evolutionary process that obliges changes in the definitions of ancestral models and introduces a new terminology" (410). A number of works have dealt with the relationship between ethnic identity and nation-states (Díaz Polanco 1997; Maybury-Lewis 1997; Roosens 1989; Young 1993), suggesting a broadened focus in the consideration of local or regional movements built on ethnic consciousness.[22]

Rather than focusing on the idea of "new ethnicities" as such, I suggest that the focus remain on the articulation of religion with projects of ethnic renewal and the relationship of either or both to the nation-state. Ultimately, as the case of the Maya movement demonstrates, the issues are distinct but interrelated. Religious practice and ethnic identity are simultaneously constructed and essential in the sense that they are often based on the perception of cultural essence defined as traditional. Understandings of the traditional as well as the constructive act of defining and redefining ethnic (and religious) identity take place in relation to social, political, and cultural forces that are larger than the group itself. This is the locus of structure in the sense used by Sahlins

(1999) and referred to by Watanabe (1999) as "procedural culture." This open-ended, processual view of culture as at once bounded and creative is consistent with a pluralistic model of religious expression and ethnicity among the Maya in Guatemala.

The next chapter provides an organizational perspective on the history of the missionary movement toward evangelization among the Maya in the early decades of the twentieth century. I then examine two Maya organizations that have been associated with political organizing and development activities from an identity rooted in both Maya and evangelical culture. The discussion is significant because it shows the engagement of evangelicals with political and social events during the last decade of the war. While not holding these groups up as direct examples of religious social movements, I do see their activities as reflective of how religious resources can be mobilized in the interest of social and political activism. Moreover, those resources are mobilized from the standpoint of ethnic identity, thus highlighting Maya-ness as a basis for mobilization. This discussion also provides a frame for looking at the interplay between culture and ethnicity in the Mam and Kaqchikel presbyteries in subsequent chapters.

4
Maya Protestantism in Guatemala

"Giving voice" should be considered one of the basic goals of good social science. . . . [M]any Latin Americans under different circumstances *have*
given voice: They have pressed for the restoration of rights that they felt
came to be denied, sought retribution for past wrongs, and asserted rights
they previously did not enjoy but to which they have come to feel entitled.
—Susan Eva Eckstein and Timothy B. Wickham-Crowley,
Struggles for Social Rights in Latin America

Missionary Beginnings and a Movement toward the Maya

Missionary Protestantism in Guatemala was not originally directed toward
the native population. The story has often been told of how liberal president
Justo Rufino Barrios invited the first evangelical missionary to the country
following a visit to New York that included a meeting with the Presbyterian
Board of Foreign Missions of the Presbyterian Church in the United States of
America.[1] That first missionary, John Clark Hill, did enter Guatemala in the
president's entourage in 1882, although the exact sequence of events and the
reasoning behind the invitation remain obscure.[2] This establishes from early
on the perception of Protestant ties to the ruling class and the concomitant
impression, which dogs the evangelical community to this day, that it is sup-
portive of the political status quo even when that status quo is represented
by repressive political powers who ignore the rule of law or impose authori-
tarian rule on their population. This is especially true of the perception of
evangelicals in relation to the presidency of Ríos Montt in 1982 and 1983 and
the atrocities of that epoch. Although I hope this study contributes to a more
complex reading of that history, this is not the moment to debate those particular charges, beyond observing that any assessment of the issue requires a
methodology that moves beyond the consideration of insider and outsider dynamics of particular congregations (or even congregational segments) in relation to their denominations and the religious field in a particular country. The
methodology also needs to attend to local and translocal relationships in assessing the role Christianity plays in processes of social change (Peterson, Vásquez,
and Williams 2001).[3]

A second issue is the rationale of the liberal governments in inviting evangelicals to Latin America in the first instance.[4] There is no reason here to depart from the accepted idea that it was part of the larger wave of modernization that went under the name of Positivism in the latter part of the nineteenth century. The idea that technological innovation, particularly in relation to transportation and communications, would revolutionize societies and contribute to social and economic progress in "backward" regions of the world is one aspect of this. In the Mesoamerican context, factors such as the perceived contribution of missionaries not only in bringing progress to the region but also in "whitening" the population of dark skin color and ignorance surely played a role. The effort to bring in lighter-skinned immigrants who would provide innovation in economic areas dated in Guatemala to the early liberal period in the decade following independence from Spain, particularly the days of the Central American Federation (formally, United Provinces of Central America, 1823–39) and, in Guatemala, the government of Mariano Gálvez (1831–38).

Sullivan-González reports how the Catholic Church was targeted by the leader of the federation, Francisco Morazán, who "exiled the archbishop to Havana, closed down most male and female regular orders, suspended the collection of the tithe, and expropriated clerical property. Marriage soon became a civil ceremony, with divorce proceedings permitted in civil court" (1998, 8). By 1837, when Rafael Carrera rose up against Gálvez in the wake of a cholera epidemic, the government had also distributed "large portions of Guatemala's arable land to a fly-by-night British colonization company" (8). Although the company was unsuccessful, Sullivan-González says that "this did not overshadow the implications of the state-initiated policy: foreigners—Protestants by faith—were making headway in an area where arable land was growing scarcer by the day" (8). At its base, liberal policy manifested an openness to other parts of the world and to modernization and secularization. The longer trajectory of this mode of thinking is particularly reflected in Guatemala's second liberal period, beginning with the liberal revolt of Miguel García Granados and Barrios in 1871. From that period until the present, the idea that progress was partially to be found in efforts to change the nation's ethnic composition has shaped the assimilationist policies that have been part of the national agenda. While the pan-Maya Movement and other forms of rhetoric such as that of interculturality (*interculturalidad*) challenge this notion today, the attack on the Maya population during the war demonstrates its pervasiveness in national consciousness. At the middle of the nineteenth century, this tendency among the Liberals makes it less than surprising that Guatemala's indigenous communities rather welcomed the Conservative rebellion that brought Carrera to power. Native communities were allowed to maintain their distinctive space in relation to the larger nation with less internal interference (Carmack 1995, 125–34).

As has been noted, the equation of ignorance and superstition was not extended to the indigenous population alone. The Roman Catholic Church was also seen as impeding progress to some degree and, in the liberal vision, as a direct threat to political power. As a result, liberal reform movements in Mexico and Guatemala were directed at breaking the power of the Roman Catholic Church in the national context. The early liberal attack on church privilege in Guatemala predates the better-known liberal reforms of Mexico, which, beginning in the 1850s, were never rolled back and became particularly intense under the revolutionary governments of the first two decades following the end of the Mexican Revolution in 1917. In Mexico this was symbolized by the fact that the Constitution of 1857, promulgated under indigenous president Benito Juárez, had no clause establishing the Roman Catholic Church as the official church or religion of the Mexican nation.[5]

In the case of Guatemala, Barrios's decree of religious liberty on 15 March 1873 opened the doors to the freedom to practice other religions.[6] In fact, a provision for toleration had existed since the Gálvez administration in 1832 and had never been stricken from the legal code (Garrard-Burnett 1998a, 11). Interestingly, the rendition of this law provided in the National Presbyterian Church's *Apuntes para la historia,* published for the centennial of Presbyterian work in Guatemala, throws a bone to the Roman Catholic Church in the form of a disclaimer that other religions would not be afforded more freedom than the Roman Catholic Church itself. In this manner, the national governments in both countries asserted their authority over the dominant religious community that had been linked to state power throughout the colonial period. Again, Sullivan-González reports that by the end of 1871 the liberals had issued decrees expelling the Jesuit community and sending the Guatemalan archbishop into exile (1998, 121).

This is not to deny continued influence by the Roman Catholic Church in subsequent time periods, but it illustrates how religious conflict has played out at the national level as well as the role of the churches in responding to that conflict. David Carey's work on Kaqchikel Maya historical self-understandings highlights the view that Barrios took on the Roman Catholic Church by using the force of other religious traditions. Carey quotes Barrios directly as evidence of his antipathy toward Catholicism: "It has been more than three centuries that [Guatemala] has been governed under the oligarchic-theocratic regimen. The government has been backward and despotic; the clergy has enjoyed the highest privilege and meddled in everything. And what have they [the people] been given in compensation for so much sacrifice? Nothing, absolutely nothing!" (cited in Carey 2001, 223, emendations in Carey).[7] Taken together, this gives some weight to Bogenschild's understanding of the genesis

of the idea of inviting missionaries, the suggestion that "Barrios' initial rationale for soliciting Protestant missionaries stemmed more from pragmatic political considerations than from affinity with (or understanding of) Protestant
ideology" (1992, 37).

In Guatemala, policies reflecting traditional liberal interests were in place
under various president-dictators until Jorge Ubico was overthrown in the
Revolution of 1944. This did not mean that the Roman Catholic Church was
in any particular overt conflict with the government or displaced in terms of
access to the reaches of government power, but church-state relations were
not a dominant theme during most of the first four decades of the twentieth century.

Important from the point of view of the historiography of Guatemalan
evangelicalism is the evangelical involvement in a nationwide literacy campaign early in the administration of Juan José Arévalo (1945–50). Although
Garrard-Burnett reports that Arévalo appointed a Presbyterian named Antonio
Guerra to lead the campaign, evangelicalism was not a component of his
"spiritual socialism," which "was grounded almost entirely in traditionally liberal, secular ideas of what constituted metaphysical enrichment" (1998a, 80).
The government itself encouraged the Evangelical Synod (founded in 1935
from the five "historical" denominations in Guatemala) that organized the
work with "a small grant of ten thousand dollars from the Presbyterian Church
in the United States" (82).[8] Work was done in Spanish and in the K'iche' and
Mam languages alongside government reading programs (82–83).[9] Participation in the literacy program has been seen as a singular example of proactive
evangelical involvement in Guatemalan politics at the national level. Apart
from the implication that evangelicals are apolitical or right-wing in political
orientation, another hindrance in this regard has been the evangelical tendency
to fragment, in part a tendency related to each individual's or group's retain-
ing the right to interpret Scripture on the basis of their particular understanding of how God's spirit is working within the community.[10]

On another level, Dennis Smith and James Grenfell suggest that the possibility of evangelical contributions to national reconciliation in Guatemala
depends upon the community's ability to address both "the lack of democratic tradition in [evangelical] churches and the lack of an ecumenical spirit"
(1999, 33). A more complete view of evangelical political involvement after
the turn of the millennium has to note evangelical involvement in some civil
society discussions relative to the peace talks between the government and the
URNG in the early 1990s and the participation of both the Alianza Evangélica and Catholic leaders in the creation of a consensus counterproposal to the
Codigo de la Niñez y la Juventud that was approved by the Guatemalan congress

in 1996. The code created considerable controversy related to family values and paternal authority in the household, and the government postponed its entrance into force indefinitely in February 2000.[11]

Early Presbyterian missionary efforts were directed toward the urban population, often the elite, in Guatemala City. Social outreach, especially in the form of schools, was a part of all the early missions, although Garrard-Burnett indicates that the emphasis was often less on education than on evangelization (1998a, 27–35).[12] Besides schools, the Presbyterians had also established the Hospital Americano by 1913.[13] Outside the capital, Scotchmer reports, one of the early Presbyterian missionaries, Eugene McBath, had been assigned to Quetzaltenango by 1903 and had begun outreach "in Spanish among both Quiché and the Mam people" (1991, 96).[14] Garrard-Burnett indicates that McBath's resignation from the mission in 1913 had to do with the mission's attitude toward the native population (1998a, 52).[15] In the Mam region, a missionary couple, Linn and Jessie Sullenberger, began worshipping in San Juan Ostuncalco as early as 1911.[16] The first truly noteworthy work among indigenous peoples was carried out by the Central American Mission (CAM) under the leadership of Cameron Townsend in the Kaqchikel region near San Antonio Aguascalientes. Townsend had begun selling Bibles in Guatemala in 1917, and by 1919 he had begun work on translating the New Testament into the local language. Garrard-Burnett notes that this was "in flagrant violation of his mission's mandate" but that the work was completed by 1929 (1998a, 53).[17]

A major chapter in the history of Presbyterian work with the Maya began when Paul and Dora Burgess arrived in Guatemala in 1913 and began working in Spanish-speaking congregations in the Quetzaltenango area the following year. Scotchmer reports that Paul pushed for someone to work with the Mam from an early date (1991, 96–98). Paul Burgess was also instrumental in a January 1921 meeting in Chichicastenango in which missionaries from several denominations formed the Latin American Indian Mission.[18] The goal of this "agency" was to deal with the evangelization of indigenous peoples from the base of policies formulated in the field rather than from offices in the United States (98–99). Work in the native languages was highlighted (despite controversy with mission agencies back home). Paul Burgess printed a translation of the Gospel of John by 1923, while Dora "directed the Quiché New Testament translation effort to completion in 1947" (101). Scotchmer says that "Paul dedicated his time to grass-roots Indian evangelization, historical and evangelistic writing, establishing a print shop and a Protestant bookstore, and the founding of the Quiché Bible Institute in 1941 (eventually located in San Christobal [sic], Totonicapan) for the training of Indian leaders in the vernacular."[19]

Apuntes para la historia reports that Presbyterian work in the departments of Quetzaltenango and Retalhuleu, part of San Marcos, and most of Suchitepéquez was directed from Quetzaltenango.[20] The work cites reports from missionary Horacio Dudley Peck in 1924 indicating that there were fourteen sites among the Mam where national *obereros* (workers) were giving pastoral attention. By 1926 Peck reported that work in the area had been divided, with him and his wife, Dorothy, working in the Mam-speaking areas, Paul and Dora Burgess in the places where the K'iche' language dominated, and James Hayter among Spanish speakers (IENPG 1982, 256–57).[21]

This discussion has examined the move toward the indigenous population and the concern for evangelization in the context of native languages (if not native culture as such). As Bogenschild acknowledges, "Presbyterian missionaries in Quezaltenango were well aware of the indigenous population in the highlands" (1992, 158). This awareness, however, was not without its own paradoxes. A factor that came into play briefly in the context of the formation of ethnic presbyteries in the second half of the century was that "[t]he missionaries were also unwilling to segregate their congregations by ethnicity" (Garrard-Burnett 1998a, 52). This was ironic not only because of the segregation that predominated on the home front at this time but also, she suspects, because "the missionaries, like many Guatemalans in the same period, considered 'Indianness' to be less an ethnic identity than a problematic social condition for which they had a remedy" (52).

This move toward the Maya population on the part of the evangelical missionaries found fertile ground in Maya communities, which had already experienced considerable disruption in the wake of liberal social and economic policy. In terms of Roman Catholicism, Garrard-Burnett credits Catholic Action, beginning in the 1940s, with having broken some of the "local hegemony of *costumbre*" in Guatemala (1996, 101).[22] The breakdown in *costumbre* is a key to understanding both village-level Catholicism and changing community authority structures in the twentieth century. Catholic Action itself was one response of the church to the continuing presence of Maya beliefs and practices in local communities, as well as to the accommodations made by the indigenous peoples of Mesoamerica during the colonial period and throughout the early first century of independence, when they were relatively free to develop their own religious traditions with some degree of autonomy from the church.[23] In the Guatemalan case, the movement seems to have fragmented into at least two branches, one focusing more on Catholic orthodoxy and another focused more on community social change. Both branches participated in efforts at social change on the local level, with the more orthodox proponents fitting more into a model of reform-oriented change and the more liberal group focused on structural change, in some cases embracing a model of revolution. More research is needed in this area, but the latter group probably began to have more affinity with liberation theology as the 1970s progressed.

Open embracing of this tendency decreased in the face of the repression of the early 1980s, particularly after the Spanish Embassy was burned following its occupation by militants associated with the Committee of Campesino Unity (CUC) in 1980. It did manifest itself (without embracing the overt language of liberation theology) in the form of groups associated with social change across ethnic lines. Other groups, such as the Guatemalan Church in Exile, continued to influence events in Guatemala after Bishop Juan Gerardi pulled all priests and religious from the department of Quiché in 1980 when they were targeted in the repression (Berryman 1994, 110–11). Such groups began to reemerge after the return to formal democracy in the mid-1980s, although associating oneself directly with liberation theology was the equivalent of having a death warrant.

Garrard-Burnett notes that Catholic Action has diverged in various countries and sometimes according to class agendas (1996, 112 n. 16). One of the primary changes in Maya communities would seem to be that associated with leadership conflict between generations, wherein the younger *catequistas* (catechists) began to usurp the traditional authority of the elders in the communal authority structure (Warren 1989). This was also one of the impacts of Protestantism in the town of Aguacatán in the western highlands, mentioned in chapter 1 (Brintnall 1979).[24] Ricardo Falla's (2001) study of conversion in San Antonio Ilotenango casts yet another light on the movement in view of social change in Guatemala in the late 1960s and early 1970s.[25]

To return briefly to the evangelical situation, evangelical growth was slow in Guatemala until it began to increase more significantly around 1960. Statistical analysis by Henri Gooren (2001, 181) suggests that Protestantism rose from 1 to 2 percent of the population in the late 1930s to perhaps 5 percent by 1960. Additionally, he reports that this period saw twelve new denominations added to the twelve already present in the country by 1935. The highest rates of growth during this period were among the Assemblies of God, who entered Guatemala in 1935, and the Seventh-Day Adventists, who had established a presence as early as 1916. Everett Wilson (1997, 143) also cites 1916 as the date for the first churches of the Pentecostal Iglesia de Dios del Evangelio Completo (Full Gospel Church of God), although it is not in Gooren's list of the fastest-growing churches during this period. Garrard-Burnett (1998a, 37) mentions the arrival of the Church of God in 1934 and the defection of a Primitive Methodist minister, Charles Furman (apparently a Pentecostal when he arrived in Guatemala in 1916), to that denomination in the same year. She reports that the historic denominations in Guatemala reacted to this upsurge in activity by forming the Evangelical Synod in 1935 and, at last, formalizing the comity agreement from early in the century (40).[26] This constituted a source of tension that continues to affect the Protestant community in Guatemala.

While growth in the historic denominations slowed or leveled off, Everett Wilson reports that "in the 1950s the Pentecostals grew from 12 percent to 33 percent" of Guatemalan evangelicals (1997, 145). This is reflective of the growth in adherents in both Pentecostal groups and faith missions throughout Latin America during the same period.[27]

For the Presbyterians, growth was moderate, and the period was one of increasing institutionalization. The denomination (along with the Evangelical Synod) supported the literacy campaign during the Arévalo administration (Garrard-Burnett 1998a, 84–85; Gooren 2001, 183; D. Smith and Grenfell 1999), though relations began to cool by the end of his term in office. When Arbenz came into the presidency, his baptism by Paul Burgess did not predispose him to favor Protestant mission activities, and Garrard-Burnett devotes several paragraphs to the way in which Arbenz's nationalism affected missionary activity by making it difficult to obtain residency and changing the credentialing process for teaching in rural schools (1998a, 88–91). Nevertheless, between 1939 and 1950 three presbyteries were added to the two existing ones, and in May 1950 the Presbyterian Synod was established.

One of the key events in the denomination took place in 1959 when the first Maya presbytery, the Presbytery Maya Quiché, was established. It was created out of the Occidente Presbytery, which had been organized in 1923 and had congregations throughout the Quetzaltenango highlands. Three of the reasons given for the founding of the presbytery are particularly interesting from the standpoint of Protestantism in the Maya wing of the IENPG. They manifest a marked tension between acculturative tendencies and the desire to respect indigenous culture that is at least sometimes present in contexts such as Guatemala, where conversion and conviviality in institutional terms clash:

1. To instruct the churches in spiritual life, because it is noted that many Maya-Quiché believers still have not put aside certain traditions (*costumbres*), some vices, and superstitions.
2. To give more attention to evangelization using the Quiché language in order to communicate the Gospel.
3. To train Quiché-speaking leaders. (IENPG 1982, 282)

The list gives more verbiage (and possibly more importance) to the need for an authentic conversion that does away with *costumbre,* but there is no real reason to doubt the concern for leadership development or the desire to preach, as it were, in the K'iche' language. A fourth reason for establishing the presbytery had to do with encouraging better cooperation between the synod and the presbytery. I assume that "the presbytery" was the new one, or at least the Maya-speaking element of the old one. The rationale highlights the fact that various issues in the synod were not understood by the K'iche', with the result that "necessary cooperation was not accomplished."

To some extent, the four reasons raise a number of issues that were still alive in the denomination when I was in the field—issues that made the IENPG something of a microcosm of ethnic relations in Guatemala as a whole. The Maya representation in the annual synod meeting was large enough to dominate the voting on any number of issues, and coalitions were often made in electing leaders and around other causes. Yet the meetings were conducted almost entirely in Spanish, and the commissioners to the meeting (ministers and elders from each presbytery) were given a book of approximately two hundred pages that consisted of minutes from prior meetings and other kinds of information for action during the five-day event. There are many ways to analyze the scene I am depicting, but from either an anthropological or a missiological perspective, the issues stated at the time of the formation of the first ethnic presbytery provide useful guides for examining the power relations within the denomination, as well as the question with which I began this work: What does it mean to be both Maya and evangelical in Guatemala?[28]

Maya Evangelical Organizations in Context

Recent examples of organizing from the standpoint of Maya evangelicals include two organizations essentially established by Maya Presbyterians: the Hermandad de Presbiterios Mayas (HPM, Brotherhood of Maya Presbyteries) and the Conferencia de Iglesias Evangélicas de Guatemala (CIEDEG, Guatemalan Conference of Evangelical Churches). They were established for different purposes. The former was focused more on internal issues within the IENPG, while the latter established relationships with a broader international constituency even as it constructed an organizational framework that dealt with social issues within Guatemala. I discuss them both in order to give examples of organizing among different segments of the Maya evangelical community during the difficult times of the war years and beyond. A subtheme is the relationship with the international community that mirrors larger tensions within Guatemala over what role (perceived or real) the international community should play in terms of post-conflict politics.

The subtheme needs to be addressed first, because it affects whether denominations like the IENPG and associated organizations can in any way be seen as representative of the tension within the country as a whole over ethnic relations and political organizing. First, an entire debate over the role of the United Nations Mission for the Verification of Human Rights in Guatemala (MINUGUA) often came down to whether the international community should have a say in the internal affairs of a country such as Guatemala as it recovers from war and experiences a lengthy period of national reconciliation whose outcome hangs in the balance well more than a decade after the signing of the final peace accord. The critique some lodged against the role of MINUGUA seems flawed given the extent of globalization in political and economic affairs and the role of international juridical institutions in attempting to mete out imperfect justice in the face of genocide and ethnic cleansing in many parts of the world.

In effect, the involvement of the international community facilitates the construction of a space for dialogue where it might otherwise be absent. Such dialogical space provides a context for both negotiation and the possibility of reconciliation in the wake of the atrocities committed in Guatemala. Negotiation takes a number of cultural forms, all of which are bolstered when there is interchange between the local and the international community—for example, *testimonios* such as those of Rigoberta Menchú and Victor Montejo that bear witness to the violence, truth commissions designed to set the record straight, and norms for human rights that have some applicability across national boundaries. Susanne Jonas (2000) and Paul Jeffrey (1998) have documented the role of the international community in bringing the Guatemalan government and the URNG to the negotiating table (cf. Sieder 1998; R. Wilson 1998).[29] This is not an argument against national autonomy or sovereignty; nor am I ignoring the possibility that international institutions can be and often are manipulated by more powerful members of the body. My perspective, however, recognizes that the global community has a role to play in processes of national reconciliation and oversight in cases where violence is rampant. Moreover, some are now making the philosophical argument in the age of globalization that the time of the nation-state is past and that more decentralized groups (ethnic, religious, etc.) will hold sway in both local and transnational fields of activity. While this remains to be seen, there is room for seeing the international community not as a monolith that seeks to impose from the outside, but as a more diffuse entity that brings great experience and alternative perspectives to bear on particular situations of violence or injustice.

Second, much of the discussion in Guatemala involves the space in which MINUGUA was allowed to function. The organization had limited power beyond its mandate to document violations of human rights abuses. Some have been frustrated by the fact that "MINUGUA didn't do anything" in response to particular cases of injustice or violations of personal or group rights. At least some of this was related precisely to the mission's role to document as opposed to involving itself directly in solving particular problems. This was an attempt to preserve the autonomy of Guatemalan institutions, but it resulted in some ambiguity regarding the role of the mission. In a state that continues to retain reserved domains of power for the military and police forces (not so far behind the scenes), this work of oversight is invaluable. In September 2003 the general secretary of the United Nations, Kofi Annan, requested an extension of the mission's mandate until the end of 2004. At that juncture, the mission, which had been decreasing in size for several years, was closed.

A final comment on the issue of international involvement comes from the larger evangelical community itself. Jeffrey records a commentary by long-time Presbyterian missionary Dennis Smith regarding the role of international funding for a particular religious group. The statement is a retrospective view on the issue of how some segments of the international evangelical community might have contributed to prolonging the war, even after it was clear that the guerrillas would never win. It can also be seen as commentary on the tendency for patronage networks to be created in relationships between people and groups living in and shaped by very different contexts. The organization in question was

> created by people in New York and Geneva who desperately needed people to talk to in Guatemala who talked like they did, because they didn't have a clue how to talk to the 97 percent of the Protestant community deeply influenced by North American fundamentalism. So those people in Geneva and New York found some local folks who were willing to spout their particular line and then they gave them a blank check to implement a program . . . and participated in Latin American professional conciliar ecumenism. It started out with several people of good faith but degenerated into an institution that became a front organization for the insurgents. (Jeffrey 1998, 95)

His intent is to provide an institutional critique of the churches, so he continues:

> When local religious groups were not able to imagine nonviolent activist alternatives of civil disobedience to confront the horror that was going on here, we convinced, with our rhetoric, a number of international church-related agencies that the revolution must be baptized. . . . It's clear to me that some international church-related organizations and especially some staff working in those organizations desperately needed to support and finance the Guatemalan revolution and desperately needed to baptize it and needed it to play guerrilla. I use that phrase because, thinking back in my own experience of the late 1970s and early 1980s, when first approached by a revolutionary organization, it was enormously seductive—especially being a foreigner and being convinced of the rhetoric of incarnation and rhetoric of solidarity and contextualization—to be asked

by local colleagues to belong to a national revolutionary movement. But what it came down to was being seduced to play guerrilla. (95–96)

This commentary is a moving reflection on the experience of living through violence and revolutionary movements as something of an outsider during Guatemala's difficult years. Ultimately, the issue is one of accountability for how resources are used in particular contexts. Responsibility wears many faces. Many who have participated in various ways in the Guatemalan revolution and subsequent peace process remain adamant that without the guerrilla movement the government (and particularly the military) would never have taken a seat at the negotiating table.

Returning to the theme of indigenous evangelicalism and the cases of the HPM and CIEDEG, it is important to note that neither organization would exist in the way in which it is currently known without support from the international religious community in the United States, Canada, and Europe. At the same time, both organizations represented Maya in Guatemala in their efforts to appropriate social space (and resources) in the very difficult years of the mid-1980s when the return to democracy presaged the possibility of organizing for social causes anew. In a sense, they form a bridge between the organizing that was taking hold in the country and was so bitterly stifled in the repression of the Lucas García and Ríos Montt years, and the organizing on the basis of culture that coalesced into the Maya Movement by the early 1990s. The key here is the upholding of Maya identity and work within the Maya evangelical community as a cultural base toward which the organizations directed their activities.

While rooted in the larger evangelical community of Guatemala, both organizations use Maya culture as something of an organizing principle and as a justification for why they exist outside of the reach and control of Mestizos. In the late 1990s the Hermandad was defined as "a union of eight presbyteries" representing five of the Maya language groups that have ethnic presbyteries in the IENPG. The description also laid claim to relations with four other presbyteries in the western part of the country and along the southeast coast; these primarily Ladino presbyteries had been fractured and reorganized following the denominational split in 1992. As a call to action and a response to the reality of Guatemalan society, the document claims that, beginning from its "Reformed Inheritance," the Hermandad has an integral concern for both the spiritual and social well-being of society.[30] The organization is said to be integrated into the context of three social forces: the religious sector, the civil sector ("without losing its cultural identity"), and the Maya sector. The latter is understood to be a religious sector in its essence. These can be understood as the spheres of interaction for the Hermandad. While specific issues and agendas have changed through time, a survey of the organization's work over the years indicates that these three spheres have been consistently present. A programmatic document produced by the Hermandad in 1985 and cited in Heinrich Schäfer's sociopolitical survey of the history of the Guatemalan Presbyterian Church provides an interesting summary of the history of the denomination's missionization in relation to other areas of human concern. It first situates the organization's philosophical concerns in relation to the events of the early 1980s and in the context of the centuries of oppression experienced by the Maya at the hands of other groups:

> In our day (1985) the consequences of those horrible situations of misery, pain, discrimination, hunger, etc. have been forcefully felt—those things that affect the great majority of the Maya descendants. . . .
>
> It is for this reason that the indigenous presbyteries of the National Evangelical Presbyterian Church unite—Quichés, Mames, Kekchíes, Cakchiqueles, and Kanjobales—in order to be present in helping our brothers who have been affected over the centuries. (Schäfer 2002, 114–15)

The text reads like a manifesto, justifying action on behalf of those who have been victimized in the past and delineating why the current actors have decided to unite their energies, and more, in response to that victimization. A critique of the blindness of the spiritual emphasis in much Protestant teaching through the decades follows.

> The Presbyterian Church came to our country 103 years ago . . . in the epoch of the triumph of the Liberal Party. The North American missionaries brought us a very spiritualist theology that only considered man as a soul with the task of saving himself from the material world in order to go to Heaven. As good foreigners they did not consider it wise to relate themselves to the social problems of the country, and they taught this to the new Christians as part of Christianity.
>
> Nevertheless, after 20 years they decided to participate in health and education activities. And it was a long time later before they participated in agricultural programs and other forms of human [social] promotion.
>
> At the same time a national leadership was coming into being, but with a reserve of limitations, a concern exclusively with spiritual service. (Schäfer 2002, 115)

Worthy of note here is the perception that the early missionaries were not initially interested in social mission and that the focus on a spirituality divorced from other spheres of human activity persists among sectors of the denomination. Also, although it is alluded to, there is no real mention here of cultural rights as an area of concern. The oppression of the Maya provides the backdrop, and the impetus is to claim space—not only within Guatemalan society but also within the context of the IENPG—to advocate for an end to oppression and violence against the Maya as a group. As already noted, part of the dynamic at work is the move by social groups (as representatives of civil society) to claim space for organizing after the repression of the late 1960s and again in the late 1970s and early 1980s when movements such as cooperatives were often painted either as Communist or as fronts for the guerrillas.

Two points about this claiming of social space can be made here. While there were certainly antecedents, two organizations mentioned in the previous chapter—GAM and CONAVIGUA—were formed at about the same time as HPM, and they even more directly manifest the tendency toward more direct political involvement. The leadership of both groups was predominantly female, and both had as their purpose finding family members who had been disappeared during the violence. While GAM (founded in 1984) had a largely Ladina membership, CONAVIGUA (founded in 1988) had its roots in the Maya population and eventually began to take on structural issues that affected Maya communities, such as forced military recruitment. Although it is often argued that silence has been a key to Maya survival during the five hundred years of conquest, these two groups were among the few voices that consistently challenged the political and social status quo in Guatemala during the 1980s. By the early 1990s, other groups were adding their voices to the protest (Falla 1992; Sinclair 1995).[31]

La Conferencia de Iglesias Evangélicas de Guatemala

Of the two Maya organizations with roots in the evangelical community, CIEDEG has maintained a more prominent profile than the Hermandad, both in terms of its broadly ecumenical approach and in terms of the presence of the organization and leaders in public forums dealing with various kinds of political crises in Guatemala since the signing of the peace. Part of this has to do with CIEDEG's former executive director and guiding personality, Vitalino Similox, a Kaqchikel Presbyterian minister who was also the vice presidential candidate for the Alianza Nueva Nación (ANN, New Nation Alliance) party in the 1999 presidential elections. The ANN placed third in the elections with a ticket headed by Álvaro Colom, who garnered 12.36 percent of the vote in the elections.

Information on CIEDEG's web site claims that the organization was formed in 1987 as the culmination of a process, begun in 1980, that was concerned with "organizing a different type of evangelical expression, with an ecumenical, pluralistic, multicultural and social service vision."[32] The phrasing indicates that considerable energy had been expended in discussion and organizational activities before "coming into the light." Antonio Otzoy, the Hermandad's former executive secretary, made a similar statement to me in regard to the founding of that organization. The implication is that, while organizational activities were taking place during the 1980s, timing was extremely important in taking the decision to openly promote activities that would be perceived as social action in a political sense. It was the return to formal democracy, signaled by the election of Vinicio Cerezo to the presidency in 1985 and the promulgation of the Constitution of 1986, that prompted the wave of more open organizing that continued into the 1990s.

Striking in CIEDEG's self-description is the focus on ecumenism and the transcending of boundaries between historical denominations, the international community, and, to some extent, the Pentecostal community. Likewise, the organization is forthright in claiming to have participated in the "process of national reconciliation" that led to the final peace. This emphasis is consistent with CIEDEG's having participated in several commissions of the Diálogo Nacional (National Dialogue) that was set in motion by 1989 as a step toward peace and national reconciliation. This step began with the establishment of the Comisión Nacional de Reconciliación (CNR, National Reconciliation Commission) on the heels of the Esquipulas II peace accord signed by the five Central American presidents in August 1987. The National Dialogue itself resulted in the Jornadas por la Vida y la Paz (Conferences for Life and Peace), ecumenical forums and public actions between 1990 and 1993. Participation in these activities showed that sectors of the Guatemalan Christian community were committed to what soon became the peace process following the signing of the Acuerdo Básico para la Búsqueda de la Paz por Medios Políticos (Basic Accord for the Search for Peace through Political Means, usually known as the Oslo Accord) between the URNG and the Guatemalan government on 30 March 1990 in Oslo. This signing initiated a round of conversations between the URNG and various sectors of Guatemalan civil society (in the CNR) that would establish some of the bases on which peace could be constructed. The immediate involvement of CIEDEG in this process was as part of the "religious sector" that met in Quito, Ecuador, in September 1990.[33]

Ongoing involvement by CIEDEG in the peace process included broadening the discussions with the URNG to form a Coordinador de Sectores Civiles (CSC, Civil Sector Coordinating Group), which included labor groups, popular and Maya organizations, groups of people who had been displaced by the war, and campesinos. CIEDEG's viewpoint is that this organization was the precursor to the Asamblea de la Sociedad Civil (ASC, Civil Society Assembly), which was actually established by the so-called Acuerdo Marco (Framework

Accord) signed between the government and the URNG on 10 January 1994. This accord set the stage for further agreements between the two sides in the conflict that culminated in the signing of the final accord at the end of 1996.[34] During this period CIEDEG participated in four consultations with ecumenical organizations designed to lend impetus to the formal negotiations that were continuing on another track.[35] When the ASC formally came into being, CIEDEG continued its participation as part of the "religious sector" as consensus documents were formulated that would be placed before the negotiating parties.[36]

The point of this discussion is to demonstrate that CIEDEG works with a strong social and political agenda that includes issues ranging from democratization and constitutional reform in the post-conflict situation to organic agriculture and community development. While it promotes itself as a conference of churches, it has been criticized as being more of a consortium of local congregations and church leaders who affiliate with the organization and some of its activities. The scope of CIEDEG's organizing and political development is less relevant to the present work than the manner in which it is rooted in Maya identity as a locus of organizing that serves to unite members in their activities within the context of contemporary Guatemala. Ethnic identity and cultural rights, then, underlie much of CIEDEG's activity and provide a trajectory for other activities. In an interview with Garrard-Burnett, Similox described his sense of the relationship of Maya Protestantism to Maya-ness and to Christianity writ large: "To Christianize cannot be the same as to Westernize. Christianity must respect all peoples. . . . It must try to be Greek with the Greeks, Guatemalan with the Guatemalans, and Maya with the Maya. And this on all planes of cultural creation. [I Cor. 9.] To say anything less diminishes and marginalizes the objective and subjective values of the Maya cultures in our environment" (1998a, 170–71, Garrard-Burnett's translation). In reflecting on these comments, Garrard-Burnett remarks that they "offer testimony to the fact that, since colonial times, religion in Guatemala has exhibited a marvelous elasticity in the hands of the faithful" (171). While much attention has been focused on this elasticity in the relationship of Maya culture to Catholicism and the *cofradía* complex, Similox is emphasizing the position of Maya culture vis-à-vis Christianity itself. The issue is not only how Christianity changes but also how Maya culture adapts in the religious context.

Ethnic identity and cultural rights, then, underlie much of CIEDEG's activity and provide a trajectory for other activities. A bulletin circulated around the time of the 1999 national elections by CIEDEG's Program of Formation for Development specified ethnicity and gender as two areas of identity and rights where democratization required the abolishment of discrimination. Regarding ethnicity itself, the bulletin says the following:

Democratic development requires that the entire marginalized population, principally the Maya population, can exercise their own and specific economic, social, political, and cultural rights as well as those corresponding to the entire citizenry of the country.

This brings with it the acknowledgment and respect of their culture, their vision of the world, their organizational forms, their language, their mode of dress, their traditions, their authorities, and especially, the right to full political participation with our own resources [*instrumentos propios*].

But true democratization in this sense will only be accomplished if the indigenous peoples—that is to say, the Maya, Garifuna, and Xinca—have full participation in local, regional, and national decision making. It will only be accomplished if they have participation in all state institutions that direct national life and if they have their own institutions that express and channel their interests toward the state. (CIEDEG n.d., 7)

The focus on broad issues such as the democratization of Guatemalan society shows CIEDEG's trajectory to be similar to those of other popular organizations as they have been described by Bastos and Camus (1995, 1996), among others. At the same time, ethnic identity and religion, including ties with international ecumenical religious organizations, are the points of departure for CIEDEG's organizing activity and for its own characteristic development work. The ties to international Protestantism are often ignored in the literature on the peace process, as is the voice of the evangelical religious community inside Guatemala more generally. While the religious community is diverse and, to be sure, often ambiguous in its pronouncements, its localized participation in the peace process and in the consolidation of democracy in Guatemala remains significant. Whether from the standpoint of social movements, democratization, or citizen involvement in general, this lack of attention is one of the lacunae that I hope to contribute to filling in this work.

CIEDEG's multifaceted role demonstrates how organizations as well as individuals have "multiple identities," an issue of increasing salience in the study of the interplay between ethnicity and religion.[37] Moreover, CIEDEG continues to work to make its voice heard in the political arena, often as part of other strategic alliances in the context of national politics, in addition to the politics of ethnic identity. An example of this tendency was CIEDEG's leadership in December 2001 and January 2002 in organizing El Foro Ecuménico por la Paz y la Reconciliación (FEPAZ, Ecumenical Forum for Peace and Reconciliation). FEPAZ was created with Catholic religious and representatives of other Protestant groups in order to draw more attention to problems surrounding implementation of the peace accords at the time of the fifth anniversary of the signing of the final accord. A joint "Celebration of the Word" was held in the Metropolitan Cathedral on 23 January 2002 (Rodríguez 2002), and FEPAZ issued public pronouncements in regard to issues such as the "Black Thursday" and the "Friday of Mourning" violence on 24 and 25 July 2003.[38] On those days, mob violence almost universally linked to the Frente Republicano Guatemalteco (FRG, Guatemalan Republican Front) virtually paralyzed Guatemala City. The violence was instigated in response to civil protests against the Court of Constitutionality's vote in favor of allowing Ríos Montt to stand for the presidency in the 2003 elections.[39]

La Hermandad de Presbiterios Mayas

Compared with CIEDEG, the HPM historically has had a more grassroots agenda. In part because of a leadership change, since 2000 its operations have been run primarily out of Quetzaltenango and not the capital. My comments here reflect the status of the organization up to and during the time of my funded field work (1997–98), when Otzoy occupied the position of executive secretary and the primary offices were in Guatemala City. Those years were not easy ones, as they encompassed the difficult period when the war slowly came to an end as well as a major crisis occasioned by a split within the IENPG in 1992, largely because of accusations that the Maya wing of the church was involved with liberation theology.

An undated manuscript produced by the Hermandad around the end of 1994 or the beginning of 1995 tried to situate the organization within the context of both the politics of the IENPG and the national society: "The general objective of the Hermandad since its beginning until today is to contribute to the demands of the necessities of the local churches of the National Evangelical Presbyterian Church (IENPG), of the Maya people, and other organized sectors that work for a just society and need our accompaniment and solidarity through both religious [and] cultural activities as well as political ones in the regions where the presbyteries are located." The document delineated violations of rights that had been committed against the IENPG by those who had left the denomination. Ethnicity clearly was a factor in the midst of the ongoing problems: "The majority of these violations were committed against Maya leaders. And specific accusations were made against Maya Presbyterians for being impure, [implying] that they were ruining the church and introducing the Theology of Liberation, for which reason they were classified as communists, etc."[40]

A list is included that documents everything from *anónimos* (anonymous threats) and verbal accusations against various leaders (including the kidnapping of a female indigenous organizer), the forced entering of houses and offices of church-related institutions, and the murder of Elizabeth Sarat Saquic in May 1994. She had been a member of a local congregation and the vice president of a local church youth organization. These events are detailed later in the document following a history of the *autoseparación* (self-separation) of a group from the IENPG following tension that began in 1985 and lasted until 1992.[41] This separation was at the root of bitter conflict within the denomination that lasted throughout the 1990s and into the new millennium, when a major coup at the annual synod meeting in 2001 replaced the executive secretary who had made some common cause with the Maya at various points during the 1990s. Some charges of corruption and misappropriation of development funds were also involved. On one level the events mirror some of the larger conflicts between ethnic groups and even the charges of corruption that take place on the national level in Guatemala. Early in the conflict the dissidents tried to take possession of some of the IENPG institutions in the western part of the country, and the particular fight over the Colegio Evangélica La Patria made its way into the court system and, occasionally, into the local press.[42]

While much more of this story is yet to be told, distance in time and a change in the position of the teller are probably requirements for the telling. From the standpoint of the Hermandad, two things stand out. One is the necessity to take a defensive posture in regard to denouncing particular acts against the larger institution and in regard to acts perpetrated against Maya leaders themselves. This issue gets at the heart of the theological import of what it means for people from different cultural backgrounds to come together in a "church." Theoretically, this has to do with the universal claims of essential humanity (or, more anthropologically, "humanness") and the manner in which such claims play out in the midst of ethnic pluralism. Second is the way the Hermandad positioned itself in regard to the IENPG, as a parallel organization with no official relationship. This made the organization suspect in the eyes of the Presbyterian Church (U.S.A.), and because of the predominant partnership mentality of the denomination and the mode of working through "partnership" agreements with the IENPG, it precluded certain avenues of funding for the Hermandad even though several local presbyteries had contact on various formal and informal levels. This was an organizing strategy by the Hermandad that also reflected to some degree the strategies in other organizations where the Maya were confronting larger structures that might need to be challenged from time to time.

During my time in Guatemala, one of the more impressive events sponsored by the Hermandad was an "Encuentro entre Indígenas Mexicanas y Guatemaltecas" ("Encounter between Mexican and Guatemalan Indigenous Peoples"), held at the Instituto Maya K'iche' (17–19 February 1998). Some twelve or thirteen Maya language groups from Mexico and Guatemala were represented, as well as missionary personnel from the United States.[43] Most of the dialogue centered around some vision of Reformed theology and the particular activities of the representatives of the various groups who participated in the *encuentro*. This was a significant meeting at the time, but to my knowledge nothing like it was repeated. In the meeting itself, I observed that the Guatemalans manifested less overt missionary connections and seemed to be able to articulate cultural demands and dimensions of their beliefs in ways that many of the Mexicans did not. At the time I attributed this to the Guatemalans' organizing experience during the war years, but I suspect a number of factors were at work.[44]

Conclusion

The story of indigenous Protestantism in Guatemala is still being written. I have emphasized the denomination with which I have done the vast majority of my work in Guatemala. The IENPG, as a historical denomination with a significant missionary history and substantial outside funding, represents a somewhat skewed story. A number of independent denominations (often Pentecostal) are indigenous both to Guatemala and to other countries in Central America, and several of the well-known neo-Pentecostal groups (e.g., El Verbo) now have mission work in other countries in both South and North America. The independence and the reach of these various churches exemplify what the literature on Christian mission history calls the globalization of Christianity, the move of the center of gravity of Christianity from Europe and North America to the global south and east.[45] As the center of gravity of the religion changes, its beliefs and practices are subject to influence and change in specific local contexts. This is a significant field of study for both anthropologists and theologians.[46]

From the point of view of the anthropology of religion in Latin America, the rise of indigenous theology requires further study. Most research in this area has been done by Roman Catholics or in relation to Catholicism and its dealings with indigenous culture. Ed Cleary has noted (personal communication) that one of the differences between Catholic and Protestant approaches to indigenous theology is that the Catholic way (typified in seven Andean research and pastoral centers) represents a more diffuse approach to indigenization than the more personalized Protestant approach centered on particular individuals (typified by Guatemalan organizations and their way of doing theology and indigenous organizing).[47] In Guatemala, the Andean mode of organizing, rooted in local culture, can be seen in the Vera Paz region among the Q'eqchi', where the Ak' Kutan Center has a substantial research and resource center that has published a series of books on indigenous identity, globalization, and even Pentecostalism in Central America.[48] On these issues, as well as other issues, the argument is that the Catholic base is larger and less personalized than the evangelical base. In this area, as in so many others, Protestant voices in Guatemala (and throughout Central America) are both more muted and more fragmented when it comes to articulating a sustained theology that embraces culture and the different meanings of indigenization in a multicultural context.

My intent has been to examine the nature of indigenous Protestantism in Guatemala by shifting the focus away from the internal relationships within a denomination and giving specific attention to two organizations that act in Guatemalan civil society from a position that is manifestly Maya and evangelical. Both CIEDEG and HPM can be situated within the religious sector of civil society, yet both also take their place as Maya organizations in the context of social movement activity in Guatemala. Because both are dependent upon international funding, they are also manifestations of global or transnational religion, which crosses boundaries and seeks to establish relationships in both directions. The difference with more traditional missionary relationships is that both organizations are controlled within Guatemala and seek resources both within and outside traditional denominational structures that would be represented by the agreements between the Presbyterian denominations in Guatemala and the United States. Particular individuals and groups from various places—Canada, Europe, and the United States—support the Hermandad, and support from the international community outside North America has likely been predominant in CIEDEG's case. Simultaneously, to a large degree, personal relations are an aspect of the structure of both organizations in that they have traditionally been guided by small groups of individuals. This is consistent with long observation of how evangelical communities and churches often develop in family networks or in conjunction with the charismatic presence of certain ministers or leaders.

It is also significant that, as of 2006, both organizations still exist, but in much weaker conditions than immediately following the signing of the peace. My understanding at this writing is that the organizational structures remain intact, but leadership changes have resulted in turnover in personnel, particularly in CIEDEG. The HPM changed personnel and moved its primary office from the capital to Quetzaltenango early in this decade. Part of the implication of this is that its reach is potentially more localized in scope, and perhaps focused more on local development activities in areas such as agriculture. In the case of CIEDEG, Similox is no longer executive secretary, and from a distance it appears that most of his time and energy is dedicated to FEPAZ, which also receives funding from a number of religious groups in Europe and Canada. FEPAZ continues to assert itself as a religious voice in national political affairs, including through the publication of works on issues such as ethics and violence (FEPAZ 2005).

These glimpses into organizational change provide a window into the trajectory of organizational leadership in nongovernmental organizations as well as into the personal lives of individuals involved in public religious life. Most such individuals do not work out their destinies on a stage as public as Similox's, but life history itself is an important tool in the study of religion, whether in local congregations or public organizations.[49] If the shifts in these organizations reflect some of the tendencies noted above, they are also indicative of the difficulties in creating self-sustaining organizations anywhere in the developing world. Transnational networks are important at particular points in time, but movements, organizations, and even personal attention spans in regard to particular agendas are transient. Understanding the implications of this for social organizing in Latin America as well as religious communities requires more scrutiny.

For my purposes, the agenda of the two organizations has transcended a preoccupation with religion alone. Both groups have sought to encompass culture as a primary part of their organizing agendas. This, in turn, has been a link with the *reivindicación* (recovering or recovery) of Maya culture so prominent in the pan-Maya movement.[50] I now turn more directly to the practice of evangelicalism at the local level among Mam and Kaqchikel Presbyterians. Examination of how such practice articulates with the organizational strategies discussed in this chapter broadens the scope for understanding the meaning of evangelicalism in contemporary Guatemala. It also returns us to the issue of the meaning of Maya evangelicalism in the community.

5
Identity in Word and Place
The Mam Presbytery

"He aquí vienen días," dice Jehová el Señor, "en los cules enviaré hambre a la tierra. No hambre de pan, ni sed de agua, sino de oír la palabra de Jehová."

"Behold, the days are coming," says the Lord God, "when I will send a famine on the land; not a famine of bread, nor a thirst for water, but of hearing the words of the Lord."

—Amos 8:11 (RSV), painted (in Spanish) to one side of the entryway of the Iglesia de Cristo in San Juan Ostuncalco

Introduction

This chapter describes the Mam Presbytery's relatively traditional approach to Maya evangelical practice. The examination is not intended as a comprehensive ethnography of what takes place in the presbytery. As a unit, Scotchmer's work (1989, 1991, 1993, 2001) provides such an ethnography, and the corpus as a whole reflects what Scotchmer saw as the construction of "an indigenous local Maya theology" (1993, 519). This theology was oriented around three "key symbols" (Ortner 1973; Scotchmer 1996), which Scotchmer identified as "*Tyol Dios*/God's Word, *Kajaw Crist*/Lord Christ, and *hermano(a)*/brother (sister)" (1989, 293).[1] In the last full article on the Mam that he published before his untimely death, Scotchmer was working on the concept of "a Maya Protestant spirituality" (1993, 507). This was reflective "of peace or harmony within three domains that dominate Maya life." These have to do with "peace with deity/ies, with the environment that sustains life, and with others in the human family," and they are as relevant to Roman Catholics and *costumbristas* (practitioners of *costumbre*) as they are to Protestants. While this is a helpful perspective, I prefer to think of an all-embracing Maya cosmology within which the person is situated. In more cognitive terms, this is a conceptualization out of which one lives in the world through "acts of symbolic communication that attempt to realize that awareness [of the transcendent] and live by its promptings" (Tambiah 1990, 6). Religious practices as well as "conventions" of family and community are worked out from within such a conceptualization. And elements of this conceptualization can erode or change when people convert or come into contact with forces of social, political, and economic modernization, including education. Likewise, when people cross international borders for political or economic reasons, aspects of the cosmology are used to re-create rhythms of life as it was lived in a different place (Wellmeier 1998; Thompson 2001).

The ethnographic analysis is framed by two aspects of the context within which Mam Presbyterians negotiate their evangelical identity. First, being evangelical does mark a definitive break with Maya religious practice embodied in *costumbre,* a break signified by conversion itself and manifested in both the material culture and the liturgical practices employed by the congregations to announce their presence in their communities. In order to examine this, I provide a generalized description of aspects of the symbolism manifest in church structures and a minimal description of the aspects of identity encoded in Mam worship as I observed it in 1997 and 1998. This description includes a discussion of baptism, which is generally understood to be the sacrament of formal entrance into the church family in Presbyterian terms.[2]

Second, the Mam context allows us to examine the relationship between Maya culture and evangelicalism somewhat away from the glare of the Maya Movement. To this end, I examine segments from two interviews dealing with aspects of religious conversion and the meaning of conversion in a person's life from the standpoint of the community, especially in relation to family and the role ancestors play in Maya lives. The inclusion of the texts reinforces the kind of experience-based ethnography that is key to my research, but the texts transcend personal experience, providing a baseline (albeit an idiographic one) for examining the interplay between Maya cultural identity and evangelicalism in both historical and contemporary terms.

At the same time, the distance from pan-Maya discourse adds a layer to the kind of analysis I conducted in my research—one situating local-level practice in multilayered contexts. For a host of reasons (geography, literacy and general educational levels, access to the capital and to other kinds of material and intellectual resources), pan-Mayanism had not penetrated the southern Mam area in the way it did other parts of the country.[3] Although San Juan Ostuncalco, the site of the office of the presbytery, is approximately seven miles from Quetzaltenango, the second-largest city in the country, one could not often buy a newspaper in the Ostuncalco plaza after noon on a given weekday.

This is not to say that nongovernmental organizations and community-based organizations are absent from the area. Both governmental and nongov-

ernmental organizations dealing with education, health, or other aspects of social life make their presence felt in rural areas throughout Guatemala's western
highlands. Still, in conversations with the leader of a small community action
organization that identified itself with Mam culture, Asociación e Identidad
del Pueblo Mam (ASIMAM, Association and Identity of the Mam People),
I was struck by how the leader, actually a schoolteacher in another community near Quetzaltenango, spoke of a sense that the Mam were discriminated
against in other organizations, such as the Committee of Campesino Unity
and Majawil Q'ij. He had been involved with both organizations in the past
and lamented the fact that ultimately they seemed to focus their energy on
issues related to the K'iche' community as opposed to the Mam. Ironically,
Majawil Q'ij is Mam for "The New Dawn." This case shows the historical
antipathy that exists between some Maya groups, and serves to highlight the
remove of the Mam community from access to power, even within indigenous organizations. Clearly, ASIMAM represents a kind of discourse within
a larger discourse. The organization worked with local community leaders,
mostly young men, to promote educational activities in the *municipios* of San
Miguel Sigüilá and Ostuncalco; one of these programs, which I attended, dealt
with conflict mediation in local communities.[4]

While others have noted some tensions within the larger movement (Otzoy 1996; cf. Warren 1998), the issue here is not the validity of pan-Maya discourse but rather the degree to which Maya in places like the Mam-speaking
municipios in the department of Quetzaltenango are shaped by such discourse
and the ethnic renewal it represents. Publications such as *IXIMULEW, Rutzijol,* and even *El regional de Xela* had significant track records in publishing on
Maya issues and Maya communities during the mid- to late 1990s, including
issues such as *interculturalidad* (interculturality). Segments of both *IXIMULEW*
and an insert in *El regional* were at times printed in Mam.[5] Given the antipathy
in both directions, it is unclear how much this information was actually consumed in the area where I did my research, especially by the evangelical community. Community organizations such as ASIMAM and governmental and
nongovernmental organizations dealing with issues such as bilingual education seemed to have a more profound impact. In the end, evangelical identity,
and Mam Maya identity as such, are to some extent not as profoundly shaped
by pan-Mayanism as are the identities of other groups such as the K'iche' and
Kaqchikel. There are surely exceptions to this generalization, as pan-Maya discourse has been profound and far-reaching on issues such as language politics
and the Accord on the Rights and Identity of Indigenous Peoples. The situation, and the practical emphases, in the Mam Presbytery are substantially different from what will be shown in the next chapter.

Setting

The Mam Presbytery was founded in 1980 as the third Maya presbytery in the IENPG. In chapter 4 I discussed some of the reasons for the founding of the first such presbytery, Maya Quiché, in 1959. Many of those reasons carried over into the Mam situation, but a symbolic factor seems to have been the failure of the primary church in the region, the Iglesia de Cristo in San Juan Ostuncalco, to prosper. A little detail on the case will provide some insight into both missionary-Mam relations and the way ethnicity played out in the Presbyterian community at the time. The larger argument, of course, is that the tensions reflected in this case are representative of village life in many parts of the highlands.

A 1960 evaluation of Presbyterian work in the Mam region highlighted five concerns: a dearth of economic support for the minister; an uncoordinated and distant relationship between the Iglesia de Cristo congregation in San Juan Ostuncalco and the Mam Center and Clinic on the outskirts of the *pueblo,* as well as "the lack of relation between the three elements"; minimal growth among the Ladino part of the church because of a lack of attention; a church that was not able to connect with the larger community because it itself had not established an identity as either indigenous (Maya) or Ladino; and a recognition that while the majority membership of the church was Mam, most of the leadership came from the Ladino sector (IENPG 1982, 295).[6] At this juncture, the lack of contact or "identification" with the community and the control issue are the primary concerns.

The de Cristo congregation was founded in 1926. By the early 1960s both Dudley Peck and Ralph Winter were promoting an integrated model in which the two ethnic groups would be united in the single congregation. The Presbyterian history records that Peck "believed that the Mam did not want to take initiatives and preferred to stay under the care and management of Ladinos" and that Winter was largely of the same mind (IENPG 1982, 294). A system was devised whereby the two missionaries and the first ordained Mam pastor, Candelario Pérez, would share leadership in the congregation until Peck's retirement in 1963. Winter left the field in 1966, and Pérez was left as the sole pastor—forty years after the church's establishment! This history indicates a bias that neither Mam people nor Ladino pastors could appropriately deal with the other group: Mam pastors could not "satisfactorily" minister to Ladinos, and Ladino pastors did not want the conflict "of having to attend to two cultures" (294). Mention is also made of Ladino youth who saw that the missionaries were drawn to native culture and for whom the "mixed" (Maya-Ladino) context was fulfilling neither culturally nor spiritually. A split in the congregation ensued, and after some conflict the Mam eventually acquired a new plot of land on which to build a church (*templo*). That was accomplished in 1976 as part of a push for a culturally appropriate ministry in the Mam context, an approach that would not begin from a perspective that viewed the Mam as "little Ladinos who must improve themselves through education and their economic situation" (295).[7]

The organization of the presbytery was formally ratified at the synod meeting of the IENPG on 15 May 1980. The concerns motivating the move toward a separate organizational identity are clearly stated in the remarks attributed to Pérez, who was the president of the new presbytery: "Brothers, our joy is your joy in this historic moment. We take up this burden and responsibility with the hope that we can continue serving the Lord together with you as brothers. Now, we go not with rebellious or angry hearts but in the love of Christ. But you can be sure that although we are your 'little brother presbytery' you are going to hear much from us as equals" (IENPG 1982, 298).

When the presbytery was organized it consisted of four churches and 724 baptized members (Scotchmer 1991, 376). At the time of my field research in Ostuncalco it consisted of more than five thousand adherents in several *municipios* (townships) west of Quetzaltenango.[8] Roughly a quarter of the sixteen churches and projects on the way to being formally organized as churches in the presbytery were in the town centers, while the rest were in *aldeas* (rural villages) (fig. 8). Additionally, many members belonged to one or another of some fifteen or twenty *congregaciones,* which often had their own building but continued to be looked after by one of the larger churches because of their small size or lack of resources.[9]

The *municipio* of Ostuncalco (population 41,140; census 2002) has been the center of Presbyterian evangelical efforts among the Mam since at least 1911.[10] On the western extreme of a large valley that includes Quetzaltenango on the east, the *cabecera* (population center) sits at an altitude of some twenty-five hundred meters above sea level, virtually at the edge of the steep, narrow escarpment running from the highlands to coffee country in the more temperate zones to ranch territory closer to the littorals near the Pacific coast. Access to broader national culture is via well-developed roads that intersect in the town. One road connects the town to Quetzaltenango, only seven miles to the east; another provides access to Guatemala's southern coastal region and Mexico after a forty-five-minute drive during which the elevation drops to temperate lands near five hundred meters in altitude along the Pacific highway that spans the rich agricultural zone. To the west, another road leads to the departmental capital of San Marcos and on to the Mexican border through a rich coffee-growing region that has been the scene of land disputes since the late 1990s. Nearly equal in importance to Ostuncalco in terms of the number of church

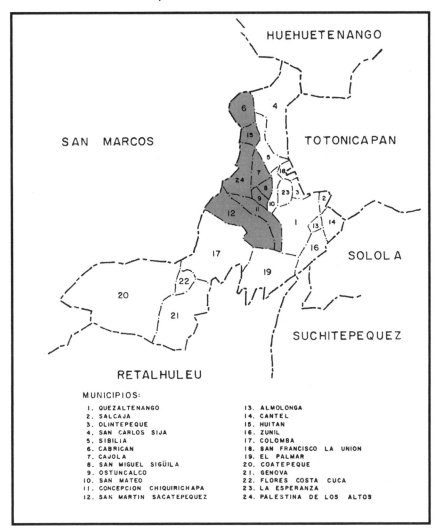

MUNICIPIOS:

1. QUEZALTENANGO
2. SALCAJA
3. OLINTEPEQUE
4. SAN CARLOS SIJA
5. SIBILIA
6. CABRICAN
7. CAJOLA
8. SAN MIGUEL SIGÜILA
9. OSTUNCALCO
10. SAN MATEO
11. CONCEPCION CHIQUIRICHAPA
12. SAN MARTIN SACATEPEQUEZ

13. ALMOLONGA
14. CANTEL
15. HUITAN
16. ZUNIL
17. COLOMBA
18. SAN FRANCISCO LA UNION
19. EL PALMAR
20. COATEPEQUE
21. GENOVA
22. FLORES COSTA CUCA
23. LA ESPERANZA
24. PALESTINA DE LOS ALTOS

Figure 8. Quetzaltenango *municipios* with Mam Presbyterian churches (after INE 1996b)

members is the *municipio* of San Martín Sacatepéquez (also known as San Martín Chileverde; population 20,712), a ten-minute drive from Ostuncalco, nearly
at the boundary between *tierra fría* (cold country) and *tierra templada* (temperate
land) on the way to the coast. Both *municipios* recorded population increases
around 24 percent between the censuses of 1994 and 2002. Additionally, both
had indigenous populations in excess of 80 percent in 1994. This compared
with just under 60 percent for the entire department of Quetzaltenango. The

percentage for the indigenous population in Ostuncalco is not much different from that recorded by Ebel from the 1950 (82.3 percent) and 1964 (80.6 percent) censuses (McArthur and Ebel 1969, 64).[11]

The area is a rugged one of mountain slopes and *altiplano* (high mountain valleys). Small to medium-sized *cabeceras* of several thousand inhabitants are surrounded by rather isolated *aldeas* or *caseríos* (hamlets). To the west of the area encompassed by the geographic bounds of the presbytery are some of the highest mountains in Central America. Traveling the high road between the *municipios* of Huitán and Cabricán at the northern extreme of the presbytery, one can often see the bare peak of Volcán Tajumulco, the highest peak in the region at 4,220 meters. To the west still further, virtually straddling the Guatemala-Mexico border, is Volcán Tacaná (4,030 meters), surrounded on its skirts in both countries by coffee *fincas* (plantations). Within the confines of the presbytery, most of the agriculture is corn farming on the highland plateaus, with corn and potatoes on the slopes. Wheat is grown in some areas, with various horticultural crops and fruit trees common in some places. Coffee is grown in the lower reaches of some of the *municipios*, while seasonal work on the *fincas* or on land owned by individuals or communities in the lowlands is common. Sheep are raised in some of the higher-altitude *municipios*. Pine and oak forests seem to predominate in those areas where trees are common, but the mountainsides are stripped of more and more trees as populations increase. Knowledge of environmental consequences is fairly commonplace, and there are efforts to preserve forestland or small stands of trees in a number of places. Besides agriculture and forest-related activities, Ostuncalco is known for its *mimbre* (wicker) furniture, and women continue to weave and sell textiles, though these are frequently sold in regional markets and not in the tourist markets so visible in other parts of the country. Economically, the department as a whole is not among the poorest of the Guatemala's departments, ranking in the top third of twenty-one departments (excluding the capital) according to a graphic contained in the conclusions of the Historical Clarification Commission (CEH 1999, 80).

Ostuncalco remains a market zone and transportation center for the western area of the department, and both the town center and roads leading into and out of the center are clogged with buses, car traffic, and the ubiquitous Toyota trucks during the Sunday morning market. Even during weekdays, as many as twenty trucks line the town square waiting to be hired for a quick job traversing the roads to other *municipios* and *aldeas* further removed from this particular center of activity. All manner of fruits, vegetables, staple goods (both highland and lowland produce trucked in from the coast), and other household items are sold in the streets until the middle of the afternoon, when the market breaks down and people return to their homes for the coming week (fig. 9).

Figure 9. Sunday market in Ostuncalco

This weekly rhythm has been central to church life in the region for decades, as many of the local congregations hold services on Sunday afternoon or evening after people have returned from their buying and selling in the market (IENPG 1982, 293).[12]

The market is one example of how in certain regards the distance from national culture, while both real and significant, should not be overstated. The region does have contact with "the outside," and this was clearly seen in the swirl of activity surrounding the festival of the Virgin of Candelaria, the primary annual celebration despite the fact that the town's namesake is Saint John the Baptist.[13] The dates of the celebration are 31 January through 3 February, but it lasts for about a week before and a day or so afterward. In the preceding days the market area and even the area around the plaza are rather *descontrolado* (unorganized). Some mechanical rides are set up, as well as a few games for cheap prizes (kicking the soccer ball, a target shoot wherein if you hit the target bearing your favorite singing group you hear them sing several lines of your favorite *norteño* songs from Mexico). Movie theaters are set up in rooms thrown together out of zinc roofing materials, and the video will surely be showing the latest in blood-and-guts violence, while outside, innumerable stalls are selling *roscas* (a crown-shaped pastry), peanuts, and other typical sweets. The indoor market seems particularly busy with all the traffic in and out of town during the week, and even the bus traffic is routed away from the town center. Speakers in the clock tower above the market blare American music a large percentage of the time, along with continual announcements regarding upcoming events. While the church bells peal the hour, some of the announcements are to thank a group of *Ostuncalquenses* who apparently now live in Arlington, Virginia, for their patronage of the festivities. On the Sunday afternoon before the *diá de la virgen,* the Dance of the Conquest is performed in front of the church, and in another section the Dance of the Bulls (some say it is the Mexican version) is taking place to the sounds of the marimba.

Clearly, migration and the "de-territorialization" of the community are in play as the community simultaneously holds onto and reshapes its identity in the face of globalization. Beyond patronage of the hometown fiesta, migration to the United States does produce considerable economic benefit for many families and communities in Guatemala's far western highlands.[14] In a number of villages in the region, two-story stucco houses are often pointed to as the result of remittances, and one elder in a Mam congregation said that he had been able to build his own home in the Ostuncalco *aldea* of La Victoria with help from his children working in Nebraska, probably in the meat-packing industry.[15]

The Shape of Evangelical Identity: Sacred Space and Worship

The description of the bustle surrounding the *fiesta patronal* (patron saint festival) provides a point of transition to the way in which evangelicals attempt to define their identity on the basis of behavior as well as belief. One Sunday afternoon during the midst of the festivities, I happened to be in the town center with a Mam minister who was waiting for a vehicle to take him to a distant congregation for a service. As I watched the activity around me, I asked my friend if evangelicals went into hiding on the actual day of the saint. He wryly replied, "No. We plan a meeting."

Ethnographic understanding of evangelical identity among Mam Presbyterians begins with the picture of small, colorful *templos* that dot the contemporary rural landscape of Guatemala.[16] Even in remote mountain areas, churches can be spotted from two mountain ridges away because of their bright color amid the earth-colored adobe houses and the occasional school or governmental building present in the larger *aldeas*. A cursory examination of the *templos* provides the initial entrée into the conceptualization of Protestant identity. Although the focus here is on Presbyterian structures, the generalizations are consistent across the spectrum of Protestantisms in Guatemala.

One interpretive key is that evangelicals of all stripes tend to form their religious identity in contradistinction to Catholicism as well as indigenous religious traditions. One can argue that the historical antipathy in the religious arena is closer to Hawkins's model of inverse images than is the ethnic dimension mentioned earlier. The oppositional quality of identity formation is inscribed on the landscape first in the mere presence of the *templos* themselves. Approaching the typically well kept edifice, one notes not only the color of the building—bright yellows, blues, occasional red or mauve, and the ubiquitous green or blue green that in some Maya contexts, such as the cemetery, has other significance—but also the absence of any cross that would identify the building as a church in the fashion of the Roman Catholic church down the path. Scotchmer, who worked in the Mam area as a missionary and anthropologist for more than twenty years, states that the mere presence of the *templo* is a replacement for the cross, "which is universally rejected by Mayan Protestants in homes and churches alike because of its centrality to both traditional Mayan and Catholic rites" (1989, 303; cf. 308 n. 4). The Protestant emphasis on conversion and the gaining of adherents might account for the more public presence of the evangelical sacred spaces as they seek to reinscribe the landscape with a Protestant presence (fig. 10).

An extension of this idea, with a more direct relation to ethnic identity, is to see the *templos* as markers of sacred space (or sacred geography) in the same manner in which Maya *encantos* (altars) are used for burning incense and the performing of ceremonies by spiritual guides or shamans. *Encantos* are often located on mountains, near caves, or even at other sacred places such as the volcanic Lake Chikabal above the town of San Martín. Such sacred spaces are well known to those who participate in Maya religious practices, and the physical act of going to a mountain peak or lake represents a commitment to a cosmology rooted in ties to the landscape that is only now beginning to be seen in what might be termed national public space. Maya ceremonies were performed in front of the National Palace during the festivities that preceded the actual signing of the final peace accord in 1996. Evangelical *templos* represent, in part, an attempt to create a public presence on the landscape. This is a more diffuse presence than that signaled by Roman Catholic buildings, which still tend to be concentrated in central locations in the center of towns and *aldeas*. This very diffuseness is a connection between the person and sacred place that spans the various religious traditions practiced in rural Guatemala.[17] At the

Figure 10. Building dedication, December 1997

same time, the *templos* announce the evangelical presence in a way that is not characteristic of the more subtle way in which *costumbrista* sites are integrated into the landscape.[18]

Further examination of the outside of the building, made either of cinder block or adobe with a plaster covering, reveals not only the absence of the cross but also the presence of another feature usually absent in the Catholic context—words. The name of the church is usually emblazoned across the portal of the door, as in Iglesia Presbiteriana Cordero de Dios (Lamb of God Presbyterian Church). Often there is also an open Bible painted beside the church's name, or on larger churches in nice letters an entire Bible verse, such as Amos 8:11 ("'Behold! The days are coming,' says Jehovah the Lord, 'in which I will send hunger to the earth. Not hunger for bread or thirst for water, but for the hearing of the Word of Jehovah'"). The primary emphasis is on the Word, but on rare occasions there might be a painted cross or even a chalice on the outside of an evangelical church. These are usually stylized and represent a more formal decorative style than on the typical evangelical church.[19]

The symbolic displacement (replacement?) continues inside the church (fig. 11). At the very front of the church, where, in a Roman Catholic setting, the high altar rises adorned by the crucified Jesus, Mary and her baby boy, and a company of the saints, there is often in evangelical churches a wall that is

Figure 11. Church interior—traditional style

blank but for a verse drawing attention not simply to words but to the Word of God that comes to the believer in Scripture. Contemporary practice in Mam Presbyterian churches varies somewhat in this regard. In a number of congregations the front wall now consists of elaborately painted murals, usually nature scenes with lakes, rivers, and mountains combined with images from the Bible—a boat full of disciples on rough seas with Jesus walking on the water toward the disciples (fig. 12). The moment depicted is not so serious as to preclude fish jumping out of the water in other parts of the mural. Elsewhere, in the midst of a mountainous landscape, an open Bible is situated to the side of Noah's ark with a rainbow superimposed over the ark. The scene affirms the theme of interconnectedness that permeates the Maya worldview. Sometimes a verse is painted in the midst of the mural—"Sing happily to God, inhabitants of all the earth" (Psalm 100:1). In the Mam Presbytery there is invariably a clock on the front wall. This is somewhat unusual compared with churches I observed in Mexico, and I have never asked anyone about the significance. Nevertheless, in view of the importance of cyclical time in Maya conceptions of the universe and the human place in the cosmos, it bears mention that one of the gifts given to the congregation at the dedication of a new *templo* in December 1997 was a clock. One hesitates to make too much of such an object, but the symbolism may transcend the evangelical worship place in

Figure 12. Church interior—contemporary style (photograph by Bea Howland)

a rather pragmatic way. In the words of Victor Montejo, "Maya thought, in terms of interrelation, is a response to these prophetic cycles that remind us that we are human and that we depend on the earth and all that exists on it" (2005, 122).[20]

The general sense one obtains from looking at the physical space where evangelical worship takes place is that identity is being reconstituted in the religious realm in response to Catholicism, which is still the most prominent institutional expression of religion. The material symbol of the cross and the iconography of the saints is replaced by a minimalist symbology revolving around God's Word, the Bible, as the foundational text for Mam evangelical identity. This is not surprising given that the root of the term *evangelical* is the Greek ευαγγελιον or evangel, which translates as "Gospel" or "Good News." This is the news, contained in the Bible, of the life, death, and resurrection of Jesus, and it remains the foundation for Protestant identity. Historically, this word-based—even text-based—approach has been juxtaposed with Catholicism's sacramental and dramatic approach to the Christian story since the Reformation. The placement of the pulpit in the center of the chancel area in Protestant places of worship has historically been intended to deemphasize Christ's sacrifice as it is presented in the Eucharist. The shift represents a move away from liturgical drama and performance—indeed, away from a literal reenactment of the sacrifice—to an approach focused on personal access to the text in the vernacular. In Guatemala's missionary history this was reflected in the decision of some of the early missionaries to provide scriptures in the indigenous languages, sometimes at the cost of conflict with their sending agencies.[21]

This symbolic reestablishment of the bases for religious community is reflected linguistically in the use of terms such as *hermano* (brother) and *hermana* (sister) in the construction of community identity in a manner that includes people with a shared faith from countries in many parts of the world. Even foreigners who presumably share the same faith are embraced by this linguistic code.[22] Scotchmer explains this code ethnographically as an extension of the "divine-human relationship" wherein God is viewed as a caring father (*qman dios*) with whom the believer cultivates a relationship of trust:

> The belief in one God leads to an understanding of mankind having been created as one family despite the differences of language, skin, and social behavior. . . . Believers then are children of God and each person is their brother and sister. . . . In fact, one can refer to an *hermano/a* for months and never know his or her name. One can say *hermano/a* to a complete stranger with the simple knowledge that he or she is a Protestant. The introduction of someone as *hermano/a* will gain a hearing quickly and practically guarantee acceptance—until there is evidence of a breach in the behavioral code for Protestants. For the Indians there is the assumption that he is now an equal with the Ladino. To be treated according to the prevailing social criteria as an inferior is not only a denial of the brother relationship, but also raises doubt about the Ladino's real belief in the God he professes to follow. This argument has won many battles within Indian-Ladino church conflicts, and in some cases has been used by Indians to gain more than an equal share politically over Ladinos. The further imagery of Jesus Christ as God's son and therefore our elder brother and example is a powerful symbol for the promotion of cooperation, unity, reconciliation, and tolerance with the Protestant church in general. (1986, 207–8)

Embodied here is the contrast between a world religion and local or vernacular religious practice wherein spirituality is integrally and intimately linked to the place where one resides.[23] Behavioral norms often delineate the extent of community boundaries by linking faith with the manner in which one conducts oneself in the daily tasks of living, especially in regard to alcohol, tobacco, dancing, and extramarital sexuality. Mam ministers and church members who deviate from the moral code are likely to find themselves under some sort of discipline, since a person's personal witness or testimony within the community is taken quite seriously within the Mam Presbytery.[24] Clearly, being adopted as a sibling serves to differentiate one group from another, and in that sense, kinship relations among evangelicals establish the boundary for the community (Cohen 1985). This evangelical community is one of a shared belief system and shared behavioral norms, norms that in some groups extend to refusing to celebrate certain religious holidays like Christmas or Holy Week.[25] The height of linguistic appropriation occurs when the converted refer to themselves as *cristianos* (Christians) in a rather exclusive sense which implies that they are real Christians and not like those Catholic *paganos* who worship images or, in the case of Maya *costumbristas,* deal with *brujos* (witches), as the various practitioners of shamanic ceremonies are invariably labeled.[26]

All of this reflects a changing of the symbolic orientation of the evangelical away from the Catholicism and *costumbre* practiced at the village level. And the rather universal claims of the evangelical community contained in this reorientation have certainly contributed to conflict and division in a number of places when people no longer support the *cofradía* system or withhold support from other community activities (Earle 1992; Marroquín 1994). The expulsion of Protestants from the town center of San Juan Chamula in Chiapas is probably the best-known case in Mesoamerica.[27]

One way to experience the new family of evangelical believers is to attend worship. Visitors familiar with the liturgy of historical denominations in North America are often surprised upon attending a worship service within the Mam Presbytery. Entering the church, one becomes slightly disoriented at the sea of color to one's left, where all the women sit, along with the majority of the children. Dressed in *traje* (the customary dress of the region), typically a dark blue *corte* (skirt) and *huipil* (blouse) that still varies according to the community of residence, they present quite a contrast with the men, who sit on the right.[28] These are usually dressed in Western clothing, including a few young men in black jackets with "Bakersfield, California" emblazoned on the back. Only in the *municipio* of San Martín do a significant number of the men still wear *traje*—sometimes with tennis shoes.

Worship services tend to have a rather informal, if consistent, liturgy and a very Pentecostal "feel" in terms of the style of prayer and the music that is played and sung. If the local musical *conjunto* (group) is present, the accordion, Spanish guitar, and plucked three-string bass can be an intriguing introduction into the musicology of the region, even if no instrument can be considered to have roots within Maya culture.[29] On another Sunday, music might be in the charge of a visiting *conjunto,* complete with keyboard, electric guitar, and two trumpet players who seem to be trying to outdo one another; this is despite the speaker system that clutters the platform area in the small *templo.* Amplification leaves the visitor without a ghost of a doubt about "being there." Regardless of which *conjunto* is playing, the immediate calm after a hymn or a selection is punctuated with a number of voices—"Gloria a Dios, Aleluya!" Although most services build toward the sermon, as is traditional in Presbyterianism, liturgical practice has clearly been shaped in the local context, where Pentecostal forms are quite prevalent.[30] Prayer is spontaneous or communal in nature, and *cadenas de coros* (chains of choruses) are common when a congregation member comes forward and leads a number of consecutive choruses, often without accompaniment. Congregation members as well as visitors are always given time to share a verse of Scripture and a brief commentary or a song. Eighty-five to ninety percent of any particular service will be conducted strictly in the Mam language, although, curiously, most of the actual Scripture reading is done in Spanish, *toj casti,* instead of Mam, *toj qyol.*[31] Some of the older women in one congregation were said to enjoy preaching in Mam because "escuchamos bien a la palabra de dios" ("we hear the Word of God well").

Baptism provides another example of evangelical practice and the struggle of Mam Presbyterians to maintain an identity distinct from Catholicism. In the presbytery, and throughout much of the IENPG, adult baptism instead of infant baptism is the standard practice. This is despite the fact that the first rite in the denomination's *Libro de fórmulas para ceremonias de la Iglesia Presbiteriana* is a ceremony for the baptism of children (IENPG 1971). Babies are brought to the church within their first few months and presented to the congregation. The minister takes the infant from the parents and says a prayer for the life and health of this new member of the family. In this context, baptism marks the believer's formal entrance into full participation in the life of the congregation. It takes place outside the context of weekly worship, in a river, a pool or hot spring, or during a trip to the Pacific Ocean, only a two-hour bus or truck ride down from the highlands. The event becomes a social as much as a religious outing as families prepare food to share following the baptisms and pile into buses and sometimes the back of pickup trucks for the trek to the baptismal site. The event itself is a ritualized experience that reinforces the kinship bonds among the *hermanos* and *hermanas.*

The rite itself would not be strange to a number of religious denominations in North America. Following a time of gathering when a layperson and the local *conjunto* lead the faithful in singing and praise, the minister comes to give the warrant for baptism, often from St. Matthew's Great or Last Commission, "Go therefore and make disciples of all nations, baptizing them . . ." (Matthew 28:19). Candidates for the sacrament are then asked questions regarding their faith commitment and their desire to fulfill the commitments baptism symbolizes (fig. 13). Lastly, the minister and several elders enter the pool wherein the candidates are brought one at a time to be admonished in the new faith, prayed over, and immersed (fig. 14). Water is then poured on the head of the new believer—three times, once for each person in the Christian trinity.[32] At

Figure 13. Preparing for baptism

the baptismal ceremony I attended, fifteen people were baptized. Coming out of the water, the newly baptized are quickly shuffled into a place were they can put on dry clothes, while the minister says a prayer with the musicians and announces that the ceremony has ended. After the ritualized hand shaking that follows any service, family groups remove food from the containers bundled in wraps that the women have been carrying, and meals are shared over friendly conversation. Soft drinks are the beverage of choice, the beer advertisements in the recreation area where the event is sometimes held notwithstanding.

To witness a baptism is to observe a combination of rather traditional evangelical practice embedded in Maya habits of life. Scotchmer says that among the Mam it is "the true sign of one's conversion" (1986, 212). One way this plays out is in the context of marriage, wherein a couple may decide to be baptized together after they are married civilly or provide evidence that they have been so married. The twofold reason for this is to keep the couple from being "baptized as fornicators" and to prevent conversion from being a cause of family division. Scotchmer also makes the interesting suggestion that marriage seems to end up functioning as a third sacrament. Marriages of a number of couples may take place first, to be followed by mass baptisms later on the same day.

Beyond these considerations, to participate in a baptism is to participate in the *fiesta* system common in rural communities throughout Mesoamerica.[33] If not in the act of baptism itself, it is in this sense of communitarianism that one

Figure 14. At the moment of baptism

can see Maya *costumbre* at work in the lives of Maya Protestants. The *hermanas y hermanos* do indeed come together in a new community. This is a celebration of new life and changed lives when viewed from the perspective of Maya evangelicals themselves. After all, as the minister has reminded those gathered, baptism "is not a commandment of man, but of God." The sacramental symbol of this shared life within the congregation is Communion, or *santa cen* (the Holy Supper), as it is called among Mam Presbyterians.

Conversion and Maya Identity

The relationship of evangelicals to Maya ethnic identity is somewhat more problematic than the overt manner in which evangelicals distinguish themselves from Roman Catholic religious practice and from the local ties that are so central to personal and group identity in Mesoamerica. Although I tend to use a person's self-identification as the primary marker of ethnic identity, the ethnographic interview provides a context wherein some of the tension between religion and ethnic identity becomes more evident. In the interview, the ethnographer not only seeks information that complements or completes observation but also seeks to revise and extend perspectives based on the views of those with whom he or she is collaborating in the field. This sense of interchange reinforces the notion of social interchange central to humanistic streams of anthropology, while it simultaneously allows for the inclusion of personal experience and narrative in anthropological research.

The possibility of self-representation in anthropological studies of religion among native peoples in the Americas is particularly important because Christianity in both its Catholic and Protestant varieties was initially imposed from the outside through missionary activities (Burkhart 1989; Tinker 1993). At the same time, students of both religion and ethnicity continue to struggle with whether it is adherence to a particular cosmology that truly gives one a particular ethnic identity. I do not propose to provide a direct answer to this question. It needs to be noted, however, that language and religion seem to be the two areas where Maya identity is most debated and contested within contemporary Guatemala, both inside and outside the Maya Movement. The Accord on the Rights and Identity of Indigenous Peoples requires the government to officially recognize indigenous languages with the assistance of the ALMG and representatives of the country's various linguistic communities. It also commits the government to "respect the exercise of [Maya] spirituality in all its manifestations, particularly the right to practice it both publicly as well as privately by means of teaching, cult, and observance. Likewise, the importance of due respect to indigenous spiritual guides as well as to ceremonies and sacred places is acknowledged" (Recopilación n.d., 8). Moreover, the accord requires an amendment to article 66 of the Guatemalan constitution "to the end of stipulating that the State acknowledges, respects, and protects" the forms of spirituality practiced by the indigenous populations in Guatemala (Maya, Garifuna, and Xinca). This was part of the package of the failed constitutional reforms of May 1999.[34]

One burden of the accord on indigenous rights was to codify the issue of cultural rights as a way of affirming collective identity. In the religious arena, the public recognition of spiritual guides and the right to celebrate ceremonies in the public sphere can be seen as an attempt to contest the more public personae of Catholic priests and Protestant ministers, as well as the social acceptability of their respective worship traditions. The anthropological literature is full of references to the concealed nature of indigenous spiritual practices, and one of the important thrusts of contemporary discourse and political maneuvering over the place of indigenous spiritual practice in Guatemala is to make such practice both public and acceptable in a "multiethnic, pluricultural, and multilingual" state. This has brought with it something of a revolution in the way Maya religious practices and those who participate in them are categorized. Maya religious practices requiring repeated actions and words become aspects of a spirituality, while the guardians of esoteric knowledge of those practices become designated as priests and spiritual guides in order to fend off the charge of being *brujos*. I have even heard of schools where people go to become such priests. My mental image of such places may not fit with reality, but the process of ethnic renewal and cultural *reivindicación* brings with it some interesting dichotomies in confrontation with marginalization and modernization.

The Mam Presbyterians with whom I worked tended to identify themselves as Mam before they identified themselves as Maya, although they noted a connection. The term *natural* (native) was still common at times, and it was never completely clear to me how some of the Mam self-identify. Part of this lack of clarity may be due to a language barrier, but I think there remains a certain degree of ambiguity related to identification with a particular place, on the one hand, and with newer terminology, such as "Maya," on the other. The emphasis on the evangelical community as a center of relationships may feed into the ambiguity, but it is related to other factors such as educational levels and experience outside of the community—at least when it comes to concerns proper to pan-Mayanism. On at least two occasions, Mam Presbyterians told me that both the war and the issue of Maya rights had to do with taking down (*bajando*) the evangelicals. In the case of the war, this had to do with the known case of a priest who was working with guerrillas. When I probed for more information on this issue, the response was that poverty was one reason for the growth of liberation theology, but a second reason was the need to counter the Protestant advance.[35] The meaning of this kind of discourse is ambiguous, but it demonstrates to some degree conflict between Catholicism and evangelicalism on an emotional level. Religious identity seems rather clearly defined, even as ethnicity is perhaps more taken for granted as an aspect of daily life—at least until ways of knowing come into conflict.

Here I provide segments of two interviews that demonstrate the interplay between Protestant identity and Mam ethnic identity. I often engaged the Mam Protestants with whom I worked in formal and informal conversation regarding the relationship between evangelical religion and Maya spirituality. Part of this conversation involved the anthropological search for what is more "traditional" among a group of people, but another aspect had to do with a nagging concern about whether conversion meant that a person had completely left another worldview and identity behind. From the standpoint of my research, it might be asked whether conversion results in a true disenchanting of the world, not so much through secularization as through being cut off from one's past and culture and thrown into the new worldview of the evangelical.

In describing what he calls a Maya spirituality, Scotchmer writes of a "crisis of belief" that turns into a "crisis of authority" leading Mam "traditionalists" to find respite in *Tyol Dios* (the Word of God) in the face of a world buffeted by change and uncertainty (1993, 510): "When ritual performance fails to cure alcoholism, lingering illness, unresolved feuding, repeated misfortune, endemic poverty, social rejection, and personal misery, there is an unavoidable crisis of belief. Questions of a very existential nature emerge that challenge not only the way one's ancestors and oneself have lived, but also what one has believed as true, acceptable, and good about one's place in the cosmos" (509). We have already seen how this shift plays out in symbolic terms. But the relationship a person maintains with other cosmologies and even folk categories of existence after conversion remains in question. This is particularly important when considering the importance of ancestors in Maya culture (and in indigenous cultures in North and Latin America in general). Most evangelicals deny going to Maya spiritual guides, but there are, for example, numerous contacts with midwives and local healers, and I even heard of one evangelical minister who was known as a *curandero* (folk healer).

The first account is a seemingly traditional account of conversion as an absolute break with the past as symbolized in the family. The second account shows the convert trying to deal with culture and tradition and somehow incorporate them into a changed worldview. They are narratives that ultimately reveal the tension between Maya-ness as embodied in the family networks and elements of *costumbre,* on the one hand, and the demands of the new faith on the other. This is played out in the experience and the perception of the family. Although not addressed directly in either case, the incorporation into a new community symbolized by baptism and the meaning of the reorientation signified by conversion and ratified by baptism are foregrounded.

Conversion as a Break with the Past

The first case involves the oldest living Mam Presbyterian minister. In 1996 he celebrated approximately the forty-fifth anniversary of his having become a "Christian." The larger interview suggested no real dissatisfaction in his preconversion life in a rural area outside the municipality of San Juan Ostuncalco. He had a friend who gave him a copy of the New Testament, which he read a little, but without much understanding. He reported trying to dedicate an entire day to reading the New Testament with the friend, "but I didn't last." He lasted half a day and began to understand a little, although "according to what I thought, I was a good Catholic and wanted to be a good Catholic." He wanted, however, "to know the truth," and he and his friend only read together. Then he said, "I set out to pray without knowing what praying was." After nearly three weeks he began to understand a prayer that he had prayed as a Catholic. He began to understand that the prayer was speaking about the death of Christ. The last section of the prayer, which he recited from memory, is:

Oh Lord, I offer you my life
and deeds and works
for the satisfaction of my sins.
I confess your goodness
that gives me the grace
for the merit
of your precious blood
until the end of my life.

Although he asked, he says he never received an answer about whether truth was in Catholicism or evangelicalism, but he did begin to understand that the prayer was speaking about the death of Christ. Then he recounts the story of his conversion.

> So that was when I made my decision to accept Christ. I asked that same person who had arrived with the Bible, or the New Testament, how does one believe in the Lord Jesus Christ? He told me, "Well, go to the church over there in San Juan, in this place, in that side of the market there. . . . And enter the church without any kind of fear, enter the church and sit down and when they make the invitation, then you raise your hand and say that you're going to accept Christ." I set out, when Sunday came, I came from there and came to San Juan, but I couldn't go in. I couldn't enter the church; I stayed in the door, but I felt something. Something of shame, something of fear. There wasn't anyone to invite me in. From there I returned. . . . Rather, I went back home. Another Sunday I went again, and the same thing happened. Then, it wasn't the same, but I stayed there standing in the door. Since I had gone to work in the *fincas,* I knew a man named Agustín Romero, and this Agustín, when he looked toward the door, when he saw me, made a sign with his hand for me to enter and told me to come in. So I had self-confidence to enter.

The conversion is a simple matter of raising his hand and being welcomed into the fellowship by the Mestizo pastor. Then he recounted the story of not knowing how he felt about his new situation, coming into contact with a prominent missionary couple in the area who hired him to help with some writing and translation in Mam, and the legalization of his marriage. His wife was ill during the legalization of the marriage, but she was transported to the mayor's office to answer questions by the missionaries.[36] She remained ill, and his father threw them out of the house that was likely adjoining the father's own property, given local patrilocal residence patterns. The minister originally did not believe that his father would throw him out of the very house that the father himself had helped build.

> But he told me a second time, so I asked him, "So papá," I said, "You really are speaking seriously?" "Yes," he said, "Yes, I'm speaking seriously." "Okay," I said, "Are you going to tell me who my father is?" I said to him, "Are you going to tell me who my father is?" "I am, but since you have disobeyed me, for that I am not your father. Get out!" So I said, "Forgive me, father. You are my father, you." He repeated, "Go and acknowledge as your parents those you have loved." "Look, papá," I said, "They are not my parents, you are my father, first God and you." "Yes," he said, "but because you disobeyed me now I'm not your father." "Okay, so it is," I told him. "Are you going to give me a month to remain in this little house, one month I ask you." . . . "Okay," he told me. I asked God to help me find a place to make the house.

There is more to this story, just as there are a number of ways to analyze the conversion discussed in these excerpts. The convert eventually found himself preaching (initially in a rather itinerant fashion), saw converts among his immediate family and community, and even achieved some degree of reconciliation with his father, who never is actually said to have converted. Yet the primary theme is conversion as a break with past traditions and even with family members who represent the ancestral traditions. A less obvious but significant issue is the role of people from other cultures—a Ladino preacher and missionaries (identified as North American in the narrative)—as those who carry the new tradition. There is something quite powerful (and a little disturbing) about the convert's father identifying the missionaries as the new parents as he throws the son out of his house. None of these themes is new in literature on conversion, and the story does not give much attention to cultural identity per se. At the same time, the central point of tension is the family network and the authority of the father within Maya culture. The tension is sustained by a worldview in which the ancestors play a key role in grounding community identity and traditions. The son's new belief system irreparably breaks this link, and the son will have to find a new home away from his family and the land that symbolizes interconnectedness in Maya cosmology.

Conversion Incorporating Tradition

A contrasting approach to conversion, and perhaps one only possible with the passage of time, is illustrated in the following narrative of a middle-aged Mam Presbyterian minister who came of age during the 1980s and struggled with family problems as well as national issues in the context of military service and repression. This minister represents a strongly biblical and Calvinistic approach to evangelicalism, and he is concerned about Pentecostal influences on the theology and practice of Presbyterianism in the highlands. He deals with Mam cultural issues through linguistic training and Bible translation, and he is very interested in theological education. In several interviews with this minister, I felt that I did not have much luck in persuading him to talk much about Maya spirituality and how that related to his evangelicalism. I often interviewed him in the company of a younger Mam layperson who was active in youth ministry and an elder in a local congregation. This latter man represented a Mam perspective that had been much more informed by life in a small urban area than did that of many of the pastors who had stronger roots in the countryside. While both men believed that Maya shamans had power, they were much more focused on the power of Jesus Christ to overcome the deleterious effects of the activities of these *brujos,* who are still credited with the power, it seems, to kill. In other words, although their worldview is oriented in a different direction, they believe other powers continue to exist and operate in the world.[37]

Perhaps typical of the researcher who does not hear what he or she might prefer to hear in the interview setting, one morning I asked a rather direct question: "Do you believe that you in one way or another still personally manage aspects of Maya religion? In any manner?" The minister replied with an answer that both surprised me and revealed a unique way of coming to terms with his evangelicalism and with an ancestor who had been quite important in his life, a *tartarabuela* (great-great-grandmother):

> In my case there is a need for more information in terms of the concept regarding faith. The last time I was remembering some of what my great-great-grandmother said, right? But one thing I'm remembering is that she said that in the case of the Maya priests, as they call them now, she said this is more recent. Likewise, she said that which is Catholic, that which is evangelical, is not of us. That came when the white people came, the Spaniards. And she said that they are not our people, they are our enemies. Along with all this [came] imposition of what is foreign— that there are priests, that there has to be Mass in the church, that one has to go to school, all of that. And the evangelical churches aren't of us, she said. Only, this was brought later. Speaking of the Maya priests, or as it is said in Mam, *ajkab',* I don't say that what they do is not ours, but it is recent as well. Except before we have this teaching that our parents and we [ourselves] have to respect God and keep with us the idea that God is present wherever we are—whether we are in the house, in the road, at work. But the idea given by the Maya priests is that we have to go to

worship God in the mountains . . . that one goes to worship in front of a rock, she said. But God is not the rock, she said. God is not there, but in all places. So in one sense, I believe that, yes, this is within Christian faith. It is possible that, yes, we are practicing part of what they practiced, right? . . .

Later when I had just begun to read the Bible, I remembered what she had told me. But a lot of what she said, I found in the Bible. [In] the case of respect, I found in the Bible that you have to have that, respect for parents, right? In the Bible it says that as well, "Honor your father and mother." And there is one God, the God, Father God. In Mam . . . *el mero anciano,* the real elder, right? But the concept is one. . . .

So I think that in some way, yes, among the people here before, there was a concept, a more clear concept of God; and perhaps religion was like that as well, with a faith in God like that in the time of Abraham. We don't know. Unfortunately, we don't have that information. . . . But the manner in which she spoke, in the light of reading the Bible, I came to a consciousness that she, while she was here on the earth, was carrying a faith in the Kingdom of God. And really, I came to believe . . . I came to believe that, yes, she also died, but she was not lost.

When I initially looked at this narrative, I examined the way this minister tried to bridge the gap between cultures—between the evangelical identity and the need to do away with past religious or spiritual traditions in the face of conversion (Samson 1999). We can take that a step further at this juncture. Even the reference to his *tartarabuela* tells us that we are dealing with a different kind of discourse. If not a *testimonio* or even some kind of a direct autobiographical account, perhaps it can be placed in the category of a kind of personal mytho-history.[38] The speaker embraces a personal spirituality even while seeking to transcend the personal (and the personally spiritual) and reconcile some of the ethnic and racial tensions that so shape culture and society in Guatemala. The discourse shows us one way in which Mam Maya Protestants can provide us with a clearer picture of the relationship between power and meaning in situations of cultural contact and conflict. The emphasis here, however, is not on the conflict so much as on the creative aspects of integrating personal and group identity, smoothing out troubling edges in the process. As Anthony Cohen writes in *Self Consciousness:*

"[C]ulture" has now to be used . . . to refer to the manifold activities and experiences of the *diverse* people whom it *aggregates*. Culture is the framework of meaning, of concepts and ideas within which different aspects of a person's life can be related to each other without imposing arbitrary categorical boundaries between them. The ingenuity and social skill of the individual is tested by the degree to which she or he can reconcile these various activities and interests, a reconciliation which implies that, while engaged in any one activity, individuals are nevertheless repositories of all their other commitments and experiences. That is what makes them unique. (1994, 96)

The tension between what is ours and what others have imposed upon us mirrors the tension between the local context and the imposition of forces of globalization upon it. But the tension is historical as well. A primary issue in the narrative is that of reconciling the tension inherent within a history of colonialism and missionary agendas that have conspired to reshape meaning, that is, personal and group self-understanding. One person who heard a version of this story went so far as to suggest that a missionary story about where God resides, a story that would have critiqued pantheistic tendencies in Maya spiritual traditions, is being reshaped and given new meaning. I read the text as a reflection of both the universalizing tendency within Christianity to insist on God's presence everywhere and in all things and the more vitalistic conceptualization in Mam cosmology wherein sacredness inheres in the relationship between people and the landscape, as well as between the generations. Time itself is measured not only in the span of a person's life but also through the continuing presence of the generations of those who sought to resolve some of the same tensions of person in community and in larger society.

In terms of conversion, the issue is how the convert actually constructs a way of thinking about faith that incorporates something of the worldview and experience of the past, including family members and, perhaps especially, ancestors or elders who are so much a part of Maya culture and of indigenous cultures in many parts of the world. The frame of reference for the transcendent has changed, but there is a need to reach out to family and community, even when those others did not or do not apprehend the world in the same terms as the convert. Here the emphasis is on the ties that bind the person (or the subject) to a place and a culture. Conversion is not a once-and-for-all event but rather a process that calls for continual reinterpretation throughout a person's life. Rather than simply a radical break with the past, here we have an effort to reincorporate tradition in a new framework.

Conclusion

While this chapter paints a view of rather traditional evangelical practice, part of its purpose is to show how such traditionalism is called into question when people come face-to-face with the radical separation that can be occasioned by conversion. This separation is manifested in the way the architecture of Mam church buildings and Mam worship services, including the ritual surrounding the sacrament of baptism, historically showed an effort on the part of the evangelical community to distance itself from the practices of both Catholic and Maya traditions. More graphic still is the sense of separation when the ties of hearth and kin are radically severed by the act of conversion. At this point, Scotchmer would seem to be correct in his assertion that "the new kinship system, while essentially redefined around the gospel and experienced within the church as an institution, shows features of exclusivity, rights, and obligations common to any family. Protestant conversion within the Mayan culture makes little sense without an understanding of the social and theological shift represented by participation and membership within this extended family" (1989, 304).

Simultaneously, the ethnographic record seems to reveal efforts to reconcile the tension between aspects of Maya-ness and the imposed religion of Protestantism. The intent is to give an accurate view of aspects of church life in the presbytery while showing how difficult it is to pigeonhole practices as exclusive of either social concern or of aspects of Mam culture. The effort to reconfigure *templo* architecture and to include a nonbelieving ancestor within the new family of the saved provides evidence that at least some of the dichotomization surrounding conversion when religious pluralism was not so common is breaking down. This may leave room for more creative expressions of religious identity in the future. And some of these expressions will reflect attempts to integrate translocal religious identity with ethnicity rooted in place. This kind of approach to Maya evangelical identity is indicative of the holism contained in expositions of indigenous worldviews emphasizing concepts such as balance (*equilibrio*), harmony, and complementarity, both in human relationships and in the interactions of human beings with the environment.[39] In one sense, such holism links the individual self more directly to a particular place and community of people, challenging the universalizing tendency within Christian discourse. Scotchmer captures the dichotomy nicely: "Unlike the culture which values the security of one last name and piece of ancestral land, one town and saint, one language and ethnic group, Mayan Protestants claim that their family includes others across every barrier without distinctions or differences between those who follow and belong to *Kajaw Crist*" (1989, 308). Elsewhere he discusses the relationship between mind (*nab'l*) and heart (*tanmi*) in Mam Protestant circles as one that "comprise[s] the social and spiritual equivalent of the person" (1993, 522 n. 18). Although this idea draws on Maya concepts, it actually highlights the autonomy of the individual Protestant who is integrated on the basis of a more holistic (or complete) sense of the individual self as opposed to a sense of self-in-place that is so characteristic of the Maya worldview.[40]

In fact, one of the burdens of this chapter has been to show that the domains "Mam" and "evangelical" are neither mutually exclusive nor necessarily dichotomized. Rather, the interactions between the two (often within the same person) embody Watanabe's "conventions of community." Ultimately, this is a more grounded perspective, rooted in the places of residence and worship, than a view of "inverse images" between Maya and Ladino. Watanabe sees identity in Santiago Chimaltenango, Huehuetenango, as both dialectical and oppositional. Acknowledging that there is a persistent opposition between the two groups, he goes on to say that "[t]his persistence entails no teleological inference of past ethnic differences because history attests to the time when a 'new world' was born in the confrontation between two old ones" (1992, 58). His sense that "otherness represents the boundary, not the substance, of ethnic identity in Guatemala" is likewise true in the religious arena. As I have shown, both through time and contemporaneously, what may be considered strictly evangelical or Maya in a direct sense can be appropriated in different ways. This is true even in the realm of social development projects alluded to in chapter 2. Even as some of this work has occasioned conflict over resources in recent years, with some people within the presbytery more interested in evangelistic activities and the building of *templos* and some others continuing to look toward community- or congregation-based projects for women, organic agriculture, or even elementary school education, the rubric of *teología integral* (integral or integrated theology) links theological concerns with human need in a manner reflective of the sense of community embodied in Maya culture.[41]

In the post-conflict situation in which Guatemalans are living, there may well be good reasons for embracing the universalizing tendencies of the Christian discourse recounted by Scotchmer. But these will not be embraced from outside the particular personal, communal, and cultural circumstances through which converts embrace evangelical practices. If sometimes a person has to leave home, kin, and country to make a new life, Maya cosmology may dictate that on some level the person take the ancestors along. Beyond the Mam Presbytery, the portrait painted, both materially and conceptually, is one that can be used in a comparative frame with other presbyteries (as I will do in the next chapter) and with other groups of evangelicals in Guatemala. As the evangelical might say, the bounds of both Maya-ness and evangelicalism do reach out into the life of the world.

6

An Activist Protestantism

The Kaqchikel Presbytery

> But the purpose of straightforward remembering is to preserve something
> that really happened. We want to have access to scenes that were real in the
> past and to somehow preserve these things in our present experience; it is
> the search for the truth of what has gone before.
>
> —Marea Teski and Jacob Climo, *The Labyrinth of Memory*

Introduction

On the afternoon of 23 June 1995, Kaqchikel Presbyterian minister Manuel
Saquic Vásquez was kidnapped on his way home from work at the Chimaltenango Office of Human Rights of the Kaqchikel Presbytery. The following
day his body was found in a *milpa* (cornfield) with thirty-three stab wounds, a
slashed throat, and torture marks. He was buried in Chimaltenango on 26 June
as an unknown person "XX." On 7 July his body was exhumed under the auspices of the United Nations Mission for the Verification of Human Rights in
Guatemala.[1] MINUGUA's Third Report from November 1995 remarks that
"The director of the Mission judged the assassination as very grave in terms
of the observance of human rights, indicating that it was not a common crime
but one destined to frighten entities and people that work in the defense of
such rights" (1995, 11).

As the first anniversary of Saquic's assassination neared, the Kaqchikel Presbytery, largely under the leadership of another Kaqchikel minister, Lucio Martínez, organized a series of memorial services in communities where Saquic
had worked and where the presbytery had established an ecumenical pattern
of ministry in the latter half of the 1980s. Martínez himself later died of a
heart attack, which some say was related to stress experienced due to threats
against his own life. The commemorative events began on 4 June 1996 and
were timed to end, on the anniversary of Saquic's disappearance, with an ecumenical religious service (*acta religiosa*) in the central plaza of Chimaltenango
and a march from the place where his body was found in the *municipio* of Parramos back to the Chimaltenango general cemetery. The march route led past
the military base where the suspected instigator (*autor intellectual*) of Saquic's

Figure 15. Marking the first anniversary of Saquic's murder

murder was the local military commissioner. While the commissioner was both known in and a frequent visitor to Chimaltenango, no action has ever been taken against him or his two sons, who were also implicated in the crime (Resolution 1996; Still 1996; A. Smith 1999).[2] Under the words "No Mas Impunidad" (No more impunity), the poster produced to announce the memorial events proclaimed Saquic a "triple martyr"—a martyr for human rights, a Christian martyr, and a Maya martyr.

The manner in which the Kaqchikel Presbytery worked to interpret Saquic's death as that of a Maya Protestant martyr provides another dimension in the analysis of Protestant religious expression in Guatemala and throughout Latin America. If the Mam Presbytery represents a Maya evangelical identity rooted in the symbolics of a historical Protestant theological tradition, and even a sometimes tenuous union of those symbolics with Mam cultural identity and cosmology, then the Kaqchikel Presbytery represents an activist evangelical identity. This activism is a direct challenge to notions of evangelicals as apolitical and inattentive to social issues. Simultaneously, it cultivates a challenge to state power and the political, social, and economic structure of Guatemalan society from a stance shaped by direct political and social involvement.

Figure 16. Poster proclaiming Saquic a triple martyr

As in the previous chapter, my approach here is to provide a limited case study. Following a description of aspects of the organizational structure of the presbytery and other aspects of the presbytery's work, I turn to a more detailed commentary on the Saquic case and the presbytery's response. The case demonstrates how a particular group of Maya evangelicals took the experience of the assassination of one of its ministers and projected that experience into the public arena in a way that highlights concerns for both Maya identity and social justice as embodied in movements for human rights in the months leading to the end of the formal peace process in 1996. In his publishing on contemporary approaches to the study of religion in the Americas, Manuel A. Vásquez has reacted to an "opposition between religion and globalization" in the work of network theorist Manuel Castells by saying that "[i]n many instances, religion thrives precisely because churches use the tools of globalization—namely, fluid transnational networks—to project their messages from the local to the global" (1999, 10). This case provides a vivid example of the presbytery's use of a translocal network in responding to a local crisis.

At the outset I should mention that the Kaqchikel Presbytery has been criticized for its approach to structural issues and direct involvement in political action. Although some initial work had begun among the Kaqchikel by Presbyterians from the capital, the history of the presbytery is tied largely to the activities of Vitalino Similox beginning with earthquake relief in the late 1970s.[3] When I was in the field, his wife, Margarita Valiente, had been *presidenta* of the presbytery for several years, and the presbytery has cultivated other connections to the international religious community that will become apparent below.[4] One leader in the presbytery even told me that it was difficult in some ways to call it a presbytery. Actual *templos* or church buildings do not typically serve as gathering places, and the discourse maintained by the presbytery is of work done in communities instead of in congregations as such. A minister from another IENPG presbytery once told me that it functions more like an "organization" than a presbytery, and that none of the ministers actually were originally Presbyterian.[5] At this juncture I report those perceptions in the interest of description, and it is not my intent to enter into any kind of polemic. It is true that some of the criticism directed toward the group from the outside reflects degrees of inter-ecclesial (and personal) animosity, but at least part of the conflict is the result of the tension created by an activist stance when religious practice moves beyond theology and doctrine. The activities of the presbytery have clearly drawn attention to the group, at times with life-and-death consequences for its members. At the same time, the fact that none of the ministers was originally Presbyterian demonstrates the fluidity of Protestant religious affiliation as well as some of the difficulties involved in the attempt to find a "Protestant" perspective on particular issues of concern.

Taken together, the Kaqchikel Presbytery's approach to ministry and its response to Sacquic's murder represent a minority current within the larger stream of Guatemalan evangelicalism. Nevertheless, the presbytery's approach is revealing as an example of how one group seeks to shape its identity in difficult circumstances and of this particular group's felt need to bring religion to bear on the post-conflict situation in Guatemala. In a broader frame of reference, it is representative of how some evangelicals approach direct social involvement in the context of organizing within civil society.

Setting

The Kaqchikel Presbytery was founded in 1987. Although it had origins in the early 1970s, work in the area took on more urgency in the context of aid distribution following the 1976 earthquake, which destroyed much of Chi-

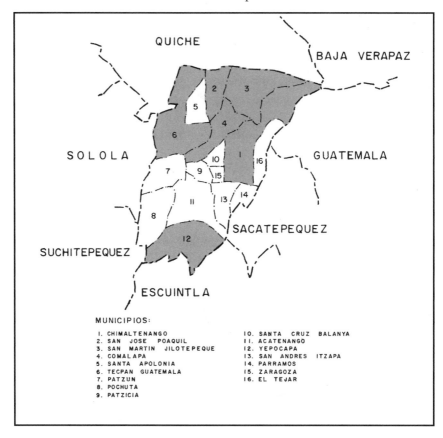

MUNICIPIOS:

1. CHIMALTENANGO
2. SAN JOSE POAQUIL
3. SAN MARTIN JILOTEPEQUE
4. COMALAPA
5. SANTA APOLONIA
6. TECPAN GUATEMALA
7. PATZUN
8. POCHUTA
9. PATZICIA

10. SANTA CRUZ BALANYA
11. ACATENANGO
12. YEPOCAPA
13. SAN ANDRES ITZAPA
14. PARRAMOS
15. ZARAGOZA
16. EL TEJAR

Figure 17. Chimaltenango *municipios* with Kaqchikel Presbyterian involvement

maltenango.[6] By 1998, work was being carried out in some nineteen *comunidades* in approximately six *municipios* in the department (Similox V. n.d.).[7] This included six congregations and an additional thirteen communities where there was no established congregation. The presbytery *presidenta* told me that the work involved approximately thirty-four hundred people in all the communities.

The presbytery's headquarters are located in the departmental capital of Chimaltenango, approximately forty-five minutes west of Guatemala City just off the improved and mostly four-lane Pan American Highway. According to the 1994 census, Chimaltenango city had a population of 44,696 inhabitants, while the department itself had 314,813. The departmental population had increased to 446,133 by 2002, a staggering 41.17 percent increase. This is a much higher percentage increase than the 23.99 percent increase the census recorded for the department of Quetzaltenango during the same time period.[8] No doubt such growth represents the demographic structure of Chimaltenango, but further investigation may reveal a connection with the availability of jobs in either agriculture or the maquila sector discussed below. Out-migration may also be lower because of both job availability and the ability to commute to and from the capital. Illiteracy for the population fifteen years of age and above was similar in both areas: 36.2 percent in Chimaltenango and 32 percent in Quetzaltenango in 1994. In both cases, the figure increased to over 40 percent in rural areas. The 1994 census identified 79.4 percent of the departmental population as indigenous.

The city of Chimaltenango is the center of an area manifesting many of the contemporary aspects of globalization. These include a transient labor force that commutes daily to Guatemala City or to a number of maquila factories that have been established between the capital and the workforce available in the region. As well, a burgeoning nontraditional agricultural export market has become an integral part of economic survival strategies for families in the region (Goldín 1999, 2001; Hamilton and Fischer 2003). Liliana Goldín has referred to the process of "re-ruralization of occupational strategies" that others have noted in various parts of Central America, as well as the concept of the "pseudo-urbanization of rural life" (2001, 36), to describe aspects of life in the area. Both terms are apt in indicating the diverse economic strategies employed by families in the area and the extent to which the movement of people in the area is tied to forces in the capital city and in other parts of the world.

Although still primarily in *tierra fría,* the area is generally lower in altitude than the Mam area, and the mountainous land, while rugged, is generally not as steep on the transportation routes near the main highway. The broader valleys and slopes between several volcanoes near Lake Atitlán comprise a rich agricultural area with a focus on both domestic and export production. Conflict over land makes headlines in the department on a fairly regular basis, notably in mid-2002 over land in a *finca* in the *municipio* of San Martín Jilotepeque. The area is also known as a rich cultural area in terms of artisan activities, such as weaving, and for the primitivist painting tradition in the cultural center of Comalapa. The city of Iximché, now an important archaeological site near the *municipio* of Tecpán, was founded in 1470 and served briefly as the center of Spanish military activities in 1524 until a rebellion broke the brief Spanish-Kaqchikel alliance. The site now is not only an archaeological site but very much a living part of local Kaqchikel culture where people go to enjoy the company of family and friends. A major ceremonial site for Maya religious practices is located in a wooded area at one end of the park-like grounds, and the area is used continually by local Maya priests who come and perform ceremonies with their clients.

Much of the city of Chimaltenango was destroyed in the earthquake, and most of the construction in the town is low and tends toward the nondescript. Residential areas impinge upon the busy market and business area in the town *centro*. The city is in many ways the true jumping-off point for the western highlands. The Pan American Highway runs through the south side of town only eight or ten blocks from the town center, and it is often jammed with cars, buses, and other vehicles plying the route between Chimaltenango and "Guate." Upon entering the town from the Pan American Highway, one cannot help but be struck by the seamier aspects of life that often accompany shifting population, including soldiers from the large military base that until recently was located on the outskirts of town. "Bars" with threadbare curtains and names like La Pasa Bien and El Buen Gusto shield the obvious from the dusty hustle and bustle of travelers moving to and from the capital or to western destinations such as Lake Atitlán, the department of Quiché, Quetzaltenango, or the Mexican border, following a six- or seven-hour ride through some of the most beautiful scenery in the country.[9]

During the war years, Chimaltenango was strongly affected by the violence. The guerrilla movement, particularly the Guerrilla Army of the Poor (EGP) and the Organización del Pueblo en Armas (ORPA, Organization of the People in Arms), was active in the region, and the local population paid a heavy price in terms of repression and displacement, particularly beginning with a massive government counterinsurgency campaign in 1981. This was in response to the military high command's "perception of eminent danger growing out of the supposition that Chimaltenango had become a center of strategic gravity for the guerrilla forces. It was an essential point for pressuring the capital and from which to declare a liberated territory, owing to the massive [local] support, and to complicate the panorama with a greater international effect" (CEH 2000, 139).[10] The strong presence of Catholic Action, which became a focus of military action as early as 1975 and 1976, probably contributed to the targeting of this area as well. Over time, such targeting surely had the opposite effect of contributing to radicalization in the region (ODHAG 1999, 225).[11]

Before moving to the analysis of the presbytery, I reinforce here the fact that the department of Chimaltenango is a center for the larger movement for cultural rights embodied in the pan-Maya movement. Fischer observes tendencies within the K'iche' and Kaqchikel wings of the movement that in some ways reflect the historical tension between the two groups and the fact that the Kaqchikel have historically been in the orb of the Guatemalan capital (regardless of location), while the K'iche' have been more tied to Quetzaltenango, "and thus a bit more isolated from first Spanish and then ladino oversight" (2001,

104). He argues that this benefited the K'iche's ability to maintain some degree of both commercial and political autonomy. While both groups pursue their goals through "organized collective action," he reports that one leader in the movement argues that "the K'iche' have traditionally been more oriented toward broadly leftist political goals, while the Kaqchikel have pursued a route of cultural activism" (104). This observation is a bit speculative, and it may reflect the difference between groups that are indeed more culturally focused and those that are more focused on class issues and, therefore, more willing to make common cause with Ladinos in social-organizing activities around land-tenure issues or economic justice.

A significant aspect of this cultural activism has been in the area of religion and Maya spirituality, and this emphasis shapes some of the activities of the Kaqchikel Presbytery to a larger degree than, for example, the emphasis on language, which receives so much attention in academic circles in North America (cf. Similox 1992; Otzoy 1997; Wuqub' Iq' 1997).[12] This is not to say that language is unimportant but rather to acknowledge the complex of cultural and social factors at play in diverse segments of pan-Mayanism as it is worked out in various contexts. In terms of religion, Fischer, while taking due note that some of their co-religionists see even language instruction as part of a slide into paganism (2001, 254 n. 2), nevertheless contends that "[a]t the local level . . . pan-Mayanism seems to appeal to both Catholics and Protestants, each of whom interpret the meaning of cultural valuation and development slightly differently" (101). There is also some tension in the formalization of traditional practices under rubrics such as Maya religion. This is especially true in relation to the words used for the renewal among those who serve as spiritual guides for their people, and who sometimes claim to be practitioners of Maya spirituality as opposed to Maya religion. As Ricardo Falla notes in the epilogue of the English translation of his study of conversion in San Antonio Ilotenango, *Quiché Rebelde,* the difference can be significant. His frame of reference is the increased number of Maya priests or spiritual guides in San Antonio: "We do not know to what extent the Maya priest in San Antonio would insist on this distinction. According to this way of thinking, Maya spirituality is an essence. It not only is shaped in rituals and prayers but permeates everything: it harmonizes nature and the humanity of living beings; it promotes consensus in decisions" (2001, 245).[13]

Violence, Peace, and Activism

With the proclamation of Saquic as a triple martyr, a new *coyuntura* (historical moment) came into being in the nexus of evangelical identity, the struggle against impunity in the area of human and civil rights, and the struggle for ethnic renewal by the Maya in Guatemala. The moment reveals elements of the evangelical community to be more engaged with their social context than has typically been acknowledged in Latin America, and it again draws our attention to particular indigenous evangelicals. Some reference to aspects of the civil war and the peace process in the Chimaltenango area are needed to better contextualize the work of the presbytery, while more clearly situating the construction of Saquic as a martyr. I limit my discussion to developments relevant to the Chimaltenango case.

Following the earthquake in 1976, much of the incoming aid appears to have been siphoned off by the military, which, according to some reports, did not distribute it properly. Other international aid, including aid from evangelical religious organizations, poured directly into local communities, sometimes creating new power bases in the process (Carmack 1979). The time immediately following the earthquake and the subsequent period of repression also heralded a period of spectacular growth among evangelical and, especially, Pentecostal churches. Sheldon Annis's (1987) seminal work on Guatemalan evangelicalism begins with an incident of preaching in the highlands shortly after the earthquake, and the CEH describes the character of Protestant growth during the repression: "Fundamentalist Protestantism helped people confront personal and local problems without bringing them so far as to confront sociopolitical problems that were out of their control" (CEH 2000, 104).[14]

By 1978 a massacre in the Panzos community in the department of Baja Verapaz signaled that a counterinsurgency was under way. The army, guided by the ideology of the national security state, targeted the Maya population as being particularly complicit with the guerrillas.[15] This was also true for priests and nuns and catechists from the Roman Catholic Church who had been active in Catholic Action and who were frequently assumed to have drunk too deeply from the well of liberation theology.[16] The infamous *patrullas de autodefensa civil* (PACs, civilian self-defense patrols) were begun as a way of maintaining military control over the rural population shortly before Romeo Lucas García (1978–82) was ousted in the coup that brought the enigmatic General Efraín Ríos Montt (1982–83) to power. Generally considered the first practicing evangelical president in Latin America, Ríos Montt was well known for delivering biblical messages on television while the army carried out its scorched-earth tactics in the highlands. Because of the high profile of his religious beliefs, his time in the presidency has skewed many interpretations of Guatemalan evangelicalism in the past twenty-five years.

In fact, Ríos Montt was the most visible constant on both the political and evangelical scene for three decades. It is generally accepted that he won the

1974 presidential elections on the Christian Democratic ticket, elections that were eventually awarded to another candidate more to the military's liking. Although he was twice prohibited by the courts from running for the presidency because of a constitutional clause forbidding a person who came to power in a coup from occupying that office, Ríos Montt was president of Guatemala's congress following the national elections of 1999, which gave the political party he continued to head in 2005, the Guatemalan Republican Front (FRG), both the presidency and nearly a two-thirds majority in the congress.

In the run-up to the November 2003 presidential election, Ríos Montt again pressed for the right to run for the presidency. His registration for the election was upheld by Guatemala's Court of Constitutionality in July 2003. The four-to-three vote in his favor was widely held to be the result of a court stacked by the FRG. When the order from the court was temporarily suspended by the Supreme Court of Justice, protests against his registration broke out in Guatemala City. In response, a number of Ríos Montt supporters, including many bused to the capital from rural areas, engaged in a series of violent demonstrations on 24 and 25 July. A MINUGUA report verified participation of FRG leaders in organizing these demonstrations. While the national police did nothing to restore order for two days, the protestors left the city at Ríos Montt's behest around noon on 25 July. The Court of Constitutionality again ordered his registration for the election on 30 July (MINUGUA 2003). In the midst of his ongoing political involvement, Ríos Montt maintained a relationship with the El Verbo (Church of the Word) congregation in zone 16 of Guatemala City, and I attended a Sunday school class he taught in March 2001. Nevertheless, his public discourse has been much less overtly religious in the years since the signing of the peace accord.[17]

In the Chimaltenango case, the different ways of relating to the guerrillas became clearer in conversations with the person who was coordinating human rights activities in the Kaqchikel Presbytery in 1998. This man had grown up largely in a coastal environment, beginning various kinds of menial activity to help support himself by age six. He considers himself Kaqchikel, although he speaks only Spanish. Following his marriage, he moved to Santa Lucía, Cotzumalguapa, where he claims his "eyes were opened" by the Jesuits. He is Episcopalian, never having actually become a catechist. While his work at the time of the interview involved organizing local human rights groups, he began training with the EGP shortly after the earthquake. He learned organizational skills from his guerrilla involvement and from further involvement with CUC. He considers most of his involvement to have been political in nature and even recounts turning in his weapon after being involved with others in letting five soldiers go rather than killing them. At various times, guerilla *normas* required that *compañeros* be killed for various acts of either omission or commission. He spent some time in hiding in an area around the *municipio* of Yepocapa, and claims to have eventually joined a PAC, which he eventually helped persuade to disarm.

I never had the opportunity to flesh out this man's life story. Besides involvement with various religious communities—Catholic, Episcopalian, and Presbyterian—his story is one of a shifting relationship with the armed revolution and a permanent commitment to community organizing. He was grateful to the Kaqchikel Presbytery for the opportunity to participate in the kind of work he was doing at the time, and he did say that by 1994 he had received threats as a result of his organizing activities, at some point even receiving the presence of an international accompaniment volunteer.[18]

In addition to the sheer difficulties of living in such circumstances, this part of his story shows the involvement of networks of international solidarity and religious activists in the pursuit of human rights and social justice in Guatemala. Furthermore, the entire sequence narrated here demonstrates how the violence intersects with issues of religion and ethnicity in the current situation. At times within the presbytery, cultural rights and identity issues are addressed in a secondary way as part of a larger discourse of human rights. This is despite the attempt of the presbytery to foreground Maya culture and an ethic more geared toward communitarianism, as will be seen below. A document produced in the presbytery called "The Manifestation of God in the Kaqchikel People" shows this tension at work. The document begins with an introduction emphasizing Maya culture as a path to both survival and liberation.

> For the Maya People, in our case the Kaqchikel Presbytery, our religion has been the base of our survival, of our resistance, and today, for our proposal in the face of the configuration of a New Guatemala— multiethnic, plurilingual, and pluricultural.
>
> Our religion and ancient Maya spirituality are the means for the rescue and construction of our identity. This will be possible to the extent that it helps us bring together all of our demands, sustain our existence in a multiethnic society and put us on the road toward our liberation and self-determination. (Similox V. n.d.)

Only two paragraphs later, in a section attempting to situate the presbytery in its social and geographic context, a more generalized demand for social and human rights is emphasized: "The political, economic, cultural and social situation demanded congruent actions as an answer to the growing and indiscriminate violation of human rights, in such a way that . . . the Kaqchikel Presbytery initiated its work as such, in the face of denunciation and protest, in the face of violations and assassinations of our fellow Guatemalans, principally and primarily Mayas."

The nature of the Kaqchikel approach to issues of human and cultural rights in a context of direct violence meant that the violence itself would become a focal point for the organization's activity and solidarity work, especially with women's groups in the area. Maya identity is projected outward in a symbolic sense, as will be seen when I return to Manuel Saquic's story below. Another aspect of this is the relationship to the international religious community, which has funded some of the presbytery's activities and maintained a consistent discourse around its activities locally with the Kaqchikel Presbytery and sometimes in response to the Guatemalan context more broadly.[19]

Another local example of the impact of the violence on life in Chimaltenango can be illustrated by segments of the autobiography of a presbytery leader, here called Gustavo. Gustavo was born in 1969, and he shows how a younger generation was affected by the war years. He left school around the time of his sixth year in primary school after seeing the *alcalde* in his *municipio* killed. Although he eventually graduated as a primary school teacher in 1989, throughout the 1990s he was involved in working with various organizations with ties to the Presbyterian Church. He reported having been kidnapped twice for brief periods during 1989. He did not elaborate on the background to those events, although they may be related to the fact that when we had the interview in 1998, he reported that former PAC members in his community saw him as an enemy ("me tienen como enemigo"). The patrol had been dissolved some four years before, but because his house is some distance from the village, he was watched (*controlado*).

While it is difficult to make generalizations based on such a brief recounting of a person's experience, it is certain that a climate of fear and mistrust continued to have an impact on community relations in years subsequent to the signing of the peace. Gustavo's "conscience was born" through study with sisters from the Roman Catholic Church, and over the years he was a catechist, an agent of the social pastorate, and a youth worker. He did not break his ties with the Catholic Church after he began to attend a reflection group with the Presbyterians.

The local texture provided here can be linked to the tenuous process of consolidating peace and democracy since the signing of the peace. I mentioned earlier the failed constitutional referendum in May 1999, which would have codified some of the mandates of the side agreements, especially in regard to indigenous rights. The "yes" vote did prevail in Chimaltenango with some 48.84 percent of the vote, and the reforms generally had more support in departments with high indigenous populations, as well as in other rural areas (De las reformas 1999).[20]

Constructing Evangelical Identity:
Liturgical Symbolism and Community

The foregoing more fully situates the narrative of Manuel Saquic's martyr-dom within the context of contemporary Guatemala, for in significant ways the crossroads of Chimaltenango mirrors the local, national, and transnational linkages between the people of the region and global social and economic pro-cesses reaching into the very households of the area. Goldín's perspective on the relationship between economic strategies and culture provides a context for assessing the Kaqchikel Presbytery's approach to political and social involve-ment: "Painfully aware of the potential of cultural loss and subjugation in the context of the expansion of capital, it seems that sectors of Maya society are struggling with understanding current developments and their implications for Maya culture and identity. As personal and community values change along-side structural conditions, there is no going back and only the new actors in the newly created landscapes can ultimately evaluate the outcomes and devise strategies for the future" (2001, 52). Without capitulating to a direct Weberian correlation between capitalism's "spirit" and an affinity with Protestantism, we can see in the activities of the Kaqchikel Presbytery concerted attention being given to evangelicalism as a local phenomenon, seeking to make an impact by crossing boundaries—between religious traditions, cultures, and even nation-states—and changing meaning in the process.

Reflecting on the churches that figure so prominently on the landscape em-braced by the Mam Presbytery, I recall my first visit to the Kaqchikel Presby-tery office in 1996. I was looking for Lucio Martínez and one of the Saquic commemoration events that was to take place in an *aldea* called Bola de Oro. The compound was closed to the small alley with a black metal door upon which the name of the presbytery was scrawled. A large gathering hall and a couple of smaller rooms were largely empty except for the representative of the national police who was guarding the compound and, presumably, pro-viding some measure of protection for threatened members of the presbytery. I briefly entered the compound and saw the office of the Defensoria Maya (Maya Defenders), the human rights office. The gathering room was arranged in a more horizontal orientation than the longitudinal view toward the chan-cel area typical of most churches in Guatemala and elsewhere. Benches were arranged in a circle around a table, and flowers were in a bucket on the floor near the table. A blackboard was on one side of the room, and on the other side was a huge banner with a picture of Saquic. The word "¡¡VIVE!!" (LIVES!) was directly below Saquic's name, and a Bible verse occupied the space below his picture: "SO JEHOVAH HAS SPOKEN: MAKE WISDOM AND JUS-TICE, AND LIBERATE THE OPPRESSED FROM THE HAND OF

THE OPPRESSOR" (Jeremiah 22:3). On the opposite wall was a banner from CIEDEG that lamented and condemned "the cowardly assassination of Pastor Manuel Saquic with a bloody act that places an obstacle in the road of the longed for peace." This was a different place, with different kinds of preoccupations, from the Mam congregations I had been working in before. Even the wall I faced as I entered, painted with a nature scene and Bible verses, seemed to give a more direct message of the link between the divine and the human in religious practice: "God takes care of the flowers. . . . Will he not take care of human beings?"

Although there are only six churches in the presbytery, even their names show a more political approach to spiritual concerns than in the Mam case. I later learned that the Chimaltenango congregation is called Ri Nabel—in Spanish, El Principio (the Beginning). The others are Nueva Vida (New Life), Caminemos Juntos (Let Us Walk Together), Esperanza en Camino (Hope in Process), Pueblo de Dios (People of God), and Embajadores del Reino (Ambassadors of the Kingdom).[21] The concern of the Kaqchikel is clearly more in the realm of day-to-day life than a strict spirituality, and the preoccupation emphasizes communitarian ideology. An organizational chart of the presbytery on the wall when I visited Ri Nabel on another occasion showed a departmental coordinating body, with representatives from each community where the presbytery was active, on the same level as the presbytery executive committee, which had representatives from each of the congregations.

At the ideological level, Kathryn Anderson's description of the shape of work in the presbytery is accurate. Anderson contrasts the bureaucratic nature typical of presbyteries with the way in which the leaders in the Kaqchikel Presbytery established their work: "They did not construct buildings or establish traditional worship services. Instead they created informal worshipping communities and community-based self-help groups, most often made up of women. They made no distinctions on the basis of religious affiliation. Those who had suffered from the violence, Protestant or Catholic, and were willing to work with their neighbours for survival and reconstruction were welcome" (2003, 132).

The emphasis on a nontraditional approach to liturgy is a particular point of contrast with the Mam Presbytery. We have already seen how the rhetoric in the presbytery tends to move away from talk of churches and toward a discourse of community. Although the authority of the minister and the centrality of the Word of God, both read and proclaimed, are important in both groups, the manner of dealing with the Word varies. In the Kaqchikel Presbytery there is to some extent a decentralization of the minister's role and a recognition of the place of the gathered community in the interpretation of Scripture. I once heard the *presidenta* of the presbytery tell a group that the

Kaqchikel did not have pulpits, essentially because such would set up an order of authority that was not a part of their indigenous culture. The better approach was the use of a circle where people could see each other face-to-face. This mode of interaction was related to the affirmation that women in Guatemala had participated in a long tradition of resistance. In that light, the issue of how to reflect on the Bible was gender-laden as well as symbolic of the nature of authority in the presbytery. The view of authority structures in indigenous culture is worthy of note, although it is a clear example of how culture is being reinterpreted in the present.

The issue of pastoral leadership in relation to the communities can also be assessed in view of the fact that the statistics compiled for the annual synod meetings of the IENPG in both 1996 and 1998 showed only four ministers in the presbytery in the period immediately following the deaths of Saquic and Martínez. One of those, whose house had been destroyed during the violence, lived in Guatemala City in a community that had been formed from displaced people in the early 1990s. Of the other three, two of them had primary responsibilities for organizations also in the capital. Some of this situation changed in 2001 when Josefina Inay (Martínez's widow) and Margarita Similox were ordained (K. Anderson 2003, 133).[22]

The approach to liturgy and the symbolism surrounding liturgy is associated with the communitarian ethic of Maya culture, but it also reflects some of the values of political organizing and the activities of groups like Catholic Action in Chimaltenango, hence the importance of some of the history cited earlier. Gustavo gave a slightly different nuance, citing a grounded process of Bible study, when I asked him about the nature of worship in his local congregation: "Reflections are what we take to be a religious activity in which we read a biblical passage. We contextualize it, asking, 'What does this say and what does it move us to do now?' In that sense, it could be done as a worship service, but more like a type of formation, discussion [or] workshop. . . . It isn't like a formal service where only the pastor speaks and that's it. Everybody is there. And . . . in relation to them, following [the reflection] we begin to talk about our necessities at home, in our *milpa,* with our children. Like that we come together to form our community."

Like the urgency surrounding so much of the activity in the presbytery, however, this localism was not viewed in isolation from either the situation of ongoing violence or from the international community upon which presbytery activists relied for support in difficult times. Gustavo put it this way when I asked him about the peace process: "Here we can't say that the peace was signed and we are at peace. No, in any moment the knock on the door can come. You hope that one receives a threat and knows that he is being watched. Otherwise, without a threat you die and it's done. So, in this sense, what we

Figure 18. March in memory of Bishop Juan Gerardi

need most is solidarity from outside." I turn now to how the presbytery dealt publicly with the violence in the case of Saquic's murder in Chimaltenango.

The Construction of a Martyr in Humanistic Perspective

The perspective of humanistic anthropology provides an experiential point of departure for understanding the self-definition reflected in the construction of Saquic as a martyr by Kaqchikel evangelicals. As the epigraph to this chapter hinted, it is precisely in the act of remembering that we see the symbolic appropriation of religion or the religious persona, even of a person's tragic death, and how such appropriation is used in the interest of cultural revitalization and political activism. This transcending of the religious sphere begins with the use of the term *martyr* itself, for the implication is that a martyr gives testimony or bears witness to something outside him- or herself (Qué es 1998). From the perspective of the presbytery, Saquic represents all those whose human rights were violated during the war and, by extension, those who continue to be victimized by impunity or by threats from forces connected to the old order even after the signing of the peace. Telling Saquic's story is part of the truth-telling aspect of remembering, an aspect accentuated in the Roman Catholic Church's project on the Recuperación de la Memoria Histórica (REMHI, Recovery of Historical Memory): "Historical memory has an important role to play in dismantling the mechanisms that made state terrorism possible and in exposing the role terrorism plays in an exclusive political and economic system. The story of people's suffering cannot be treated as if it were pages in a book. The distortion of events and of accountability for them elevates the risk that new ways will be found to legitimize the instigators of the war, placing Guatemala's future in grave jeopardy" (ODHAG 1999, xxxiii).

Historical memory, then, provides an important foregrounding for ethics in an age when the nation-state continues to be the arbiter among competing groups, groups who, nevertheless, continue to resist repression and abuses of power. Anthropologically, the question becomes one of examining how a perspective on culture "stresses both the flow of experience and the transfiguration of that experience into cultural forms" (Richardson and Dunton 1989, 76). While pointing in the direction of a constructivist view of culture, such a perspective remains tied to experience in place. In honoring Saquic's memory, *experience* and *transfiguration* are the operative words for the Kaqchikel. The cultural form is that of a local martyr with a specific ethnic and religious identity. Unlike fellow Central Americans Archbishop Oscar Romero in El Salvador and Bishop Juan Gerardi, the latter of whom was beaten to death in the garage of his home in Guatemala City on 26 April 1998, two days after presiding over the release of the report of the project on the Recovery of Historical Memory, Saquic is not remembered through his texts or through the weight of an institution as powerful as the Roman Catholic Church.[23] Instead, he is transfigured in the memory of his own community as it tells his story from out of the silence of his absence in their midst.[24] The narrative itself to some extent transfigures the person. Although Saquic was known for involvement in human rights, and while he identified with the Maya community of which he was a part, some who knew him have suggested that his own sense of himself as an evangelical was lived out in tension with aspects of Maya religious practice. Even in the service of just causes, one's image and the things one stood for in life might be differently reinterpreted (or reappropriated) in death.

Saquic's martyrdom was accented in the public activities of the Kaqchikel Presbytery in Chimaltenango in the months leading up to the formal end of the war. Undoubtedly, the need to grieve and to hold onto something of a life that exuded hope in difficult circumstances played a role, but remembering a person is not the only purpose for the narration of the martyrdom of Manuel Saquic. The narrative of Saquic's death focuses attention on the role religion can play in the social and political contexts that impinge on the Kaqchikel Presbytery, as well as on the concerns of the Maya and others who lived through the violence of a counterinsurgency war.[25] When his former colleagues highlight Saquic's work as a human rights activist, they draw attention to the coalescence between Saquic's work at the time of his death and the way in which his memory is appropriated.[26]

In the arena where Saquic is understood as a Maya and Christian martyr, the terms of the discussion are already being pushed into a more extensive social milieu. The very use of the terms *Maya* and *Christian* reveal the presbytery's appropriation of identity in a direction that transcends the Kaqchikel community in Chimaltenango and includes the entire Maya community in Guatemala and perhaps in Mesoamerica as a whole. Because he was an evangelical pastor, the use of the term *Christian* is particularly significant. Proclaiming Saquic a *martir cristiano* situates his narrative in a context wherein the term *cristiano* is used for all followers of Christ and not solely for those who have converted from Roman Catholicism or from Maya spiritual traditions. When I attended one of the memorial services in honor of Saquic mentioned at the beginning of this chapter, the service actually began in the cemetery of a small *aldea* where Saquic and other members of the presbytery had been involved in community development activities. People seemed to feel comfortable sitting among the graves and flowers while pastors commented on Saquic's life and the crime that had been committed. The assemblage of some fifty or sixty people then walked into the local Roman Catholic church, which had two of the posters plastered on the front door. Although the priest seemed slightly disinterested, twice confusing Saquic's name, the church was filled with people who had not been in the cemetery and who seemed to be appreciative not only of Saquic's work among them but also of the work of the Kaqchikel Presbytery in their midst. A few years later I was drawn to this dramatic sign of ecumenism when I heard that Presbyterian churches in Guatemala City refused to open their doors for commemorative services when Bishop Gerardi was murdered.[27]

The Kaqchikel Presbytery has taken and refocused not only Saquic's death but also a key term in religious discourse, and it has placed both at the service of an agenda that is ecumenical in nature. This agenda was designed to have a political impact in the days when Guatemala lurched toward the signing of the peace and beyond. Such an impact was political on two fronts. As a proclamation of identity and presence, a refusal to keep silent in the face of the worst kind of threat that occult powers with ties to the military could deliver, the mere telling of the story was an effort to challenge those who would try to mute concern for human and cultural rights within the peace process.[28] On the religious front, the construction of Saquic as a *martir maya* as well as a *martir cristiano* represented an embracing of Maya cultural and religious traditions, even as it linked people from different Christian traditions both inside Guatemala and in the international community.

This process of reinterpretation transcended Guatemala, reaching into other countries and then returning in various ways to the local context of Chimaltenango itself.[29] Immediately after Saquic was killed, the call went out to churches in North America for people to stay with his family and with other

Presbyterian leaders, both Maya and non-Maya, who had received threats after having demanded a clarification of the events—a clarification that, apparently, will never come. As people from three denominations in the United States and Canada stayed with Saquic's widow and children as well as with other families, the story began to be recorded and told in the North American context. Besides the testimony from the companions and occasional news reports, the most accessible retelling of the story for the religious community in North America was perhaps the book written by United Church of Canada minister Jim Manly, *The Wounds of Manuel Saquic: Biblical Reflections from Guatemala* (1997). The book has thirty-three devotional chapters, one for each of Manuel's stab wounds, with titles such as "Time of trial," "Dos Equis" ("Double X"), "Forgiveness and impunity," "Blond Jesus," and "In all cultures, among all peoples."[30] The work extends the narrative of Saquic's death by highlighting more inclusive concerns for human rights and respect for cultural (and religious) differences by people who would seek to accompany the Maya in their pilgrimage of faith and struggles against impunity. For some in the international ecumenical community, the idea of accompaniment gained theological significance as it translated into simply "being with" people in difficult and threatening circumstances rather than "doing for" them in contexts that outsiders could hardly begin to fully understand. In these ways, Saquic's story and the remembering of Saquic in the telling of his story became living expressions of transnational Protestantism.

The remembering of Saquic's life and martyrdom also became part of the narrative of the Kaqchikel Presbytery as it sought to bring together people in the department of Chimaltenango and to inscribe the landscape of the city with signs of hope appropriate to Maya culture and to the historical moment in which the population lives. After the signing of the peace agreement, the presbytery and CIEDEG were instrumental in erecting a monument in the central park of the city of Chimaltenango. The "Monument in Memory of the Martyrs" (Son Turnil 1997, 67) is a statue of a Maya woman in customary dress breaking a rifle raised above her head (fig. 19). Beneath her are the names of those who sponsored the memorial, as well as two sentences from writings sacred to some Maya Christians: the Popol Wuj, the creation story from the K'iche' Maya (sometimes called the Mayan Bible), and the Christian Bible (fig. 20). The first sentence deals with the issue of origins: "From the east we have come and to the east we shall go." The second was chosen from the Gospel of Matthew: "Blessed are the peacemakers, for they shall be called the sons of God" (Matthew 5:9). It is inscribed on the pages of an open book similar to the manner in which open Bibles are painted on the front of evangelical churches in the countryside. The emphasis is on self-knowledge, the incorporation of ethnic and religious identity, and the need to be active in the struggle

Figure 19. Monument to martyrs, Plaza Central, Chimaltenango

for peace. The monument serves as a memorial: "In homage to the thousands
and thousands of martyrs, Maya Kaqchikel and non-Maya, who struggled for
peace with social justice and who were kidnapped, disappeared, tortured, mas-
sacred and assassinated by the repressive forces during the last 36 years."

Saquic's name, along with that of one Joselino Xoyon, is given for the "departmental capital" within a list of names on one side of the monument, each
name given "for" (*por*) the village with which the victim is identified. The
monument projects Saquic's martyrdom into the experience of others who
suffered and died during the armed conflict. Names provide the evidence of
the narrative of suffering and martyrdom in particular places, even as Saquic's story and the stories of Guatemalan exiles have spread the history of the

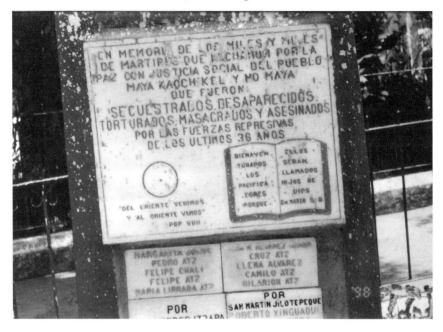

Figure 20. Monument inscription, Popol Wuj and Bible

war into various spatial, even transnational, contexts.[31] Religion here is rooted in place, with the Popol Wuj being adopted to represent Maya spirituality in a pan-Maya sense and the Bible being used as an integral part of the process of recuperating historical memory in the sense that those martyred are understood to be peacemakers. The cultural and religious identity of those named is lodged not solely in the experience of martyrdom but in the sacred words appropriated by the Kaqchikel and by religious people from North America and elsewhere who crossed boundaries to physically accompany the Maya in their efforts to fight against repression. The words from the Popol Wuj and the Bible graphically illustrate the intention to hold on to both Maya-ness and evangelicalism as two important aspects of identity among Kaqchikel evangelicals.[32]

On Religion, War, and the Nature of Church

The construction of Manuel Saquic as a martyr in the midst of Guatemala's struggle to implement a just and lasting peace focuses attention on issues of religious change in Chimaltenango. As a political statement linking evangelical practice to human rights and a strong affirmation of Maya identity, his story challenges the perception of evangelicals as apolitical or fundamentalist in terms of their response to social issues. Nevertheless, Saquic's story is only part of the diverse evangelical presence in Guatemala, and some in other segments of the evangelical community question whether their religion is being co-opted for a radicalized political agenda.

There are many reasons for raising such questions, and they are often part of political interests specific to the one raising the questions. Still, some criticism revolves around Similox's high profile. I have already mentioned his place as vice presidential candidate for the New Nation Alliance (ANN) during the 1999 presidential elections. The ANN was created after a split from the Frente Democrático Nueva Guatemala (FDNG, New Guatemala Democratic Front), which came in fourth in the 1995 elections; it included the political party of the former guerrillas of the URNG, which had been formed after the signing of the peace accord. The ANN fractured after the 1999 elections when its former presidential candidate, Álvaro Colom, left to form another political party, and the URNG element began to function as an independent party. This gives evidence both to the difficulty that left-of-center parties experience in maintaining their constituencies and to the fragmentary nature of Guatemalan politics, in which no governing party has returned to the presidency in a succeeding election since the return to democracy in 1985. Similox took what amounted to a leave of absence from CIEDEG and from the exercise of ministry (as required by Guatemalan law) during the electoral campaign. In interviews I conducted with him he consistently stated that he sees such political involvement as an extension of the need for Christians to be involved in society in a constructive manner.

Beyond such issues and concerns, the narrative of the martyrdom of Manuel Saquic refocuses our attempts to make sense of religion and war in the local milieu. Saquic is no longer with us to speak for himself, and he left no legacy of written texts or oral discourses as others did, such as Oscar Romero, the 1989 Jesuit martyrs of San Salvador's Central American University, or Bishop Gerardi in Guatemala. He is remembered not on the basis of his own words but through a reconstructed narrative that sheds light on the experience of many others who were martyred during the Guatemalan conflict. Taking into account the different social positions of the martyrs themselves, the discussion necessarily has to deal with how symbols are appropriated, by whom, and to what end. Anna L. Peterson's study of martyrs and martyrdom in El Salvador during the 1980s provides a helpful framework for comparing such symbolic appropriations in different situations. Peterson reports distinctions between martyrs who were "pastoral workers," "ordinary people," and "political martyrs." Sometimes called "martyrs of the people" or "popular martyrs," the latter category includes people who do not acknowledge faith and yet sacrifice their lives in the struggle for justice. Because this mirrors the practice of Christian values, Peterson invokes Karl Rahner's term "anonymous Christians" for those in this group (Peterson 1997, 103–7). When narratives of martyrdom are created and told about particular individuals, the narratives themselves become "a resource that provides ordinary people with a language, values, and patterns of thought and behavior" (127).

In this vein, attending to the narrative of Saquic's triple martyrdom brings together a number of threads in terms of the intersections among religion, ethnicity, and violent conflict in Guatemala and elsewhere. Unique in the Saquic case is the evangelical community's appropriation of the Roman Catholic tradition of saints and martyrs and the link established between local or community-level experience and ecumenical practice extending to the international religious community that responded to Saquic's assassination. Both Peterson and Mary Christine Morkovsky, who also analyzed Roman Catholic experience during the civil war in El Salvador, show how martyrdom has been understood in Central America in terms of Christian spirituality. As Morkovsky explains: "The spirituality of martyrdom explores the paradox of losing one's life in order to save it. Accepting a death neither planned nor chosen declares the absolute supremacy of love, manifests hope in future happiness, and witnesses to faith in something not yet possessed. It is an honest and necessary response to a world of sin and death given by those who will to free it" (1993, 539–40; cf. C. Alvarez 1990, ch. 4). This response is interpreted in theological terms such as salvation, liberation, the Kingdom of God, and resurrection, but it extends directly to the everyday arenas of survival, resistance, and political activism. Peterson refers to a particular Roman Catholic organization that "incorporates political analyses and goals in its interpretation of martyrdom and resurrection" (1997, 150). In the interpretation given to Saquic's death, theology, culture, and activism all come together: "The communitarian traditions of pre-Hispanic Mesoamerica, in which the dead live on in the community, coincide with Catholic moral teaching to make sacrifice possible and resurrection plausible" (150).

Ultimately, the argument can be made that in the end the focus has to return to Manuel Saquic. About one and a half years after his assassination, he was present when the peace agreement was finally signed in Guatemala. He was transfigured as a martyr in the eyes of those who carried his image on a banner into the capital city—an ecumenical, evangelical martyr for human rights and for the cultural integrity of the Maya peoples (fig. 21). While his presence was only one part of the collective memory of the people gathered in the Plaza Mayor on that day, the interpretation of Saquic as a martyr demonstrates yet another aspect of the manner in which Protestantism is being constructed in Guatemala in the face of violence and impunity.

The significance of Saquic's death and the manner in which he is remem-

Figure 21. Manuel Saquic, "Presente," during the signing of the peace accord

bered in the Kaqchikel Presbytery transcend the tragedy surrounding those events and permit a glimpse into the manner in which Kaqchikel Presbyterians have created an identity for themselves since Guatemala's return to civilian government in the mid-1980s, even before the presbytery was formally organized. Gustavo told me that he converted to Presbyterianism because he was attracted to the kind of commitment he saw within the presbytery. He was somewhat disappointed when it became clear that the Presbyterian denomination as a whole did not share those commitments. For him, the church should be involved in spiritual, cultural, economic, and political issues. As he lamented that when human rights violations take place the national church often does not say anything, he made it clear that the actions of the presbytery are not simply an involvement of the church in politics or an effort to use the church for political ends. "We are the church," he said. "[This is] our way of understanding the church."

Conclusions

Contextualizing Maya Protestant Practice

> I dare to make the assurance that Guatemala will never be a "disenchanted" country; mystery, miracles, and magic flower on top of all beliefs, even the most "rationalized" such as Protestantism: Pentecostal and neo-Pentecostal evangelicals bear witness to that.
>
> —Pilar Sanchíz Ochoa, *Evangelismo y Poder*

> As a Mayan anthropologist and writer, I am contributing to the present Mayan renewal. I believe that anthropologists must contribute to the self-determination of the indigenous people that they study. This may be a more difficult task for foreign anthropologists; but in my case, being a Maya, I can see the multiple ways in which I can contribute to the auto-representation of my people. . . . The multiple voices of the contemporary Maya should be heard, because they are no longer silent or sunken in centuries-old amnesia. We remember who we are and where we come from as we fashion our hopes for the future.
>
> —Victor Montejo, "The Multiplicity of Mayan Voices"

Religious Practice among Mam and Kaqchikel Presbyterians

In August 2005 I made a brief research trip to Guatemala, and for the first time I heard someone refer to the *acuerdos de paz* (peace accords) as the *recuerdos de paz* (remembrances of peace). The grim humor in the remark stayed with me after I returned home as indicative of how much of the euphoria and hope surrounding the end of the war had dissipated in the following decade. Everyday concerns about violence and security (in a personal and economic sense) and disillusionment with governmental corruption and inefficiency in successive administrations certainly raise questions about the new pluricultural Guatemala that was envisioned during the negotiations leading to the end of the conflict and in the immediate aftermath when significant change in economic and social structures seemed like a viable possibility. The context provided by the peace process continues to frame a significant portion of my own research agenda (note, for example, the passage of the new Framework Accord for the

Fulfillment of the Peace Accords, also in August 2005).[1] At the same time, the burgeoning religious pluralism documented in this work demonstrates how the ongoing study of religion in Guatemala can redirect our attention toward the spaces for change that exist within the broader political and social narratives that continue to shape the post-conflict situation.

The question with which I began—What does it mean to be both Maya and Protestant in Guatemala?—focuses attention on one of those spaces: the space where evangelical religion intersects with Maya culture and identity in the lives of Maya evangelicals. There is, of course, no single way of being either Maya or Protestant, and I am reminded of the insight Berger claimed when he acknowledged that he had been wrong (along with many others) to think that "modernity necessarily leads to a decline in religion" (1998, 782). The insight had to do with pluralism and the way it "undermines the taken-for-grantedness of beliefs and values." In beginning his discussion along those lines, Berger remarks that "pluralism influences not so much *what* people believe as *how* they believe it." The "how" of religious practice is the space wherein Mam and Kaqchikel Presbyterians live out their identities as Maya Protestants. By attending to their practices, this book makes a small contribution to letting us hear from that multiplicity of Maya voices to which Montejo refers in this chapter's second epigraph.

Hearing those voices is not only about fashioning hope for the future, however. Sanchíz Ochoa's suggestion that Guatemala will never be "disenchanted" has some affinity with my concern for re-enchantment in view of the pluralism of Protestantisms in Guatemala and the intersections of Maya identity with evangelical practice. There can be little doubt that a process involving the reworking of religious meaning is taking place on many levels in contemporary Guatemala; this can be seen not only in the Protestant presence but also in the midst of the *reivindicación* of Maya culture and Maya spirituality that challenges at every turn the tenets of both Roman Catholic and Protestant manifestations of Christianity. Yet Sanchíz Ochoa and Berger remind us that there is more going on in Guatemala than meets the eye. From the anthropological perspective this borders on a truism, but it is helpful in gaining a more nuanced reading of evangelical practices in Guatemala and in Mesoamerica more broadly. In theory, Mam and Kaqchikel groups who are the subjects of this work represent the most rational wing of Protestantism—ascetic Calvinists with connections to a long missionary history in Guatemala. Part of what makes them unique is precisely their identification with their indigenous heritage and the effort, however tenuous at times, to integrate that renewed heritage into Protestant practices that can be offered back to the communities in which they live and work. At the most fundamental level, the ethnographic move enables us to look beyond secularization and below globalization to gain a sense of how people "make do" and reconstruct patterns of subsistence and meaning in the midst of a context that is quite often fraught with uncertainty.

In attending to the "how" of Maya evangelical practice, this work highlights the way in which the interplay between religion and ethnicity articulates with larger scales of interaction. As Manuel Vásquez and Philip Williams note in their introduction to an issue of *Latin American Perspectives,* "The task here is to continue to be attentive to specificities of local, national, and regional histories and power relations while embedding them in transnational and global dynamics" (2005, 19).

To be sure, I have tried to situate the examination in the context of Guatemala's history of violence and in the light of the missionary origins of Protestantism, particularly Presbyterianism. As far as the IENPG is concerned, the formation of the Maya Quiché Presbytery in 1959 signaled that segments of the IENPG had begun to organize and challenge the institutional structure of the denomination from an ethnic standpoint. The Mam and Kaqchikel presbyteries are part of that trajectory, although the interpretation in relation to ethnic renewal is complex because the move was assisted, at least in part, by the missionary presence that had been so strong in the western highlands.

Uncertainty remains a key for the examination of religion in Guatemala. The post-conflict situation cannot be considered a time of peace and harmony. On several occasions one minister in the Mam Presbytery told me that although the peace had indeed been signed, the situation was not secure. The memory of the violence and the palpable uncertainty of the present were not softened in his comments:

> It is not real; instead, it is a negotiated peace. This is a general evaluation. Why would the *comandantes* sign if they were struggling for peace? It is a trick to the people up 'til now. Everything remained in silence, in peace, and it is not possible to complain. It cannot be carried out, and the poor continue suffering. There are thousands of orphans and widows, overall, [among] *el pueblo maya,* the indigenous. [President] Arzú signed the peace accord in order to attract foreign investment. . . . The Guatemalan structure is bad. In 1980, this was never said. If one said this, you didn't wake up. This is a brief commentary. We are not free. Things can change.

There are many threads here, and one of the characteristics of religion as it is worked out in human experience is its power to move people as they respond to changing circumstances. My work emphasizes the need to take a local perspective as we seek to understand such responses in all of their layers of "situatedness." Whether we anthropologists speak of resistance, revitalization or renewal, or some kind of "resacralization of the profane" (Garrard-Burnett 1996), William Swatos and Kevin Christiano are correct, I believe, in insisting that "we are standing within 'new paradigm' rather than 'old paradigm' sociology of religion; that is, that our understanding of spirituality-religion-sacredness finds its root in the limitless dissatisfaction that is a species characteristic of *homo sapiens*" (1999, 224).[2]

This resonates with the humanistic perspective I have adopted as another part of the frame for this work. Dissatisfaction can be read in this sense as more existential than as a capitulation to a crisis-solace model of evangelical expansion.[3] Dissatisfaction takes many forms, including experiences of dislocation and crisis, but it can also be seen as a kind of restlessness that pervades human activity and acts as an impetus to the reformulation of meaning.

This reformulation of meaning has been significant in Latin America, and Steigenga has gone so far as to affirm that "the interactions between Christianity and indigenous religion in the past forty years gave rise to the basis for an insurgent consciousness framed within an identity both Christian and Indian" (2004, 238). On the local level, the Mam and Kaqchikel presbyteries highlight differences in the way people situate themselves in light of the demands of their evangelical religious beliefs. In both cases a communitarian ethic rooted in Maya culture underlies the reformulation and the construction of identity as it intersects with Protestantism. In the Kaqchikel case such reformulation is more public, and it manifests itself as a direct protest against a repressive political context at the level of the nation-state. As protest, religion serves as more than a survival mechanism for those living in the midst of massive social change and responding to such change from a somewhat marginal social position. Religious practice and the religious community itself become important aspects of a commitment to the context itself, part of the effort to create something new out of the profane history of murder and disappearances, even as that history is embodied in a case like that of Manuel Saquic.[4] In the process, the Kaqchikel have cultivated a more visible network of international connections as they have responded to the violence directed at their community. This network has, in turn, influenced theological reflection in the United States and Canada as supporters of the presbytery have reflected upon the meaning of solidarity and accompaniment with people in contexts vastly different from their own. Such theology needs to be studied alongside reflection growing out of the Kaqchikel community itself (cf. Otzoy n.d.).

The situation of the Mam Presbytery is more ambiguous, but the presbytery's less overt political orientation may make it the example that best shows the effort to adapt local culture to evangelicalism. Both Scotchmer and Greenberg, who worked on healing and illness in the Mam *municipio* of Cajolá, suggested that people in the region converted because somehow the older meaning systems ceased to make sense. As opposed to the ideology of Catholic Action, which still supported elements of an "egalitarian and communal flavor" associated with traditional religious practices, "Evangelical Protestantism . . . is clearly separated from the Ajiox [*costumbre*] and the Catholic ideologies. Not only do they remove themselves from socio-political activities in the village, but they also reject the concomitant economic constraints and obligations as well. This places them on a 'new path' which provides them with new power, protection and well-being" (Greenberg 1984, 253).

To the extent that this is correct, the question of why the new religion makes sense needs to be examined more in-depth. In *Holy Saints and Fiery Preachers: The Anthropology of Protestantism in Mexico and Central America* (2001), coeditor Alan Sandstrom argues that economic changes are largely to account for "the turn to Protestantism" in Mesoamerica. "The new and uncertain context changes the pragmatic material factors to which individuals must adjust in order to survive and thrive," he continues. "These changes in turn make the old identities obsolete and open the way for new and innovative solutions to the problem of making a living and finding a meaningful place in an evolving social system" (2001, 278). Sandstrom argues for "a materialist explanation that links macro-level analysis with human agency, that focuses on how and why people adjust to the new economic conditions of their lives" (278). I highlight this because, despite the materialist emphasis, it is very similar in some regards to my theoretical approach linking ethnography and practice theory to local and global frames of analysis in the anthropology of religion (cf. Vásquez and Marquardt 2003, chapter 2).

In essence, Sandstrom argues that Protestantism constitutes a type of "third ethnic group" with an oppositional identity that, in turn, contributes to the fragmenting of Mesoamerican communities. From two different directions, the Protestant presence has had a direct impact on "Native American" religious resistance (e.g., reduced alcohol consumption during rituals) and on "Catholic-affiliate" efforts "to reduce the Native American elements in systems of folk Catholicism" (279). Sandstrom is acutely aware of the complexities surrounding conversion and the implications of conversion at the community level. I simply add to the discussion by noting that while conversion to Protestantism creates division in many communities, the Protestantisms themselves diverge tremendously in their impacts on local communities.[5] While in the Guatemalan case this may have something to do with the longer history of Presbyterianism in the western highlands, the presbyteries clearly show the possibility for community as well as personal revitalization.

Referring to a posthumous article by Scotchmer in the same volume, Sandstrom argues that it is doubtful that "religions like Protestantism have a greater ability than local religions to satisfy the spiritual needs of a people" (2001,

286). He goes on to say that "[t]he Protestant package was developed in a totally different social context to address a totally different set of needs" (286). This perspective in some degree reflects his research in the state of Veracruz in Mexico, and his argument that the "change [to Protestantism] must be understood on a number of levels from the macroeconomic to the psychological" (277) is compelling from the methodological standpoint.

In the end, conversion brings with it no clear path to either renewal or community fragmentation. Watanabe's work in Santiago Chimaltenango showed that tensions between traditionalists, catechists, and evangelicals in part resulted in a rise in the number of people who claimed not to have any religion (1992, 202). Beyond the tension between the groups, at the time his research was done, outright fragmentation had not taken place, and members of the community continued to negotiate their relationships on the basis of their membership in it (212–16). At the same time, a significant number of people are claiming to have returned to the practice of Maya religion, especially from Catholicism.

Re-enchantment, Renewal, and Maya Protestantism

In 1993 Scotchmer remarked that though it was probably "too early to document, Maya Protestantism that follows a *revitalization* model may play a crucial role in Guatemala's future given its growth among the disenfranchised and its dynamic for creating an indigenous local Maya theology" (1993, 519). This model was drawn as a contrast with "the ladino-dominated *assimilationist* church and ascribed to by those who have succeeded economically as Protestants." The latter was a model that did "not speak to the poor and the disenfranchised Mayas who are discovering their collective misery" (510). These words were written as the peace process was still taking shape on the horizon and about the time that the Maya movement as such was beginning to find its voice and to articulate its demands more directly within the political life of the nation. On the national level the revitalization that subsequently took place had more to do with culture and cultural rights than it did with economic inequality or religion per se.

From the standpoint of evangelical religion among the Mam, revitalization remains a localized phenomenon. Ultimately, the concern has to go beyond what it might mean for a person to be both Maya and Protestant in the present moment. Any consideration of the interplay between Maya ethnicity and Protestant religiosity has to address issues of religious, social, economic, and political change in response to the forces of globalization reaching the village level throughout Latin America. This is especially true because the Presbyterians of the Maya presbyteries discussed here remain in largely rural or *municipio* environments. Religious practice remains tied to place and to community, although the communities have shifting boundaries in terms of belief. To the extent that there are transnational ties, the community boundaries, both religious and pragmatic, are expanding to include more extended families of *hermanas y hermanos.*

Even if the religious landscape has been changed in response to evangelical ideology, the interpretation of that ideology ultimately resides in the hands (and minds) of Mam Maya Protestants themselves. Such reinterpretation is reflective of the ongoing political and social struggle in Guatemala wherein the Maya are continuing to revitalize their culture even as some organize for more direct political power. At an even more localized level, it is reflective of how culture itself is shaped in response to the meaning-making activities of people who struggle to make sense of the complexities of their own lives.

Here, again, the Kaqchikel case brings the issue more sharply into focus. Gustavo, whom we met in chapter 6, spoke more directly of the need to build bridges between representatives of the old and the new traditions in his own community: "In this sense we reflect on a biblical passage but we also contextualize it with Maya customs. In our group, in our reflections, two Maya priests regularly come. They don't have any problem being with us reflecting on the Bible, and neither do we have any problem with participating in a Maya ceremony. So, when we say, 'The Bible says this,' they say, 'Ah, but our ancestors also said this.' That is to say, the two things, the Maya and the Christian, always go in the same hand. It isn't good to do this, but it has turned out that way with us, and this is our way of walking [*nuestro caminar*]."

I asked Gustavo why he said it "isn't good to do this." He replied: "I say that because perhaps it isn't good to mix everything up. [Still] as an example there are Christians that don't want anything to do with what is Maya, and there are other Maya who don't want anything to do with what is Christian. But we use both. For that reason we are seen as odd, well, everyone sees us as strange. For that reason, I sometimes say, 'Man, what you're doing isn't good.' But it is giving us results, so this is to say that it is good. [I say that] to question myself in order to keep walking." He is clearly using the term *Christian* in the more familiar ecumenical sense we are accustomed to in North America. But this ecumenicity also embraces the cultural and cosmological aspects of Maya-ness in a direct statement that Christianity and ethnic identity need to be brought together.

Revitalization does not have to take a form as dramatic as in the Kaqchikel case. The social and political activities of Mam Presbyterians reflect a style of interaction with local communities that may be more conceptually in line with *costumbre* than their Protestant religious affiliation indicates. During the 1999 national elections, at least three Mam *municipios* in Quetzaltenango elected *al-*

caldes who had direct connections with the Presbyterian community in the area. They were not running on the same kind of ticket or for the same party. The full implications of this would have to be analyzed historically, but it represents a level of acceptance, and possibly even trust in evangelicals, that certainly did not exist at midcentury when the older minister was thrown out of his father's house for converting and for consorting with the missionaries. It is also a contrast with Kaqchikel Presbyterians running for national political office or opting to open offices for the defense of human rights, a powerful and dangerous symbol of social involvement.

On the surface, then, the Mam case is less clear in terms of the response to Maya culture. Yet if fifty years ago a minister was reduced to asking God to help him build a house for himself and his wife, it is a change when another minister two generations later wrestles with the idea of how to include a non-Christian grandmother in the company of the saved. Culture reflects the manner in which our experiences transform our self-understanding and the interpretations we make about the world and our place in it. In the midst of great change for Mam Maya Protestants, the past is not left totally behind. The new community still has to have room for the ancestors. "I came to believe that, yes, [my grandmother] also died, but she was not lost."

Re-enchantment and renewal of identity are conscious acts in the face of historical circumstances, and the complexity revealed in ethnographic descriptions of Mam and Kaqchikel Presbyterians in vastly different circumstances demonstrates that the process occurs in many ways. In the religious realm, re-enchantment provides new meaning in the personal and communal spaces of the lives of Mam and Kaqchikel Protestants even as it provides new impetus for cultural and political movements that are changing the face of the Guatemalan landscape, the place the Maya call the Land of Maize, Iximuleu.

Appendix: Statement on the National Day for the Victims of the Armed Conflict

Coordinadora Nacional de Viudas de Guatemala
CONAVIGUA

Email: conavigua@intelnet.net.gt   Tels: (502) 253-7914
8ave. 2-29 Zona 1, Guatemala, Ciudad   Fax: (502) 232-5642

DÍA NACIONAL DE LAS VICTIMAS DEL CONFLICTO ARMADO.

LA COORDINADORA NACIONAL DE VIUDAS DE GUATEMALA CONAVIGUA

A LA OPINIÓN PÚBLICA NACIONAL E INTERNACIONAL.

1. Que este 25 de febrero se conmemora una vez mas el Día Nacional de las Victimas del Conflicto Armado Interno, fecha en que se dió a conocer el informe de la Comisión del Esclarecimiento Histórico C.E.H., fué un momento Histórico para reafirmar que hubo genocidio contra los pueblos indígenas, que se violó nuestros derechos individuales y colectivos, que el ejército se ensañó contra los pueblos indígenas y especialmente contra las mujeres para dejar huellas imborrables en nuestra memoria como mujeres.

2. A cinco años del informe Memoria del Silencio los gobiernos anteriores no mostraron voluntad política para impulsar el Plan Nacional de Resarcimiento, las Victimas sobrevivientes en especial las mujeres estamos en una situación de extrema pobreza, sufrimos el desempleo y la discriminación, la mayoría de nosotras no hemos superado el miedo, la angustia y la incertidumbre por no saber el paradero de nuestros esposos, padres, hijos u otros familiares.

3. CONAVIGUA plantea la necesidad para que el actual gobierno cumpla su compromiso de garantizar la participación plena en la Comisión Nacional de Resarcimiento, así mismo que se garantice un presupuesto para las mujeres viudas y huérfanos como también garantizar la seguridad de los familiares, los trabajadores y los antropólogos forenses en el trabajo de exhumaciones.

4. Como mujeres victimas animamos a las mujeres a estar organizadas, a no dejarse engañar y manipular por falsas promesas de parte de personas o grupos que pretenden aprovecharse de nuestro dolor y de la pobreza en que vivimos.

CONAVIGUA reafirma su compromiso de luchar por un Resarcimiento Justo y Digno para las Victimas de la Guerra, así mismo reafirmamos nuestro compromiso de seguir buscando a nuestros familiares en los cientos de cementerios clandestinos dejados en nuestras comunidades, y de luchar por la búsqueda de la Justicia NUESTROS MARTIRES NO TIENEN PRECIO, SU SANGRE DERRAMADA BROTARA EN LA LUCHA POR EL RESPETO A LA VIDA Y A LA IDENTIDAD DE NUESTRO PUEBLOS.

¡¡VIVA EL 25 DE FEBRERO DÍA DE LA DIGNIDAD DE NUESTROS MARTIRES
CONAVIGUA PRESENTE!!

Guatemala, 25 de Febrero de 2004.

Notes

Prologue

1. I use the terms *Protestant* and *evangelical* (*evangélico*) interchangeably. From the perspective of the missionizing churches of the North, the general term for non–Roman Catholic Christians in Latin America was *Protestant*. This usage reflected some of the early connections with immigrant churches in the region and with the denominations that had early missionary activities there. In formal usage, however, the term refers to denominations that grew out of the Protestant Reformation in the sixteenth century. A number of groups that established a presence in Latin America by the first two decades of the twentieth century were not Protestants in this formal sense. As I observed in prior work in Mexico, a common mode of self-identification is simply to say "Soy evangélico" (I am evangelical), while the term *Protestant* is rarely used. *Evangelical* basically means "person of the good news" (Gospel) or of the Bible. At the outset this establishes the evangelical community as people of the Word. But even this picture is complicated, since most evangelicals in Latin America (70–80 percent) are Pentecostal (*pentecostál* or *pentecostés*). In the case of the groups with which I conducted the majority of my research, Presbyterians are both Protestant and evangelical, and some even incorporate Pentecostal-like practices in their worship.

2. Tekum is usually known by the name Tecún Umán. There is considerable controversy over his actual existence, and some in the Maya community believe that the legends surrounding his actions in the battle with Alvarado embody a negative portrayal of the Maya people. See Lovell and Lutz (2001, 50–51) and the section they reference in Warren (1998, 154–56).

3. I also tend to use the terms *Mestizo* and *Ladino* interchangeably. In Guatemala and Chiapas, *Ladino* is the common term for non-Maya, Spanish-speaking people whose ancestors are both European and Amerindian. As a cultural term it typically refers to people who adopted Spanish dress, and in that sense it includes Maya who had "assimilated" to Spanish culture. Ladinos did not become commonly recognized in Guatemala until the 1830s and 1840s. The term sometimes seems to refer to a poorer segment of the Hispanicized and "white" population (see the discussion in Hendrickson 1995, 30–33). In Mexico and the southwestern part of the United States, *mestizaje* is frequently used in a political sense to denote the mixing of cultures that results in a new race, *la raza*. The critique from the indigenous side is that this denigrates aspects of culture in Mesoamerica arising from the original cultures of the region. The tension

between Maya and Ladinos is well captured in the etymology provided by some of the Mam Maya with whom I worked. On more than one occasion I was informed that the word *ladino* came from *ladrón,* the Spanish word for "robber" or "thief." Moreover, in Guatemalan discourses of ethnicity, the evocation of the Ladino often implies one who does not have a culture. This has been a source of considerable debate over ethnicity in recent years in the light of Maya cultural activism.

4. For sources relevant to Latin America, see Willems 1967; Lalive d'Epinay 1969; Bastian 1986, 1992; Martin 1990; Stoll 1990; and Garrard-Burnett and Stoll 1993. For Mesoamerica, especially Guatemala, see Nash 1963; Roberts 1967; Bastian 1983, 1990; Sexton 1978; Garrard 1986; Scotchmer 1986, 1989, 1991; Annis 1987; Garrard-Burnett 1990; Garma Navarro 1989; Goldín and Metz 1991; Earle 1992.

Chapter 1

1. A presbytery is the administrative grouping of congregations located in a particular geographic area. Like the term *Presbyterian,* it comes from a Greek word meaning "elder." The governing body of the presbytery (which is also called the presbytery) is composed of elder and clergy representatives from the congregations in a particular region. Sometimes the regions can overlap if presbyteries are formed along ethnic rather than strict geographic lines.

2. Some of the reasons for the absence of reference to evangelicals in the social movement literature are understandable, the newness of the movement being paramount among them. Eckstein's opening chapter in her edited volume on social movements in Latin America does mention Protestantism, noting its sectarian character, its political conservatism, and its potential to provide a space for challenging dominant social orders in particular cases (2001b, 31–32). One chapter in the work deals primarily with liberationist Catholicism (Levine and Mainwaring 2001). In her epilogue, Eckstein acknowledges that "[e]vangelicalism became a social movement of sorts" (2001a, 395), but her brief discussion emphasizes the disempowering aspects of the movement, ties to conservative politics, and individualism, especially in the case of Pentecostalism, which makes it more amenable to neoliberal economic agendas. I am not unsympathetic to aspects of evangelicalism that reflect these tendencies, but the story told here shows the case to be much more complex. Burdick (1998) addresses specifically the relationship of Pentecostals to the Movimento Negro in Brazil, arguing that the former might provide certain kinds of symbolic resources that could be mobilized by the latter. Religion as a whole receives scant attention in the two major anthologies on social movements in Latin America (Escobar and Alvarez 1992; Alvarez, Dagnino, and Escobar 1998).

3. Watanabe provides a helpful summary of the issues and identity politics surrounding Mayan languages in Guatemala (2000, 236–38). In June 2003, legislative decree 24-2003 of the Guatemalan congress amended article 7 of the Law of the Academy of Maya Languages (decree 65-90) to make room for a representative from the Chalchiteka community (primarily in the municipality of Aguacatán) on the superior council of the academy. This had the effect of recognizing Chalchiteko as the twenty-second Maya language. In the prior month, decree 19-2003 gave official recognition to Maya, Xinca, and Garifuna languages while maintaining Spanish as the official language as such. This decree provides for the translation of laws and other kinds of communications into the languages of the various linguistic communities acknowledged in the law.

Provision is also made for state institutions to report on the usage of services by members of the various communities. I have yet to read any commentary on this particular law, but it is on the surface a step in the direction of acknowledging Guatemala's pluricultural character (cf. García Ruiz 1997).

4. See also Watanabe's discussion of the population issue (2000, 227–28). Another piece to the issue of Maya demography is the continuing predominance of rural residence by the Maya population. Guatemala remains more rural than many other countries in Latin America, where the total urban population approaches 75 percent. Rurality pays significant dividends in maintaining culture and lifeways, but it also limits access to crucial resources in areas such as education, health care, and access to jobs.

5. Like *modernity, secularization* is a much-debated term these days. Casanova's (1994, 19–39) discussion of the "three separate moments" of secularization is a good beginning point for investigation. The "decline of religion" is only part of the story.

6. Regarding Maya self-determination, Warren notes that Mayanists "face the paradox of having to assert claims in a universalistic language that does not recognize the cultural specificity of their concerns" (1998, 31).

7. Berger (1967) long ago noted that religion plays both a world-maintaining and a world-constructing role in the lives of adherents. Turner criticizes Berger's phenomenological work for focusing too much on social order and aspects of the legitimation of social order rooted in religion and thereby "demolishing Weber's central interest in power" (1996, 170). While I would not completely dismiss this criticism, I see differential foci on power (embedded in structure and the material bases of culture) and meaning (embodied in the self and ideology) as complementary rather than oppositional. Furthermore, the social construction (and preservation) of meaning can be a powerful force for social change as well as legitimation in contemporary societies. I do not at all accept Morris's conclusion that (as opposed to structural Marxism) "hermeneutics and symbolic anthropology lead only to interesting cul-de-sacs" (1987, 328).

8. In his seminal essay "Religion as a Cultural System," Geertz compares the religious worldview to that embodied in other perspectives through "which men construe the world—the common-sensical, the scientific, and the aesthetic" (1973b, 111). Of the "religious perspective," he writes that "[r]ather than detachment, its watchword is commitment; rather than analysis, encounter" (112). There is plenty of space here for linking the person to the larger context, despite the criticisms that have been leveled at Geertz's definition. Although Geertz has been criticized for the lack of attention to power and the power of discourse in the constitution of religion (Asad 1983, 1993), the concentration on meaning remains crucial for understanding the ideological role religion plays in shaping society and culture. In *Holy Terrors: Thinking about Religion after September 11,* Bruce Lincoln (2003, 1–8) discusses Asad's critique of Geertz, arguing, pace Asad, that it is possible to consider a "universal definition of religion." He turns the discussion more in the direction of Asad's concern with practice by suggesting that "[a] proper definition must therefore be polythetic and flexible" (5) even as it attends to the four domains of "discourse, practice, community, and institution," aspects that "can be developed and emphasized to differing degrees and can relate to the others in various ways" (7).

9. In addressing these issues, I am informed by theoretical and methodological approaches that grow out of the interpretive anthropology of Clifford Geertz (1973c), with its focus on "thick description" and meaning, and the perspective of practice theory associated with the work of Sherry Ortner (1989, 1994; cf. Bourdieu 1977,

1990). As sources for examining the production of discourse and narrative in the study of religion, both practice theory and Robert Wuthnow's (1992a, 1992b) cultural sociology provide frames for conceptualizing the nexus between theory and ethnography, or between actors and social structure. Wuthnow advocates a "production of culture" approach in the study of religion, a perspective that opens space "between private and public expressions of culture" (1994, 24). Ortner's description of practice theory (and she resists providing a formal definition) privileges the place of action and the acting person in the study of culture. While this Weberian turn is grounded in the realities of asymmetrical power relations more properly associated with Marxist theory, for Ortner change is more gradual than revolutionary, and it involves meaning as well as power relationships (1994, 399). This kind of perspective holds cultural action to be significant (if not always interesting) in its most mundane aspects, even as it reaffirms the plurality of sites for cultural production.

10. Representative sources for discursive approaches to culture include the work of Fairclough (1992) and, in Mesoamerica, Hanks (1996). More narrative-oriented sources for the region include Reck (1983, 1986), B. Tedlock (1983, 1991), D. Tedlock (1983), and Sosa (1997). The testimonial genre (e.g., Menchú 1984; Montejo 1987; Perera 1993; cf. Falla 1993) provides another perspective on these various methods of analysis. Interestingly, recent studies of evangelical practice in Latin America have not focused as strongly on these forms of discourse. This is remarkable given Protestantism's status as the quintessential "religion of the Word," although Brusco (1996) makes the well-taken point that (personal) testimonies are important sources for anthropological studies provided they are seen as tied to the processes of conversion to a new faith out of which they arise. In the North American context, Harding (1992, 1994a, 1994b) has focused on rhetoric and the public discourse of prominent televangelists to analyze certain strains of "fundamentalist" Christianity.

11. Religious practice and change among the Maya has been addressed in a number of ethnographic and ethnohistorical studies in Guatemala. See Bunzel 1959; Colby and van den Berghe 1969; Oakes 1951; Brintnall 1979; Warren 1989; Watanabe 1990, 1992, 1996; La Farge 1994; R. Wilson 1995; Falla 1995; Carmack 1995; Carlsen 1997; Tarn 1997. Most of the studies that have focused directly on Protestant religiosity as an aspect of religious pluralism at the local level have been articles or dissertations. They are increasing in number and reflect an interdisciplinary cast of investigators. See Nash 1963; Roberts 1967; Reina and Schwartz 1974; Sexton 1978; Annis 1987; Evans 1990; Scotchmer 1986, 1989, 1991, 1993, 1994; Goldín and Metz 1991; Garrard-Burnett 1990, 1996, 1998a, 1998b; Bogenschild 1992; Earle 1992; A. Adams 1999, 2001; Chiappari 1999, 2002; D. Smith 1991; Steigenga 1999, 2001; Grenfell 1995; Reep 1997; Cantón Delgado 1998; Sanchíz Ochoa 1998; Alonso 1998; D. Smith and Grenfell 1999. At the same time, more historically focused studies on the Roman Catholic Church provide a broader frame for the consideration of social and cultural forces at work in the religious arena in contemporary Guatemala. See R. Adams 1970; Calder 1970, 1997, 2001, 2004; Chea Urruela 1988; Sullivan-González 1998.

12. Absenteeism was less pervasive in the two national presidential and congressional elections held since the referendum, but in some analyses those elections continued to represent formal democratic trappings and not the more involved processes of establishing political structures that respond to the needs of the citizenry by allowing for both participation and access to power within Guatemalan society (cf. Diamond 1999; Chase-Dunn, Jonas, and Amaro 2001). The rural-urban split and the contrast between

primarily rural Maya and largely urbanized Ladinos were also factors in the defeat of the referendum. For detailed treatments of the referendum, see Jonas (2000, chapter 8), Warren (2002), and Carey (2004).

13. Adherents to communities such as the Seventh-Day Adventists, Latter Day Saints, and Jehovah's Witnesses might loosely be considered evangelicals in this schema. Scholars tend to characterize them as sects, and that would make them sects (in the social science sense) of Christianity. Others are adamant that they are not Christian because they purport "to complete or correct the Judeo-Christian revelation contained in the Bible" (Alonso 1998, 220). See also chapter 3, note 18.

14. The term *folk Catholicism* has often been used in the literature to describe the overlay of Spanish religious traditions on the indigenous cultures of Latin America. For the most part, I use terms such as *costumbre* or, occasionally, *Maya Catholicism* to emphasize the Maya-ness of such practices in the Guatemala highlands.

15. This is also the case in other places in Mesoamerica. Perhaps the most frequently cited instance of communal divisions has been in the Tzotzil Maya town center of San Juan Chamula in the Mexican state of Chiapas, where the traditional hierarchy has expelled both evangelicals and "Word of God Catholics" to enforce unity within the community. The case is complex and also linked to forces originating outside the community, such as connections with the former ruling Partido Revolucionario Institucional (PRI, Institutional Revolutionary Party). Through these connections the traditionalists have maintained a monopoly on alcohol sales and soft drinks, and this has reinforced their claims to the authority to uphold unity in the community. For the outlines of the conflict and reference to other sources, see Kovic (2005).

16. The following either focus on or address this tension from the standpoint of various religions in different locations, sometimes beyond the community level; the religious groups at issue (and therefore the kinds of tensions) vary, and the story is often one of adaptation or accommodation as well as conflict: Brintnall 1979; Annis 1987; Warren 1989; B. Tedlock 1992; Scotchmer 1991, 1994; Watanabe 1992, 1996; Carmack 1995; R. Wilson 1995; Carlsen 1997; Cantón Delgado 1998; Gossen and Leventhal 1999; Falla 2001.

17. Religion does contribute to the dynamism within cultural systems by fomenting both social change and resistance. See particularly studies of missionization and conversion or world order perspectives, e.g., Lincoln 1985, Roof 1991, Hefner 1993, and Kaplan 1995. Sources for Mesoamerica include Gossen 1986, Clendinnen 1987, Burkhart 1989, Stephen and Dow 1990, Evans 1990, Gossen and León-Portillo 1993, Goldín and Metz 1991, and Carlsen and Prechtel 1991. Classic studies of religious revitalization and change include Wallace 1956 and Worsely 1968. Kehoe 2006 is a recent ethnohistorical study from native North America.

18. There is some overlap here between constructivist and essentialist approaches to ethnicity, whether from the native or the anthropologist's point of view. If the immediate concerns of my research are more consistent with so-called instrumentalist approaches to ethnicity, I am informed as well by more substantive approaches to ethnicity. Arguments related to a particular kind of "blood" and ancestry remain significant in the discourse of ethnicity (Geertz 1973a; Hoeben and Hefner 1991). Ancestors are, after all, the bearers of culture and lifeways.

19. See Cahn's (2003) insightful work based in Tzintzuntzan, Mexico, where efforts are made to keep harmony in the community through the affirmation that "all religions are good."

20. Warren (2001) provides a moving example that embraces generational perspectives on both ethnic renewal and religion in the context of the pan-Maya Movement in the community where she has worked for three decades. For historical perspective on similar issues, see also Brintnall 1979, LeBaron 1993, Warren 1989, and Calder 2004.

21. See Garrard-Burnett's (2004) effort to examine how the statement can be seen in the light of Maya theological projects of inculturation. Clearly, there is overlap between the projects in which we are engaged.

Chapter 2

1. Colby and van den Berghe also note that the Ladinos conceive society in a more dichotomous framework than the Maya, who recognize different languages and places of origin (1969, 180).

2. I use the words *tradition* and *traditional* in the sense employed by David Gros (1992, 8): "a set of practices, a constellation of beliefs, or a mode of thinking that exists in the present but was inherited from the past." Toward the end of his work, Gros remarks that "the reappropriation of tradition is, in itself, no alternative to an immanent critique of modernity. It is only a means to broaden and deepen the methods of immanent critique by tapping into a wealth of material that normally lies outside its range" (135). Tradition implies continuity with the past and perhaps an alternative epistemology. Debates about authenticity and legitimacy are held in abeyance.

3. Approximately 70 percent of the membership is said to be Maya. This has important consequences for interethnic relations within the institution, and they have not been well explored from an academic standpoint.

4. These figures are from the 2002 census, which makes the Mam the fourth-largest Maya community and now lists the Q'eqchi' community, with over 850,000 people, as the second largest. These positions are reversed from much prior information related to identity and language use. The census also recorded information on the language in which people above the age of three learned to speak. Q'eqchi' was still second on the list (over 700,000), Mam was third (over 475,000), and Kaqchikel was fourth (just under 450,000). These data are particularly interesting in showing the number of Kaqchikel Maya who did not learn to speak Kaqchikel as their first language yet who self-identify as Kaqchikel. The K'iche' community, with over one million people, is the largest Maya group in Guatemala.

5. Two of these trips were related to my own activities in a relationship between the Mam Presbytery and Albany Presbytery, an analogous group in my own denomination. The video *Precarious Peace: God and Guatemala* was produced by Rudy and Shirley Nelson, respectively Associate Professor Emeritus in the English Department of the University at Albany and an independent writer. It deals with the involvement of the international religious community in Guatemala's peace process and presents a panoramic view of contemporary religious pluralism in the wake of the signing of the final accord. The project received funding from the United States Institute for Peace. In each of these involvements I embodied a kind of active participant observation either directly or indirectly with the groups that are the subject of this research. I also was able to broaden my own horizons in terms of issues related to the story told in these pages. Visiting a coffee *finca* (farm) in the southern part of the department of Quetzaltenango established by former guerrillas and conducting an interview with the director of the

Catholic offices that deal with land issues in the Diocese of Los Altos provided more texture for reflecting on the current Guatemalan situation.

6. The Mam Seminary is an extension of the IENPG's national seminary located in San Felipe, Retaluhleu. Guatemala was a primary site for the development of Theological Education by Extension (TEE) in the 1960s, and the seminary has several sites where courses are given in various of the denomination's presbyteries. Education reaches the level of the *licenciatura* (bachelor's) degree in theology, but most of the education is done with a practical focus at lower levels, including literacy (in San Juan Ostuncalco) in Mam.

Chapter 3

1. See Montejo 1987 for another *testimonio* from the war zone.

2. Besides her work (1988) on the refugee crisis of the time Manz (2004) recounts the history of the village of Santa María Tzejá during the violence and the subsequent efforts by villagers to reestablish the community. It is a significant addition to the literature on the war and the manner in which the Maya are dealing with the aftermath.

3. Guatemala is unique in that two peace commissions were established following the war. The report of the Human Rights Office of the Archdiocese of Guatemala (ODHAG), the Proyecto Interdiocesano de Recuparación de la Memoria Histórica (REMHI, Recovery of Historical Memory Project), was released in four volumes under the title *Guatemala: Nunca más* on 24 April 1998. See ODHAG (1999) for the English summary of the report. The Comisión para el Esclarecimiento Histórico (CEH, Historical Clarification Commission) "was established by means of the Oslo Accord of 23 July 1994 in order to clarify with complete objectivity, equity and impartiality the violations of human rights and violent acts linked to the armed confrontation that have caused suffering to the Guatemalan population" (CEH 1999, 11). Completed largely under the auspices of the United Nations, the report was released early in 1999 and concluded that 93 percent of all violent acts it had documented during the war had been committed by the military or by paramilitary organizations. Guerrilla forces accounted for 3 percent of the incidents, while the perpetrators of 4 percent of the acts could not be determined.

4. Victoria Sanford's *Buried Secrets* (2003), based on her involvement with the Guatemalan Forensic Anthropology Team and collecting the stories of survivors of army atrocities, is a moving and often courageous story of the experiences of the survivors of the violence whom she interviewed. Sanford challenges Stoll's thesis that Maya in the Ixil region were caught "between two fires" during the conflict, as well as the work of Yvon Le Bot (1995) and Ricardo Falla (1992). The primary critique is that binary formulations of the army against the guerrillas (who could not defend the local populations in the communities where they worked) deny agency to the Maya, who sympathized with the guerrilla cause. Ultimately, this binary argument is said to silence Maya voices, especially those of women. The version of the conflict reported by these authors (and others) is said to merely repeat the "official discourse" of the army, which justified the atrocities in the first place. Sanford also highlights structural injustice that the CEH underlines as the root cause of the violence (210).

From the religious standpoint, structural violence was one of the primary themes that emerged from the Latin American Bishops' Conference in Medellín in 1968, which provided some of the underpinnings for liberation theology. At the same time, it has frequently been cited as the root cause of revolutionary movements in Latin America since at least the 1960s. My concern is with the tone of Sanford's discourse, which focuses on how particular types of analysis conspire to silence "the other"—in this case, victims of violence. We certainly need to be aware of such issues, and this was one of the strengths of postcolonial and subaltern studies, as well as a strength in Sanford's emphasis on telling the truth as we do memory work in post-conflict situations. At the same time, we need to be more tolerant of scholars who have different social locations and approach issues from different frameworks. None of the scholars named supported the army or the Guatemalan government during the violence. Falla, in particular, saw his task as one of accompanying the CPRs, and taking that rather more religious idea into account might put a different light on his work, even if some of his analysis does not go far enough at certain points. I also understand that the Stoll–Rigoberta Menchú controversy is part of the issue here, as Sanford makes clear. Nevertheless, all of us who research and write in the midst of post-conflict societies are involved in processes of deciding which voices will be heard, even when telling truth or "speaking truth to power." A recognition of this might go a long way toward bringing some tolerance back into our discourses with each other, much as Sanford highlights at the end of her work the potential for tolerance in Maya communities working out their own histories.

5. While there is no doubt much truth to this argument, the sheer diversity of evangelical expression and its relationship to efforts at Maya cultural revitalization in some quarters make any generalization tenuous. This is an area for further research regarding the shape of evangelical presence in Guatemala, and contributing to this discussion is one of the goals of this book. See also Manz's discussion of these same issues, including comments on the relations between foreign anthropologists and the Maya (2004, 9–12).

6. Unless otherwise noted, translations from Spanish sources are my own.

7. The party also garnered two seats in the Guatemalan congress.

8. Zapeta's stance on many issues in the movement in the subsequent decade would lead many to question his credentials as a spokesperson for the movement. See Warren (1998, 228 n. 30).

9. England's date for the establishing of the ALMG is 1991 (1995, 129), but it appears that the academy was actually founded in October 1986 (Cojtí Cuxil 1996, 36; Fischer 1996, 66). Cojtí (1996, 26) mentions a Government Accord 1046-87 in November 1987 that put into place a unified writing system for Mayan languages as well as congressional approval for the ALMG in March 1987 (36). He also notes that the vote in 1990 was on legislative decree 65-90. The effect was to make the academy officially funded by the government. Fischer notes how the funding languished during the early 1990s and the ambiguity created by the official status accorded to the ALMG (66–67). England's articles (1995, 1996, 2003) and the work of Judith Maxwell (1996) are helpful summaries of the ALMG's history and its role in recent Guatemalan history as well as of the role of linguistics in the Maya nationalism movement in Guatemala.

10. In this vein, Hale (1994) has analyzed groups active by the time of the 1991 "Encounter of Two Cultures" as those that had a particularly cultural (i.e., Maya) agenda and those other organized groups that had a more overt goal of providing space for political organizing and that tended to cross boundaries. He includes Rigoberta Menchú's visible participation in the *encuentro* as an example of the latter. From the standpoint

of Marxist social theory, the emphasis is on either class or culture, depending upon the viewpoint of the participant. See further discussion in Bastos and Camus (1996) and Otzoy (1996).

11. *Merriam-Webster's Collegiate Dictionary* (11th ed., 2004) gives the date of first usage for the terms *nationalism* and *nationalistic* as 1844 and 1866, respectively. The first usage of the adjectival form of *nationalist* ("of, relating to, or advocating nationalism") is given a date of 1884.

12. The UN asked Stavenhagen to carry out a special investigation on the situation of Guatemala's indigenous population in 2002. See the findings of his report in UN Economic and Social Council (2003).

13. In this section of his work, Palmer contradicts Anderson's interpretation of Latin American nationalism, at least in regard to Guatemala and Costa Rica. He faults Anderson's use of the 1838 breakup of the Central American Federation as an appropriate beginning point for nationalist self-consciousness. Some of this rests on the lack of overt revolt against Spain in the region. He quotes a comment of Anderson's that during the wars of independence in Mexico and South America, many Creoles were dead or financially ruined: "This willingness to sacrifice on the part of the comfortable classes is food for thought" (1990, 37). Then he responds: "In Central America, however—or, rather, the Captaincy General of Guatemala—the dinner is a rather frugal one: there simply were no wars or movements for independence in this the most backward of Spain's American colonies" (38). While this is a helpful and important clarification in regard to Central America, it does not have to be seen as undermining Anderson's entire argument.

14. See Ebel's discussion of the *intendente* system, which assured Mestizo control of the municipal government in highland communities during the last decade of the Ubico dictatorship (1972, 162–63).

15. Still, the dichotomy may have been somewhat overdrawn. Interaction between rural and urban centers as well as with *el norte* (to which many Maya migrate on a regular basis) certainly changes the shape of the peasantry even as it calls into question yet again the idea of "self-enclosed" communities. On migration in both Maya and Ladino contexts, see Moran-Taylor (2003).

16. See Urban and Sherzer (1991) for a helpful introduction to "folklorization" and "exoticization" in dealing with indigenous Latin American cultures.

17. I use this number as a secure baseline in part not to overstate the evangelical population. Some scholars who share my concerns continue to argue for an evangelical percentage of around 30 percent.

18. As far as I can tell, the figure does not include nominally Christian groups who have been characterized as sectarian by other evangelicals, such as the Seventh-Day Adventists, Jehovah's Witnesses, and the Mormons. In much of Mesoamerica, conversion rates and percentages of Protestants relative to national population are actually higher in indigenous communities.

19. I note here the absence of the broad and very important Brazilian literature in this overview.

20. The comparative reference here is to an essay in *Crosscurrents in Indigenous Spirituality: Interface of Maya, Catholic, and Protestant Worldviews* (Cook 1997). Cook's work is marred by poor editing and an introduction that focuses too much on a narrowly essentialist view of Maya culture instead of setting the tone for what the volume really contributes to understanding the religious panorama in Mesoamerica from either the cul-

tural or the more theological side. An evangelical scholar with an affinity for liberation theology, Cook was an important interpreter of the changes facing the Latin American Protestant community for the better part of three decades. The book remains an important contribution to interreligious dialogue in Mesoamerica.

21. The anthropological literature refers to shaman-priests who, depending on the circumstances, assume roles both in responding to individual needs and as lineage heads in varying degrees (B. Tedlock 1992, 52–53). The relationship between the upsurge in training new Maya priests and the authority of the mother-father is unclear. While the term *Maya priest* is used in discourse designed to give more credibility to the role of the ritual specialist in Maya spirituality, many prefer to use the term for day keeper, *ajq'ij*. In Spanish, the term *guía espiritual* (spiritual guide) is becoming more common. These options avoid the use of terms such as witch (*brujo*) or shaman, although the latter is not offensive. Both *ajq'ij* and *ajitz* have K'iche' origins. The Mam have two terms for the religious specialist; *ajkab'* is the general term, and the supposed practitioner of black magic is called *ajitz*. Even evangelicals who believe that the latter have no direct control over their own lives acknowledge that they do have power, even the power to kill. An older term used in at least the *municipios* of Concepción Chiquirichapa and Ostuncalco was *ajpkab.'* Finally, *ajb'ech* refers to a person who deals with *copal* (flowers). The reference there is to the burning that is characteristic of Maya rituals. The rituals are often called *ceremonias* today, but Chiappari (1999, 40) says that the generic term in Totonicapán is *quema* (burning).

22. For an ethnohistorical perspective on the Maya case see Restall (2004).

Chapter 4

1. This was the northern group of Presbyterians who divided into northern and southern constituencies at the time of the Civil War. The then-named Presbyterian Church in the United States of America united with the United Presbyterian Church in North America in 1958. The resulting United Presbyterian Church in the United States of America reunited with the southern Presbyterian Church in the United States in 1983; this reunion was named the Presbyterian Church (U.S.A.).

2. Bogenschild provides a helpful summary of the invitation and the surrounding context. Protestant pedagogical expertise in education seems to have been a larger part of the decision than has usually been recognized (1992, 34–44; cf. Zapata Arceyuz 1982).

3. A few other Protestants sought to make inroads in Guatemala prior to 1871. The most prominent exemplar was the Bible colporteur Frederick Crowe, who entered Guatemala City in 1843 after having been in the Verapaz area for a time. His presence was eventually the cause of considerable controversy, and he was escorted out of the country in April 1846 (IENPG 1982, 21–36). Garrard-Burnett links Crowe's presence to that of other ministers and colporteurs who entered Guatemala between 1827 and 1846 with "British imperial expansionism" (1998a, 7). On another level, their presence is indicative of the earliest wave of evangelical religious presence in Central America.

4. This issue was raised in discussion with James Wessman in relation to archival work he has done regarding the conflicts between some of the earliest Presbyterian missionaries in Guatemala.

5. The historiography of the Mexican church in relation to the state in the nineteenth and twentieth centuries is extensive. Relations between church and state were

again addressed in reforms to the Mexican Constitution in the early 1990s. See Metz (1994) on contemporary Protestantism and Camp (1997) for Catholic developments, as well as relevant bibliographic material on a number of issues.

6. Barrios followed Miguel García Granados in the presidency. Granados was the first to occupy the position following the liberal victory in 1871. Although Barrios actually won an election in mid-1873, he seems to have assumed the presidency at the very end of 1872, when Granados vacated the office under some pressure (Handy 1984, 61–62). The detail is important, since Barrios is credited with the decree in favor of religious freedom in March and the elections were not held until later in the year.

7. Carey also notes that the judgment about Barrios's efforts in this regard varied according to the religious persuasion of those he interviewed.

8. I believe the reference is actually to the Presbyterian Church in the United States of America, mentioned at the beginning of this chapter. Historical denominations in Guatemala are the first five denominations with missionary work in the country—the Presbyterians (1882), the Central American Mission (1896), the Church of the Nazarene (1901/1904), the California Friends (1902), and the Primitive Methodists (1914). The Friends are now associated with the Evangelical Friends International—not the American Friends Service Committee familiar to many academics. The first four of these groups early on (1902) established a comity agreement specifying the area of the country where each group would work (Garrard-Burnett 1998a, 29–32, 177 n. 27). The agreement was not formalized until 1936. The 1914 date for the Primitive Methodists is Garrard-Burnett's. She does not cite a source, and other sources give 1921 as the date the beginning of their work in Guatemala.

9. Arévalo himself was presented with a copy of the New Testament in both Mam and K'iche' in 1946. See photograph in P. Burgess (1957, 46).

10. In the theological community, this has sometimes been referred to as the "Protestant Principle." See Tillich (1957, 163).

11. See Steigenga (1999, 2001) and Samson (2007) for further analysis of evangelicals and Guatemalan political processes.

12. The discussion in these pages is insightful in terms of situating a conflict between Edward Haymaker and Albert Bishop, the most formidable personalities in the early missionary activities of the Presbyterian Church and the Central American Mission, respectively, as a portent of the modernist-fundamentalist debate that engulfed North American Protestantism in the early decades of the twentieth century. The Presbyterians were clearly on the modernist side of the divide and were "the most ideologically committed to the development of secular institutions" (Garrard-Burnett 1998a, 33). The importance of this divide among the Guatemalan historical denominations on into the twenty-first century cannot be overstated. The dispensationalism promoted by the Central American Mission and its founder, Cyrus Scofield, had a profound impact on the course of evangelical history in the country, in part through the impact of their Bible institute, founded in 1929 (now Seminario Teológico Centroamericano [SETECA, Central American Theological Seminary]). The idea that God's intentions for the world unfold in a series of "dispensations" tends to be associated with premillennialist views predicating Christ's reign on the imminent end of human history. The corollary to this kind of thought is the need to prepare for the end rather than for involvement in the world. This is one root of the lack of political involvement by evangelicals, as well as confusion surrounding the term "fundamentalism" (see Marsden 1991; Schfer 1992, 32–35). In analyzing Guatemalan fundamentalism, Bogenschild

(1992) emphasizes fragmentation between missionaries, various "pietistic" movements among such as the Adventists and Kramerites, and nativistic impulses on the part of native converts reacting against missionary colonialism. Bogenschild's work is focused on the western highlands and primarily around the work of Paul Burgess.

13. I am using the date from IENPG (1982), although Garrard-Burnett dates the hospital to 1910, in addition to the founding of clinics in various locations before 1920 (1998a, 33).

14. Bogenschild cites Salcajá, Cantel, Olintepeque, and San Carlos Sija as other areas visited by the missionaries working in Xela between 1910 and 1913. The only formally organized congregation in the region until 1919 was the Bethel congregation in Xela (1992, 160). Guatemalans were active with the missionaries from an early date; while not ordained, these "national workers" did a fair amount of work throughout the area.

15. McBath and his spouse, Anna Halloway McBath (whom he met while she was associated with the Central American Mission in Guatemala), lost a son from diphtheria in Quetzaltenango in 1911. The connection this event gave them with the people of the area is one of the reasons why McBath is said to have wanted to begin a school for the native population. The couple retired (briefly) to Almolonga in 1913. In another irony of missionary lore, McBath is credited with bringing horticultural knowledge to Almolonga (IENPG 1982, 89–90).

16. While the story of Edward Haymaker, the Pecks, and the Burgesses assumes a larger place here and in the history of indigenous Protestantism in Guatemala, the Sullenbergers also lived in Guatemala for more than forty years. A study of the long-term missionary tenure of several Presbyterians in Guatemala would be an interesting undertaking. Bogenschild (1992) bases much of his work on the Burgess correspondence, and Scotchmer (1985) has produced a brief ethnohistorical analysis based on an analysis of Haymaker's own writings. To date, the Pecks have received much less of this kind of attention. Two of their children remain involved with the Mam community in Ostuncalco. A more extensive comparative study on the various perspectives on working with the indigenous population would also be instructive.

17. The work actually seems to have been published in 1931. Townsend was the founder of the Wycliffe Bible Translators, now known as the Summer Institute of Linguistics. For a longer discussion of his career, see the chapter on Townsend in Stoll (1982) and the recent work by Todd Hartch (2006), *Missionaries of the State*.

18. Townsend also figured in this meeting (see Mulholland 1997).

19. This is not the place to rehash the history of the Burgesses. Their missionary service ended in 1957, and both died in retirement in Quetzaltenango, Paul in 1958 and Dora in 1962. In addition to what has been recounted here, Dora collaborated in publishing a Spanish translation from K'iche' of the Popol Wuj (D. Burgess and Xec 1955) after the couple reportedly discovered the Ximénez K'iche' Spanish manuscript in the Newberry Library in 1945 (Dalquist 1995, 144–46). The text had actually been located bound with another manuscript by Adrián Recinos in 1941 (Recinos, Goetz, and Morley 1950, xii). Paul was also largely responsible for writing and editing the *Historia de la obra evangélica presbiteriana en Guatemala* (P. Burgess 1957) on the seventy-fifth anniversary of the denomination's work in the country and a biography of Justo Rufino Barrios (P. Burgess 1972). In another interesting sidelight of his full life, he is said to have baptized Jacobo Arbenz (Garrard-Burnett 1998a, 89; Dalquist 1995, 155). The Dalquist volume (1995) has interesting pieces of information about the couple, but it is written as a sympathetic portrayal of Paul Burgess the missionary.

20. Many older sources refer to Quezaltenango instead of Quetzaltenango. The former appears to have been the spelling until recent years. I preserve the older spelling only in quotations where it is so used. Some foreigners with long experience in the highlands will still refer to "Quez." More common in daily speech are references to "Xela," from the Maya name for the city, Xelaju.

21. The Pecks are the primary figures from the Presbyterian mission among the Mam. They remained in the region until 1970 and contributed linguistic texts in the Mam language to the larger academic community as well as Dudley's dissertation on Mam shamanism (Peck 1970). Based on their work, a Mam hymnal was produced in 1927 and a New Testament was published by the American Bible Society in 1939.

22. Elsewhere she says that Catholic Action came to Guatemala in 1935. Like the Protestant missions, its activities were initially confined to the capital (Garrard-Burnett 1998a, 104).

23. *Costumbre* refers most literally to tradition, or to patterns of religious and social practice that have been handed down through the generations. Discourse related to *costumbre* typically makes reference to *antepasados,* or ancestors who have passed the traditions to succeeding generations. In general terms, *costumbre* involves private ceremonies that center on sacrifices where *copal* incense, candles, and other offerings are burned in a ritual fire. The more public aspects of *costumbre* are those involving cargo systems or *cofradías* that care for images of Catholic saints. In the classic model of the Mesoamerican civil-religious hierarchy, men served alternating terms in the *cofradía* and civil offices until attaining the title of *principal* within the community. Both the *cofradía* and *costumbre* represent the mixing of pre-contact and Spanish religious practices, although the syncretism is more obvious in the case of the *cofradía*. In addition to studies emphasizing the breakdown of the traditional authority structures that were legitimized in the *cofradía* system, other recent work has viewed *costumbre* as a space of resistance and adaptation for native communities (Carlsen 1997). From the standpoint of Maya ethnic renewal, what might be called the purification of *costumbre* has become an important issue.

24. The clash of generational leadership has been well studied, but it remains a topic of interest in the context of community studies that more than ever view the local indigenous community as interconnected with national and even transnational culture. The study of the individual or family associations with particular religious communities within individual life spans and within families through generations is an underutilized method for understanding religious change in Latin America. Such a method can be particularly useful in the study of Protestant growth in the region and in the study of the different ideological tendencies current within the Roman Catholic Church. See Warren (2001) for an address to this issue in the context of her long work in the Kaqchikel community of San Andrés Semetabaj.

25. But see Watanabe (1992, 171–75) for a discussion of the breakdown of the cargo system in Santiago Chimaltenango, a Mam-speaking community in Huehuetenango. He relates this to changes in the way in which the legitimation of political authority took place in the community through the formalization of individual land titles, which severed the authority of the *principales* to manage land tenure in the community. The shift could also be seen when the Guatemalan government decreed that the community was an *aldea* of a neighboring community in 1935, and a young Spanish speaker was chosen to lead the delegation to go to Guatemala City to negotiate for a return to the prior status.

26. The date for the founding of the Evangelical Synod in *Apuntes para la historia* is March 1936 (IENPG 1982, 45).

27. Wilson's article is also important for highlighting the importance of Guatemalan leadership—both Ladino and Maya—among the Pentecostals.

28. Another document on the origins of the presbytery I have in my possession, written by a missionary from the Church of Scotland, puts some of the issues in more direct ethnic terms. Of the two reasons cited for forming the presbytery, one had to do with Ladino jealousy in the face of missionary wealth. While slightly unclear, the implication seems to be that the missionaries planted the seed of the ethnic presbytery as a way of dealing with that conflict. The indicated tension still exists. When I went to the field, any North American or European who worked with the denomination would be assumed to be with one side or the other in terms of moral and other kinds of support. The second reason cited in the missionary document is that the Maya did feel discriminated against. The next ethnic presbytery, among the Q'eqchi', was not founded until 1978. The Mam Presbytery was the third ethnic presbytery to be founded, in 1980.

29. Jeffrey's work is complementary to Jonas's. Jeffrey is a longtime Methodist missionary in Central America with a vocation in journalism. Because of his long residence in the region, he has extensive contacts with representatives of both the Roman Catholic and the evangelical community. He is a regular contributor to *Latinamerica Press* and has published in the *Christian Century* and *National Catholic Reporter*. The work cited here makes an essential contribution to understanding the religious community's involvement in the Guatemalan peace process. This role, particularly as far as evangelicals are concerned, is often neglected in the scholarly study of the steps leading to the events of 29 December 1996. Jeffrey does not neglect the role of Maya spirituality in his account, and from the anthropological perspective he adds a view of local groups claiming their voice within the larger discussion. This has implications not only for the Guatemalan situation but also for the understanding of local organizing in transnational context. See also Calder (2001).

30. This is a reference to the Reformed theological tradition, which has roots in the part of the Protestant Reformation that took place in Switzerland, especially under the leadership of John Calvin. A number of Presbyterian and Congregational, as well as Reformed, denominations in Europe and North America trace their roots to this tradition. As a result of missionary activity, these denominations, in turn, have founded churches throughout the world over the past 150 years.

31. This is not to ignore groups (e.g., the Committee for Campesino Unity) that have been involved in land issues since before the violence. The key in singling out these two organizations, both of which have maintained a high profile, is the element of gender.

32. The home page is http://www.geocities.com/Athens/Delphi/3127/; accessed 23 December 2003. My description is from that date. A perusal of the site in late April 2004 showed changes that more heavily accentuated Maya culture.

33. Details of involvement here come primarily from Son Turnil (1997, 10–21). The story is clearly from the viewpoint of CIEDEG and its leadership. Nevertheless, the organization is criticized in some quarters for having co-opted the evangelical position in some of the meetings designed to have broad public participation in laying out the framework for discussions leading to peace accords. The more theologically conservative Alianza Evangélica did participate in the Quito meeting, but its involvement in the CNR was curtailed for reasons that remain obscure to me. For more detail about

the entire process, see the second chapter, "The Mined Road to Peace," in Jonas (2000). In Jonas's discussion of the peace process, only a couple of references deal with the involvement of the evangelical community.

34. Between the Framework Accord and the final accord, which brought the conflict to an end, were a series of "side" agreements on substantive issues having to do with various aspects of Guatemalan society such as agrarian issues, indigenous rights, democratization, and the role of the armed forces. The first of these accords, signed in March 1994, was the Global Accord on Human Rights. This accord is noteworthy for guaranteeing human rights while future agreements were being discussed and for inviting the UN to send an "observer mission" to monitor human rights violations on the ground. Ultimately, MINUGUA became the most visible symbol of the international community's involvement in the post-conflict situation.

35. Jeffrey reports that "church representatives from inside Guatemala were largely excluded, in part because of opposition from popular organization leaders who controlled the local organizing committee" (1998, 20).

36. Jonas says that the consensus model developed among the diverse actors represented by the ASC was unique. She also claims that the major part of its activity was over by the end of 1995 (2000, 140).

37. While leaving this issue for the moment, I should note that CIEDEG itself was rooted in the activities of the Consejo Cristiano de Agencias de Desarrollo (CONCAD, Christian Council of Development Agencies), which was created to manage relief aid in the wake of the devastating earthquake of 4 February 1976. Another group from this period, less formally organized but representing a space of resistance to the repression of the Guatemalan state in the early 1980s, was the Confraternidad Evangélica. Berryman says that it challenged Ríos Montt's "use of personal religiosity to garner support for the government" (1994, 121). Koll links the Confraternidad to the EGP, remarking that some missionaries "saw support for organized revolutionary efforts as consistent with their understand of the demands of the gospel" (2004, 350).

38. A web site describing the United Church of Canada's involvement with Guatemala claims 10 April 2002 as the date of "the first meeting" of FEPAZ. This may be true in a formal sense, but Similox's presentation at the 23 January meeting was designed to put the agenda on the table within the ecumenical community. The CIEDEG connection and Similox himself seem to predominate in FEPAZ. Pronouncements from both organizations are released simultaneously, and these are preserved in links on CIEDEG's web site cited in note 32.

39. In the months following President Oscar Berger's inauguration in January 2004, Ríos Montt was placed under house arrest for his alleged culpability in these events.

40. When the document referred to here was written, some eight presbyteries were associated in the organization. By the time I ended my field work, the four Q'eqchi' presbyteries had formed their own Q'eqchi' Association. Although it continues to exist, I have little information about the current functioning of that association. The Hermandad continued to have relationships with the Mam, Q'anhob'al, Kaqchikel, and Maya Quiché presbyteries. The Hermandad also works with some women's groups in the highlands. The Maya Quiché Presbytery split into two presbyteries in 2002.

41. Schäfer (2002) documents aspects of the conflict in the early years. The violence exacerbated the ethnic and theological tensions discussed in the text. Scotchmer recounts an event from the 1981 annual synod meeting of the IENPG when a leader from the Q'eqchi' Presbytery stood before the assembly to tell the chilling story of a

threatening conflict with Ladino landowners in the area of the presbytery. The other Maya present joined him at the front of the meeting space "until all the Indian delegates stood facing the remaining assembly of *Ladinos,* a few missionaries and visitors" (1989, 306). Scotchmer goes on to recount the fate of the commission formed to investigate the situation, including the disappearance of three Maya leaders. The families apparently were able to continue to use the lands in question, and Scotchmer concludes that "the crisis never degenerated into an ethnic conflict as sociocultural patterns would have dictated" (306). While this is perhaps true in that context, ethnicity seemed to be at the core of many of the denomination's conflicts in the 1990s.

42. The *colegio* has been a prominent part of the educational infrastructure of Quetzaltenango since the early 1920s. It was eventually returned to the IENPG, although another evangelical school founded near the market area on the western side of the city was one fruit of the conflict.

43. In the Presbyterian Church (U.S.A.), missionaries are now called "mission coworkers" as a recognition of some of the vagaries of past missionary activities. The Presbyterian Church (U.S.A.) works internationally under a guiding rubric of "partnership." This is supposed to imply that U.S. personnel in either short- or long-term relationships with local agencies are guided by formal agreements that provide structure for the way in which the relationships take shape on the ground. Many connections, particularly by individual congregations and groups, continue to be made outside the formal denomination-to-denomination arrangements. Personal contacts between individuals often result in congregation-to-congregation ties or even relationships between congregations and other kinds organizations. Such ties are part of the wave of transnational religion. Ease of travel and communications more generally means that personal and group contacts can at best be channeled and not controlled by denominational entities. See Koll (2004) for detailed information about solidarity networks and partnerships between the Presbyterian Church (U.S.A.) and Central American religious organizations during the 1980s. Her section on the IENPG (311–95) provides significant information that helps fill in gaps around the subsequent history and the types of relationships that have developed between groups in the United States and Guatemala.

44. For recent studies on Protestantism among the Maya in Yucatán, see Kray (1997) and Forand (2001). Forand gives considerable attention to Presbyterians, and her findings differ in several regards from my own. See also her discussion of marriage arrangements between Maya Protestants and Catholics (Forand 2002).

45. The literature on this topic is growing. For a recent assessment, see Jenkins (2002). Both missiology and the history of missions have become viable fields of study in Bible colleges, seminaries, and divinity schools.

46. Stoll is often misinterpreted on this point. While he does note the Guatemalan evangelical community's ties to the Religious Right, he acknowledges that the connection was both complex and in many ways not as determinative as others argued (1990, 305–31).

47. Cleary (1997, 2001, 2004) has laid significant groundwork for understanding indigenous theology as it has played out in Latin American Catholicism. He has been a consistent scholar of religious change in both Catholic and evangelical contexts, as well as on human rights agendas.

48. Although it is more personalized, the activities of José Serech and the Centro de Documentación e Investigación Maya (CEDIM, Maya Documentation and Research Center) in Guatemala City belong on this fairly short list.

49. See Gossen (1989) for a study of the trajectory of a Protestant leader involved with community level politics in Chiapas.

50. On one level the basic meaning of *reivindicación* is to rediscover something, but in the case of aspects of Maya culture the sense of the term moves beyond that notion to a concept of reclaiming something. Though spelled as "revendicate," there is apparently legal language in Louisiana civil law that gives more texture to the term, for in that context it means "to bring an action to enforce rights in (specific property) esp. for the recognition of ownership and the recovery of possession from one wrongfully in possession." This definition surely fits the way in which the Maya Movement is responding to cultural appropriation and the efforts on the part of the Guatemalan state to assimilate the Maya peoples. For more information, see the entries for the respective terms at www.dictionary.com.

Chapter 5

1. Scotchmer uses an older (i.e., not standardized) orthography for Mam words. I studied the newer orthography and will use that (except for long or double vowels) on those few occasions when the need arises in reference to my own work. For example, in this quote *Kajaw* would become *Qajaw,* with q- as the second-person possessive. In the article cited, Scotchmer gives the meaning of *Kajaw Crist* as "Christ Our Lord, Owner, Guardian" (300). The attempt is to capture both the Christian sense of Christ as Lord over a person's life (in both the Maya and Christian senses) and the notion of the Spanish *dueño* (owner), which can be applied to the mountain spirits who inhabit the sacred landscape in the Maya world. See Scotchmer (1986, 201–2) for a discussion of this issue in relation to sacrifice and the saints, including Jesus. For more on the mountain spirits (*witz*) among the Mam, see Watanabe (1992, 76–79); among the Q'eqchi', see R. Wilson (1991) and A. Adams (2001).

2. I use the word *sacrament* comfortably with Presbyterians, and in the historical Protestant context more generally, but with trepidation in terms of other evangelical groups. Baptism can fairly well be said to be universal among evangelicals, and most groups at some time or another celebrate the Lord's Supper or Communion. The latter, while important, is given much less attention, and one can probably argue that conversion itself sometimes has a symbolic significance comparable to baptism. Speaking in tongues (glossolalia) and being filled with the Spirit have sacramental overtones in Pentecostal settings. Defining such concepts, as well as concepts related to positions of authority within the congregation (e.g., elder) is an important part of doing ethnography with evangelicals in Mesoamerica.

3. I am using "southern Mam" to refer primarily to the region and language of the Mam in the department of Quetzaltenango, as opposed to Huehuetenango and the area to the west of Ostuncalo on to the Mexican border. This is generally the division followed by the Summer Institute of Linguists and their "Ethnologue" reporting (http://www.ethnologue.com). Most dialects are identified by the community where they are spoken (cf. England 1983; B'aayil and Ajb'ee 1997).

4. Indicating how organizations change over time in Guatemala, a Google search of ASIMAM on 2 October 2006 revealed that it is a civil organization composed mostly of women. Still located in San Miguel Sigüilá, it seems to focus on community development, including the sale of textiles. See http://asimam.tripod.com/index.html.

5. *IXIMULEW* was published in varying arrangements through time by CECMA,

Siglo-Veintiuno (at the time probably the second national daily newspaper), and Cholsamaj; *Rutzijol* by the Centro Maya SAQB'E in Chimaltenango; *El regional* under its own auspices as a weekly in Quetzaltenango. On visits to Guatemala subsequent to my long-term field work, I got the sense that *IXIMULEW* was no longer being published and that *El regional* was not using Maya languages the way it had in 1997 and 1998.

6. The tension between church agendas and the clinic and the center was very much a live issue when I was in the field. Some of the tension was related to local patronage networks, but it remains complicated by outside interests who still desire to cooperate with the Mam in their work, especially in the social arena. Gender is also a factor, and the clinic director was a single woman with social work training who had a long track record of success in outreach and educational efforts among Mam women.

7. It is important to note that this historical sketch was mostly likely written by David Scotchmer, who was intimately involved in the unfolding of these events and the establishment of the presbytery. He gives a slightly different version with a few more details in his dissertation (1991, 371–76). Scotchmer's formal tenure as a missionary among the Mam ended in 1982. He once told me that he had been warned about being on military's "list."

8. In this case, adherents include baptized members (adults), people in membership training (*catecumenos*), and children. The thirteen churches that brought statistics to the presbytery meeting of January 1998 had a total of 5,171 members. The 2,176 children recorded in these numbers are significant in terms of the future demographics of the region.

9. The distinction between *iglesias* (churches), *proyectos* (projects), and *congregaciones* (congregations) is fundamental to church organizing in the area. I generally use *church* to refer to either a building in a particular place or the gathered congregation that meets there. I refer to church buildings themselves as *templos* (literally, temples).

10. Census figures from 1994 here and in the next chapter are from INE (1996a, 1996b). Numbers from 2002 can be accessed at the site of the National Institute of Statistics: http://www.segeplan.gob.gt/ine/censos2003/index.html.

11. Despite the preponderance of the Mam population, a K'iche'-organized "pan-Indian political movement called Xel-hú" (Ebel 1992, 177) provided assistance in the 1976 election of "the first Indian mayor in the modern history of San Juan Ostuncalco" (178). The history is a complicated one in which the Maya apparently were able to manage a parallel town council through the first quarter of the twentieth century (174). From Ebel's description, the town was beset by religious, ethnic, and other factional conflict beginning in the 1950s. Some of this conflict was accentuated by political party maneuvering during the 1960s. The mayor elected in 1976 was unable to serve out his term amid various accusations made against him, although he was replaced by another Maya from the town council. Ebel also documents some of the violence that engulfed the town in the early 1980s and muses about the possibility that "growing religious pluralism . . . continues to reduce the historic political tensions and factionalism in the town" (191). By the early 1990s the son of one of the Mam Presbyterian ministers was mayor, and he reported conflict with the local priest in an interview I had with him in 2001. The priest (a K'iche' who learned to speak Mam) seemed to have changed his attitude somewhat, and the former mayor was working on establishing a bilingual school. Overt conflict between the ethnic groups seemed to be in abeyance during my time in the field.

12. Although some classes in the Mam Seminary are held on Sunday morning when families will already be in Ostuncalco, the grounds for the complex (including a small house formerly used by missionaries and a few other rooms occupying about a quarter of a city block) serve as a parking space for church members and others who do not wish to leave their vehicles on the crowded streets.

13. The life-size figure of La Candelaria is enshrined in a glass case in the center of the chancel area in the town's Catholic church. Her clothes are changed periodically, and during the time of the festival in her honor, lines of the faithful ascend a small set of steps placed near the case, greet her, and make their petitions. During most of the year this kind of access is not granted. A number of other saint figures are in niches along the walls of the nave and the transept. These figures include at least three of Jesus, including El Señor Sepultado (Lord in the Tomb), a life-size image of a bloodied Jesus lying as if in a sepulcher that is common in churches in many parts of Guatemala. A replica of El Señor de Esquipulas, which often has candles burning in front of it, is centered along one wall, and a small image of John the Baptist, the town's titular saint, hangs on a wall in the area approaching the chancel and demarcating the altar area from the seating of the congregants. Ears of dried maize and pieces of *tela* (native cloth) are encased with some of the images. In reflecting upon these images, I am reminded of a quote from Charles Wagley recorded in one of Scotchmer's articles, to the effect that people in Santiago Chimaltenango view Christ and the saints as native, while mountain spirits ("Guardians") are perceived as Ladino (1986, 202). The arrangement of images in Catholic churches changes with some degree of frequency.

14. Remittances from migratory workers now compose the single largest source of foreign exchange in Guatemala. Of course, there are other consequences and potential consequences. Although I cannot verify the information, I have heard reports that in some communities nearly 50 percent of the male population has made the trip northward. Besides the usual documented problems of making the journey—abuse by *coyotes* (migration guide, smuggler), the possibility of being detained along the way, the possibility of illness in unfamiliar circumstance—the cost is exorbitant. Michelle Moran-Taylor (personal communication) reported costs of $3,600 to $4,500 (Q28,000 to 35,000) in 2001. Land is often sold to obtain the fare.

15. This can be compared with Horst's useful discussion of land pressure and seasonal migration within Guatemala in the mid-1960s (1967, 161–67).

16. Description in this section makes use of composite portraits born out of observations in the field.

17. See A. Adam's (1999, 125–26) discussion of the relationship between the mountain spirits (*Tzuultaq'a*) among the Q'eqchi' in the Verapaz and "the regional highland-lowland prestige pattern" (125). Although higher concentrations of evangelicals live in the lowlands, the larger church structures are built in highland areas.

18. Hostnig (1991, 169–70) provides a chart with the names of ninety-nine sites in the *municipio* of Ostuncalco that have a relationship to Maya ceremonial practices.

19. Scotchmer reports that a missionary's suggestion of putting a cross on a newly constructed building for the de Cristo congregation in San Juan was rejected (1986, 207). A Star of David appeared, but it was simply because the design was aesthetically pleasing.

20. This practice is not so common within the Catholic churches of the area. In 1999, however, I did see a clock high up on the *altar mayor* of the main church in San

Juan Ixcoy, a Q'anjobal *municipio* far up in the Cuchumatán Mountains in the department of Huehuetenango.

21. The theological foundation for this implies an even more profound shift, because "the Word" in Reformed theology refers to the Bible, to Jesus as the word God "speaks" to humankind, and to the literal act of proclaiming the word in preaching. A. Adams (2001) provides a good discussion of language and the interplay of Q'eqchi' and Christian conceptualizations of heated language and the heart. Included is a discussion of Bible translation among the Q'eqchi'. She notes that the Gospel of John, which begins, "In the beginning was the Word . . . ," assumed a certain primacy among translators (2001, 217).

22. Non-Christian anthropologists who spend a lot of time in evangelical communities are sometimes embraced in this way. I always assumed that the community held out hope for a conversion. I even recall one conversation with an anthropologist who said that he had preached when given time in a church service, despite not really having any particular religious beliefs.

23. The term *hermano* does seem to have other kinds of common usage in colloquial talk, but so far I have not been able to discern whether there is some ethnic or larger communal base for that usage. It reflects the way in which someone might say "man" in English or the way a friend of mine in Mexico used to say *carnal,* which as a term for friendship in the context of this study might be translated as "flesh of my flesh."

24. A summary of statistics for the presbytery that I obtained for the period from June to December 1996 listed twenty-nine people in the "reconciled" category and twenty-six who were "disciplined."

25. The young student who helped me with Mam while I was in the field was a Pentecostal, and he explained the Christmas prohibition by pointing out that since Christ came just once there was no point in celebrating his birth every year. The Holy Week prohibition is more clear, given the generalized Latin American focus on Good Friday and all the Catholic traditions surrounding that time.

26. I noted this in the Huasteca region of Mexico (see Samson 1994), and the generalization still holds. It breaks down in situations when ecumenical unity becomes important, but it may be that people with historical Protestant roots are more comfortable with the more inclusive discourse than are other evangelical groups. From a sociolinguistic viewpoint, this might simply be part of the dynamic of conversion, a way of marking a changed status and appropriating common discourse to the needs of the community.

27. See Watanabe on similarities between the approach of Maryknoll catechists and evangelicals in their approach to *costumbre* (1992, 201–2). He also notes that "local factionalism and interpersonal differences" contributed to sectarianism in the community where he worked. This point cannot be made strongly enough in regard to religious tension in Guatemala. Buffeted by the ethnic divide, the history of violence in which anyone under forty-five has spent his or her entire adult life living through the war and the uncertain post-conflict years, and the shifting nature of the economy in the wake of structural adjustment in the 1980s and the advent of neoliberalism in the 1990s, there are plenty of reasons for conflict. On the other side of the coin, local populations are also now accustomed to living with a kind of religious pluralism that was not common before the 1970s.

28. This was also true in the more indigenous (Nahua) congregations I visited in the

Huasteca region. See Palka (2002) for a study of the right and left domains, including their association with gender in both ancient and contemporary Maya culture. In his commentary on the Popol Vuh, D. Tedlock (1996, 217 n. 63) mentions that both male and female diviners "are symbolically androgynous, female on the left side of the body and male on the right."

29. Missionaries, both Roman Catholic and Protestant, banned the marimba as being too closely associated with traditional Maya religion. It has made a comeback in a number of contexts, and cassettes with evangelical marimba music can be found in any weekly market.

30. This raises the question of the appeal of Pentecostalism within indigenous culture. Services did vary somewhat in the Mam Presbytery, but concerns were voiced about the Pentecostalization of Reformed worship practices. The reasons for this Pentecostalization of Presbyterianism have not been examined. In addition to hearing the more usual kinds of arguments about Pentecostal services being more exciting or having more appeal in a context where orality is valued, I was told that when people migrated to the coast for work there were few Presbyterian churches. That would make an interesting thesis for a research project.

31. Scotchmer also noted this and attributed it to the prestige factor of Spanish. I mostly accept that interpretation, although I was once told that it might have something to do with the nature of the available Mam Bible translation itself. It was Peck's translation based on an early version of Reina-Valera Spanish translation—sort of a Spanish King James Version. In at least one congregation I was told that elements of the service had to be in Spanish so that some people could understand it. See J. Hill and Hill (1986) for an insightful discussion of purity and power codes in language use in another Mesoamerican context.

32. The form described here is interesting in that the person is immersed and then water from the pool is poured on his or her head three times. One almost gets the sense that elements of both immersion and "sprinkling" are being preserved. The whole issue of why Presbyterians immerse at all is an interesting one. This was another case where the assumption might be made that the shift in practice was designed to differentiate evangelicals from Catholics. Scotchmer says that either form was acceptable (1986, 211). Bogenschild (1992, 240–43) records an interesting incident in his study of "fundamentalism" in the southwestern part of Guatemala, where Paul Burgess, as early as 1922, was forced to allow congregations to opt for their own style of baptism. Eventually, Burgess was forced "to drop the practice and replace it with a 'presentation ceremony' for newborns" (243). Bogenschild assumes that the particular case had to do with the involvement of a person with exposure to the Central American Mission but that the interest in immersion also had to do with more literal interpretations of the Bible. He also is concerned with allowing room for local interpretations (as opposed to missionary colonialism) in regard to issues such as baptism (personal communication, 23 March 2004). In such theological issues it is important to be clear about whether such inculturation involves "native" interpretations in the Guatemalan sense more generally or in the particular context of indigenous culture.

33. I am extending this idea from Maurer's discussion of the festival tradition as a "sacrament of harmony" (1996, 43–47). The concept grows out of Catholic notions of inculturation, but it provides an insightful view of the Mesoamerican response to Christianity, including the downplaying of the Mass and the Eucharist.

34. The legislative decrees mentioned earlier stopped short of "officializing" Maya

languages, and a number of constitutional changes required by the peace accords were derailed with the failure of the referendum. See Jonas (2000, chapter 8) for a detailed examination of the referendum and the surrounding political climate.

35. To a certain degree, this is logical when one reflects on the history of Catholic Action as a renewal movement that went off into more radical directions. Liberation theology was also a movement in its own right in many places. See Chea Urruela (1998) for a discussion of the different currents in the Guatemalan Catholic Church between the mid-1950s and the early 1980s.

36. The assumption is that the missionaries are the Pecks, but this is not made clear.

37. While outside my purposes here, the connection made by evangelicals between sorcery and Satan or the Devil should not be overlooked in either a literal or a metaphorical sense.

38. Although her example comes from the Huichol culture and not the Maya, Myerhoff notes how "[t]erms referring to those beyond great grandfather become metaphorical and are used to signify the 'very ancient ones' or ancestors" (1974, 67). In that context, ancestors are central to a cosmology in which both ritual and kinship are evoked in the interest of continually linking the present generation to the ancestors and to the ancestral homeland. The peyote hunt is a literal return to that homeland, Wirikuta, and at the same time it recapitulates the cultural sequence of Huichol subsistence patterns.

39. This trinity of characteristics related to Maya spirituality and what one might on another level call a Maya ethos comes largely from Antonio Otzoy. I spent a fair amount of time in conversation with Antonio over the months when I was in the field, and I also heard him talk to visiting groups from North America about Maya spirituality on a number of occasions. Fischer's work (also in the Kaqchikel context) refers on several occasions to the notion of balance or even "reciprocal balance" in Maya culture (2001, 147–48). Practical cycles such as agriculture and cosmic cycles such as the calendar round are linked in such a way that the "consensual norms are perpetuated in changing circumstances" (148). See also R. Hill and Fischer (1999). A. Adams (2001) also discusses the concept extensively in relation to Q'eqchi' evangelicals.

40. Of course, this sense of self-in-place is being challenged on a number of levels through migratory practices in which many Maya now reside on a more or less permanent basis in the United States. Yet there is also the tendency to reinforce ties with the home community in Guatemala not only through remittances but in some cases through re-creating patron saint festivals in the new home. The issues here revolve around the deterritorialization and reterritorialization of religion (Vásquez and Marquardt 2003) as well as transnational religious networks. See Williams and Steigenga (2005) for recent work in this area.

41. In the summer of 2006, the long-term director of the Mam Center, José "Chepe" Romero, died of an apparent suicide resulting in part from his struggle with Parkinson's disease. He had been removed from the directorship of the Mam Center several years before as part of a struggle over leadership within the presbytery that has only been referred to briefly in the interstices of the description I have provided here. This was obviously a blow to a person who had been very active in the presbytery leadership since the 1970s. Chepe was credited with steering a course between guerrilla and government forces during the early 1980s that allowed the Mam Center to remain open for the duration of the conflict.

Chapter 6

1. See Samson (2003) for more details on Manuel Saquic. I am grateful to the editors of *Le Fait Missionnaire, Social Science and Missions* for permission to use material from that article here. The chronology of Saquic's death draws on Manly (1997, xiiv), MINUGUA (1995, 10), and Amnesty International (1996).

2. Various newspaper reports and press releases indicate that at the time of his abduction Saquic had been working on the case of the Kaqchikel Presbyterian elder and human rights activist Pascual Serech, who had been murdered in August 1994. Earlier in the month of his death, Saquic is said to have witnessed the abduction of yet another Kaqchikel Presbyterian linked to a local human rights commission.

3. Historical references to the origins of the presbytery are largely from Koll (2004). Another manuscript in my possession ignores some of the earlier antecedents to the presbytery's founding and focuses more directly on relief work following the earthquake (Similox V. n.d.). No doubt some of the international connections in the presbytery date to that period.

4. A son of the couple, Ronaldo, was coordinating mental health work and working in human rights in the presbytery during my time in the field. He studied psychology in the university, and in one talk I heard him give to a visiting group of First Nations Peoples from Canada, he said that the university education he had received was something that committed him to serve the community. Margarita's background is somewhat atypical as well. She is a K'iche' who married into a Kaqchikel family. Additionally, she ran for the national congress with the Frente Democrático Nueva Guatemala (FDNG, New Guatemala Democratic Front) in the 1995 elections, placing third.

5. I have not been able to verify this, but I do know that both Manuel Saquic and Lucio Martínez had roots in Pentecostal contexts. Former catechists also seem to be numerous in the presbytery in an area that was known for involvement with Catholic Action. This shifting affiliation is one of the issues that complicates assessments of the number of evangelicals in Guatemala and elsewhere in Central America.

6. The confluences in the trajectory of the presbytery with CIEDEG and the HPM as discussed in chapter 4 are significant. All three organizations are tied to the Chimaltenango Presbyterian context.

7. The same document reports that the presbytery was to expand its activities to seven other *municipios* during 1998. I do not know the extent of presbytery activity beyond the late 1990s.

8. It is also considerably higher than the national population increase of 34.87 percent, from 8,331,874 to 11,237,196.

9. Hale says that the "bars" were frequented by indigenous soldiers from the military base and that most of the women were Mestizas from El Salvador (1999, 314). The base was finally closed in early 2003, and the land was returned to representatives of the Pedro Molina Rural Normal School, from which the land had been taken in 1980 (*La hora,* 10 de Enero de 2003).

10. The conclusions to the CEH identify seventy massacres in Chimaltenango, placing it third on the list, behind Quiché and Huehuetenango. Exhumations of bodies in the department were ongoing in the middle of 2005.

11. Thinking about Catholic Action and the subsequent development of liberation theology and other forms of activist Catholicism should probably begin by ac-

knowledging their roots in a movement for church renewal and reform of the Roman Catholic Church before Vatican II. In some places the impetus of the movement was to provide an alternative to communism in the decades leading up to and after World War II. The emphasis on the development of community leadership created tension within many communities when the younger leadership began to replace the community elders who had been the traditional focus of power and authority, frequently with legitimation through the cargo system. As mentioned in chapter 4, there seems to have been a division in many places between those who continued to focus on internal church and spiritual matters or community development activities in the local context. Other analyses attend to currents within the church as a whole, some related to the presence of foreign priests and religious workers after the mid-1950s. "Traditionalist" and "developmentalist" tendencies are identified, with the developmentalist group basing their thought on Catholic social teaching. Following the Latin American Bishops' Conference (CELAM) in Medellín in 1968, more attention was given to structural injustice or structural sin, and the possibility of an option for revolution became more viable. The lines are not hard and fast, and the developmentalist wing of Catholic Action provided adepts for a more radicalized vision that, in some cases in Guatemala and elsewhere in Latin America, supported guerrilla activity. For further information on this complex of issues see Cleary (1985), Chea Urruela (1988), Le Bot (1995), and Calder (1997). Carmack (1992a) provides a more detailed account of the impact of Catholic Action at the community level.

12. Linguistic training for both Maya and North Americans has been the focus of OKMA (Asociación Oxlajuuj Keej Maya' Ajtz'iib'), a training course and center largely associated with the work of Nora England, and of Tulane University's summer program in the Kaqchikel language associated with Judith Maxwell.

13. The discourse around such issues changes as the movement becomes more widespread and responds differentially to influences from other religions and secular discourse, including that originating with intellectual voices in the Maya Movement itself. Chiappari (1999, 136) provides the example of a Maya priest in Totonicapán who participates in an "association of Maya priests." The man is opposed by some of the other priests in the area, in part because he is against the use of alcohol in ceremonies and sorcery.

14. This statement is accurate in describing a "crisis-solace" model of evangelical growth. It also illustrates how evangelical expression in Guatemala is often painted with the broad brush of fundamentalism and sectarianism because of its frequently apolitical nature.

15. The full extent of Maya support for the revolution is debated (R. Adams 1992, 286–87). A helpful distinction is sometimes made between "political" supporters of the guerrillas and actual combatants. It is clear that the guerrilla movement was not able to protect local communities from the fury of the army when the response came. Stoll (1993) uses the rubric "between two armies" to describe the situation in which the villagers found themselves in the middle of one of the primary zones of conflict. For the impact of the violence of the early 1980s on Maya communities, see Carmack (1992). See also the analysis in Le Bot (1995).

16. The reach of the Roman Catholic Church's communications network also played a role in situating the church in a mediating position between the on-the-ground situation of the communities and outside entities assisting with local problems. Progressive Catholics were involved in the formation of the Committee for Campesino

Unity (CUC) and were often targeted for repression, most memorably in the burning of the Spanish Embassy they had occupied in 1980. In the same year, the Catholic diocese in the department of Quiché was effectively closed by then-bishop Juan Gerardi. This led to the creation of the Guatemalan Church in Exile, located in Mexico, which issued pronouncements on Guatemalan events throughout the rest of the decade (Berryman 1994, 110–11). M. Taylor (1998) discusses the problems that liberation theology poses for those concerned with indigenous culture and spirituality. By the time I began regular field work in Guatemala in the mid-1990s, the term *liberation theology* was rarely, if ever, used in public by Guatemalans. A Maya evangelical told me on several occasions, "They accused us of liberation theology, but we didn't even know what that was."

17. When the administration of Oscar Berger took office in January 2004, Ríos Montt was placed under house arrest (Helweg-Larsen 2004).

18. These were people (usually from the United States or Canada in the Kaqchikel case) who simply lived for varying periods of time with Guatemalans whose lives had been threatened.

19. As in other parts of Central America in the wake of the Central American revolutions of the late 1970s and 1980s, the international community's involvement in Guatemala is extensive and often controversial. In the case of the Kaqchikel Presbytery, the human rights coordinator whose story I related earlier was receiving some sort of a salary, as well as help for educating some of his nine children. Although I do not know the outcome, he indicated he might lose his salary by the end of 1998 because of a lack of international support. A whole discourse of solidarity and, in a more theological vein, accompaniment has surrounded these activities. Numerous North Americans since the mid-1980s have participated in various kinds of "cultural immersion" experiences in Guatemala as a result of religious and social-justice-oriented perspectives on international relations. For an examination of how this has played out that involves members of the Kaqchikel Presbytery, see Anderson (2003). The interplay between religion and identity in these kinds of activities cannot be overstated, but it requires a more systematic analysis on any number of levels. In other contexts, such as the Mam Presbytery, the focus might be more on establishing relationships and helping with various kinds of development projects—health care, access to potable water, and agriculture.

20. The figure cited here is probably below 50 percent because of blank or otherwise invalid votes. In addition to the source cited, Jonas (2000, chapter 8) provides a thorough examination of the factors that conspired against the reforms and the viciousness of the "no" campaign. Warren justifiably highlights the fact that the absenteeism rate "was not unusual for a national referendum in a nonpresidential election" (2002, 177 n. 2). At the same time, this was in many ways not a typical referendum, and the process, as well as the vote, draws attention to the difficulties of consolidating democracy in post-conflict Guatemala.

21. A denominational source named this congregation Sembradores del Reino (Sowers of the Kingdom).

22. Anderson claims that they were the first women ordained in the IENPG. I have some information that a Ladina woman, Veronica Girón, was ordained earlier by the Occidente Presbytery. My understanding is that she is not serving in a pastoral role, as are the Kaqchikel women (Karla Koll, personal communication).

23. Romero is the most famous martyr in the revolutions of Central America. After assuming the archbishopric in San Salvador, he was outspoken in the defense of human rights from a pastoral perspective. He was assassinated on 24 March 1980 while say-

ing mass in a hospital. Gerardi's murder became a test case for the scope of impunity in Guatemala's culture of violence. Four convictions resulted from the case in June 2001, but by October 2002 word came out that the convictions had been thrown out on appeal and that there would have to be a new trial. In a paradox that sometimes seems to characterize Guatemala, this came on the heels of a single conviction in the case of the murder of anthropologist Myrna Mack. Mack had been killed in 1990, and her sister struggled for more than ten years to have the "intellectual authors" of the crime convicted. In 2004 the administration of President Oscar Berger admitted government culpability in Mack's murder. Guatemala's Supreme Court did uphold the Gerardi convictions in February 2003.

24. The dialectic between presence and absence has been explored from various standpoints. See Richardson (1994) for an ethnographic approach to speech and text wherein silence creates the space for intersubjectivity. Hale (1997, 824) sees the attention given to collective memory in Guatemala as having two specific purposes: recovering "history lost" and "creat[ing] hopeful images that might help people to transcend what history has wrought." Antonella Fabri (1995, 154) considers the role of memory in testimonials as a counter to the "monumentality of the official construction of history." REMHI advocates various forms of monuments as ceremonial tributes or "symbolic reparation measures" to victims (ODHAG 1999, 316). In addition, the CEH advocates a "national day for the dignity of the victims of the violence" (CEH 1999, 51). Some groups have begun to celebrate this day on 25 February, but to my knowledge, no legislative decree has been passed to that effect. The date was chosen because it is the date on which the CEH report was released in 1999. See the appendix for a statement issued by CONAVIGUA in 2004 as a form of political pressure.

25. The work of former priest Phillip Berryman (1984, 1994) demonstrates the intersection of religion and revolution in Central America during the 1970s, 1980s, and early 1990s. Jeffrey's work (1998) is a concise and useful introduction to the role of both Roman Catholic and Protestant religious groups in the Guatemalan peace process. The work also includes a critique of involvement in the revolutionary movement in Guatemala that implicates foreign religious institutions and activists. Calder (2001) highlights religious involvement in the peace process in its ecumenical aspects and in the strengthening of Guatemala's civil society.

26. For another approach to remembering as a way to address concerns with injustice and otherness, see the first chapter in M. Taylor (1990). Elsewhere, Taylor (1998) reflects on the notion of *desencarnación* (defleshment) in the context of interviews with Antonio Otzoy. Otzoy attributes the term to his grandmother as she reflected on the implications of the violence for the Maya. The article examines the cultural response of the Maya to *desencarnación*.

27. I should note that I have no information about the reasons for the decision. It would have been a symbolic statement, given that the most visible Presbyterian church building is directly behind the national palace, a place that probably marks the relationship of Protestantism to the power structure in the early years. It is doubtful that such a prime piece of real estate would have been available without some governmental intervention.

28. See Yashar (1997) for a discussion of the interplay between military agendas and popular movements during this period.

29. It should be noted that Saquic's death took place in the midst of bitter divisions within IENPG. Much of the tension within the IENPG can at least initially be seen

as a microcosm of Guatemala in terms of ethnic conflict and the "culture of violence" that grew out of the war years. As late as 1999, three consecutive moderators of the IENPG's annual synod meeting had received threats of bodily harm (A. Smith 1999).

30. The book itself is an example of the transnational religious connections emanating from missionary activity in recent decades. Proceeds from its sale are dedicated "to the Division of World Outreach, The United Church of Canada, for continuing human rights work in Guatemala" (Manly 1997, xv).

31. See Steinberg and Taylor (2003) for a more expansive discussion on the spread of memorials over Guatemala's post-conflict landscape.

32. A plaque at the base of the back of the monument, bearing the date of 20 October 1998, is dedicated "In Honor of the Compañero Rolando Moran Ricardo Arnoldo Ramírez de León for His Irreplaceable Contribution to Peace, Unity, and National Reconciliation." I did not note this during my first visit to the monument, and I suspect it was placed there in honor of the former guerrilla commander following his death in September 1998. The plaque's presence illustrates a connection between some of the guerrilla ideals and the hopes attached to the peace process embodied in the monument.

Conclusions

1. The text of the law, decree number 52-2005 of the Guatemalan congress, can be found at http://www.derechos.org/nizkor/guatemala/doc/leymarco.html; accessed 9 March 2006.

2. The article referenced here and Casanova (2001) provide helpful background for the discussion of secularization theory and its relationship to religion as it is manifested in the midst of globalization.

3. See Heelas and Haglund-Heelas (1988) for a critique of "deprivation" as a reason for conversion.

4. This is not to deny the role of forceful or charismatic leadership, either local or foreign in the case of missionaries.

5. An important comparative case is that of Mam Presbyterians in Chiapas. Hernández Castillo documents how Presbyterianism became a "component of ethnicity" (2001, 45). In the early decades after the Mexican Revolution, the Protestant churches were not persecuted in the way the Roman Catholic Church was as the government tried to enforce secularization and assert state authority. Missionaries supported the use of the Mam language, and in general Presbyterianism seems to have provided a space from which the Mam could selectively embrace Protestantism and resist some of the encroachments of the state. Hernández Castillo acknowledges that, simultaneously, there was "a reproduction of dominant values related to the respect for the state and the reproduction of the political system" (47).

Bibliography

Adams, Abigail Elizabeth. 1999. Word, work and worship: Engendering evangelical culture between highland Guatemala and the United States. Ph.D. diss., Univ. of Virginia.

———. 2001. Making one our word: Protestant Q'eqchi' Mayas in highland Guatemala. In *Holy saints and fiery preachers: The anthropology of Protestantism in Mexico and Central America,* ed. James W. Dow and Alan R. Sandstrom, 205–33. Westport, Conn.: Praeger.

Adams, Richard N. 1970. *Crucifixion by power: Essays on Guatemalan national social structure, 1944–1966.* Austin: Univ. of Texas Press.

———. 1992. Conclusions: What can we know about the harvest of violence? In *Harvest of violence: The Maya Indians and the Guatemalan crisis,* ed. Robert M. Carmack, 274–91. 1988. Norman: Univ. of Oklahoma Press.

———. 1994. A report on the political status of the Guatemalan Maya. In *Indigenous peoples and democracy in Latin America,* ed. Donna Lee Van Cott, 155–86. New York: St. Martin's Press.

———. 1995. *Etnias en evolución social: Estudios de Guatemala y Centroamérica.* Mexico City: Universidad Autónoma Metropolitana.

———. 1998. Problems political, professional, and technical in Guatemalan ethnic demography. Paper presented in the 97th Annual Meeting of the American Anthropological Association. Philadelphia.

Adams, Richard, and Santiago Bastos. 2003. *Las relaciones étnicas en Guatemala, 1944–2000.* Antigua, Guatemala: CIRMA.

Alecio, Rolando. 1995. Uncovering the truth: political violence and indigenous organizations. In *The new politics of survival: Grassroots movements in Central America,* ed. Minor Sinclair, 25–45. New York: EPICA/Monthly Review Press.

Alonso, Pedro Luis. 1998. *En el nombre de la crisis: Tranformaciones religiosas de la sociedad Guatemalateca contemporánea.* Guatemala City: Editorial Atemis-Edinter.

Alvarez, Carmelo. 1990. *People of hope: The Protestant movement in Central America.* New York: Friendship Press.

Alvarez, Sonia E., Evelina Dagnino, and Arturo Escobar, eds. 1998. *Cultures of politics/politics of cultures: Re-visioning Latin American social movements.* Boulder: Westview Press.

Amnesty International. 1996. Guatemala: Summary of Amnesty International's concerns (January 1995–January 1996). Amnesty International Report AMR 34/03/96. www.amnest.it/alib/aipub/1996/AMR/23400396.htm (accessed 23 July 2003).

————. 2005. No protection, no justice: killings of women in Guatemala. Amnesty International Report AMR 34/017/2005. http://web.amnesty.org/library/index/ENGAMR340172005 (accessed 7 May 2006).

Anderson, Benedict. 1991. *Imagined communities.* Rev. ed. London: Verso.

Anderson, Kathryn. 2003. *Weaving relationships: Canada-Guatemala solidarity.* Waterloo, Ont.: Wilfrid Laurier Univ. Press.

Annis, Sheldon. 1987. *God and production in a Guatemalan town.* Austin: Univ. of Texas Press.

Arias, Arturo. 1990. Changing Indian identity: Guatemala's violent transition to modernity. In *Guatemalan Indians and the state, 1540 to 1988,* ed. Carol A. Smith, with Marilyn M. Moors, 230–57. Austin: Univ. of Texas Press.

Asad, Talal. 1983. Anthropological conceptions of religion: Reflections on Geertz. *Man* 18:237–59.

————. 1993. *Genealogies of religion: Discipline and reasons of power in Christianity and Islam.* Baltimore: Johns Hopkins Univ. Press.

B'aayil (Eduardo Pérez), and Ajb'ee (Odilio Jiménez). 1997. *Ttxoolil Qyool Mam/Gramática Mam.* Guatemala City: Cholsamaj.

Baez Camargo, G., and Kenneth G. Grubb. 1935. *Religion in the Republic of Mexico.* London: World Dominion Press.

Barbero, Jesús Martín. 2001. Secularización, desencanto, y reencantamiento massmediatico. In *Al sur de la modernidad: Comunicación, globalización, y multiculturalidad,* 173–82. Pittsburgh: Instituto de Literatura Iberoamericana.

Bastian, Jean Pierre. 1983. *Protestantismo y sociedad en México.* Mexico City: Casa Unidad de Publicaciones, S.A.

————. 1986. *Breve historia del protestantes y revolución en México, 1872–1911.* Mexico City: Casa Unidad de Publicaciones, S.A.

————. 1990. *Protestantes, liberales, y francmasones: Sociedades de ideas y modernidad en América Latina.* Mexico City: Fondo de Cultura Económica.

————. 1992. Protestantism in Latin America. In *The church in Latin America, 1492–1992,* ed. Enrique Dussel, 331–50. Tunbridge Wells, Kent, and Maryknoll, N.Y.: Burns & Oates and Orbis.

————. 1993. The metamorphosis of Latin American Protestant groups: A sociohistorical perspective. Trans. Margaret Caffey-Moquin. *Latin American Research Review* 28 (2): 33–61.

————. 1998. The new religious map of Latin America: Causes and social effects. *Cross Currents* 48 (3): 330–46.

Bastos, Santiago, and Manuela Camus. 1995. *Abriendo caminos: Las organizaciones Mayas desde el Nobel hasta el acuerdo de derechos indígenas.* Guatemala City: Facultad Latinoamericana de Ciencias Sociales.

————. 1996. *Quebrando el silencio: Organizationes del pueblo Maya y sus demandas (1986–1992).* 3rd ed. Guatemala City: Facultad Latinoamericana de Ciencias Sociales.

Benavides, Gustavo. 1998. Modernity. In *Critical terms for religious studies,* ed. Mark C. Taylor, 186–204. Chicago: Univ. of Chicago Press.

Berger, Peter L. 1967. *The sacred canopy: Elements of a sociological theory of religion.* New York: Anchor Books.

————. 1998. Protestantism and the quest for certainty. *Christian Century* 26 August–2 September:782–85, 792–96.

————. 1999. The desecularization of the world: A global overview. In *The desecular-*

ization of the world: Resurgent religion and world politics, ed. Peter L. Berger, 1–18. Washington, D.C., and Grand Rapids, Mich.: Ethics and Public Policy Center and Eerdmans.

Berger, Peter L., and Thomas Luckmann. 1966. *The social construction of reality.* Garden City, N.J.: Doubleday.

Berryman, Phillip. 1984. *The religious roots of rebellion: Christians in Central American revolutions.* Maryknoll, N.Y.: Orbis.

———. 1994. *Stubborn hope: Religion, politics, and revolution in Central America.* Maryknoll, N.Y.: Orbis; New York: The New Press.

Bogenschild, Thomas E. 1992. The roots of fundamentalism in liberal Guatemala: Missionary ideologies and local response, 1882–1944. Ph.D. diss., Univ. of California, Berkeley.

Bourdieu, Pierre. 1977. *Outline of a theory of practice.* Trans. Richard Nice. Cambridge: Cambridge Univ. Press.

———. 1990. *The logic of practice.* Trans. Richard Nice. Stanford, Calif.: Stanford Univ. Press.

Brett, Roddy. 2006. *Movimiento social, etnicidad, y democratización en Guatemala, 1985–1996.* Guatemala City: F&G Editores.

Brintnall, Douglas E. 1979. *Revolt against the dead: The modernization of a Mayan community in the highlands of Guatemala.* New York: Gordon and Breach.

Brown, R. McKenna. 1996. The Mayan language loyalty movement in Guatemala. In *Maya cultural activism in Guatemala,* ed. Edward F. Fischer and R. McKenna Brown, 165–77. Austin: Univ. of Texas Press.

Brusco, Elizabeth. 1996. Religious conversion. In *Encyclopedia of cultural anthropology,* vol. 3, ed. David Levinson and Melvin Ember, 1100–1104. New York: Henry Holt.

Bunzel, Ruth. 1959. *Chichicastenango: A Guatemalan village.* Ed. Marian W. Smith. Publications of the American Ethnological Society, 23. Seattle: Univ. of Washington Press.

Burdick, John. 1998. *Blessed Anastacia: Women, race, and Christianity in Brazil.* New York: Routledge.

Burgess, Dora M. de, and Patricio Xec, trans. 1955. *Popol Vuh* (version of Francisco Ximénez). Quezaltenango, Guatemala: n.p.

Burgess, Paul. 1957. *Historia de la obra evangélica presbiteriana en Guatemala: Bodas de diamante.* Quetzaltenango, Guatemala: Tipografía El Noticiero.

———. 1972. *Justo Rufino Barrios.* Trans. Ricardo Letona-Estrada. San José, Costa Rica: Editorial Universitaria de Guatemala.

Burkhart, Louise M. 1989. *The slippery earth: Nahua-Christian dialogue in sixteenth-century Mexico.* Tucson: Univ. of Arizona Press.

Cabrera, Mario Rolando, and Arlena D. Cifuentes. 1997. *El proceso de negociaciones de paz.* Guatemala City: Ediciones Nueva Era.

Cahn, Peter. 2003. *All religions are good in Tzintzuntzan: Evangelicals in Catholic Mexico.* Austin: Univ. of Texas Press.

Calder, Bruce. 1970. *Crecimiento y cambio de la Iglesia Católica Guatemalteca, 1944–1966.* Guatemala City: José de Pineda Ibarra.

———. 1997. Influencia extranjera en la Iglesia Católica. In *Historia general de Guatemala, tomo VI (Epoca contemporánea: De 1945 a la actualida),* 279–87. Gen. ed. Jorge Luján Muñoz. Guatemala City: Asociación de Amigos del País and Fundación para la Cultura y el Desarrollo.

———. 2001. The role of the Catholic Church and other religious institutions in the Guatemalan peace process, 1980–1996. *Journal of Church and State* 43 (1): 773–97.

———. 2004. Interwoven histories: The Catholic Church and the Maya, 1940 to the present. In *Resurgent voices in Latin America: Indigenous peoples, political mobilization, and religious change,* ed. Edward L. Cleary and Timothy Steigenga, 93–124. New Brunswick, N.J.: Rutgers Univ. Press.

Cambranes, Julio Castellanos. 1985. *Coffee and peasants in Guatemala: The origins of the modern plantation economy in Guatemala, 1853–1897.* Monograph no. 10, Institute of Latin American Studies. Stockholm: Universitet Stockholms.

Camp, Roderic Ai. 1997. *Crossing swords: Politics and religion in Mexico.* New York: Oxford Univ. Press.

Cantón Delgado, Manuela. 1998. *Bautizados en fuego: Protestantes, discursos de conversión y política en Guatemala (1989–1993).* La Antigua, Guatemala, and South Woodstock, Vt.: CIRMA y Plumsock Mesoamerican Studies.

Carey, David, Jr. 2001. *Our elders teach us: Maya-Kaqchikel historical perspectives: Xkib'ij kan qate' qatata'.* Tuscaloosa: Univ. of Alabama Press.

———. 2004. Maya perspectives on the 1999 Referendum in Guatemala: Ethnic equality rejected? *Latin American Perspectives* 31 (6): 69–95.

Carlsen, Robert S. 1997. *The war for the heart and soul of a highland Maya town.* Austin: Univ. of Texas Press.

Carlsen, Robert S., and Martín Prechtel. 1991. The flowering of the dead: Mayan notions of sacred change. *Man: Journal of the Royal Anthropological Institute* 26 (1): 23–42.

Carmack, Robert M. 1971. Ethnography and ethnohistory: Their application in Middle American studies. *Ethnohistory* 18 (2): 127–45.

———. 1979. Analysis antropológico de los effectos de terremoto en occidented de Guatemala. In *Historia social de los Quichés,* 399–426. Seminario de Integración Social Guatemalteca, no. 21. Guatemala City: Editorial José de Pineda Ibarra, Ministerio de Educación.

———. 1981. *The Quiché Maya of Utatlán: The evolution of a highland Guatemala kingdom.* Norman: Univ. of Oklahoma Press.

———. 1990. State and community in nineteenth-century Guatemala: The Momostenango case. In *Guatemalan Indians and the state: 1540–1988,* ed. Carol A. Smith with Marilyn M. Moors, 116–36. Austin: Univ. of Texas Press.

———, ed. 1992a. *Harvest of violence: The Maya Indians and the Guatemalan crisis.* 1988. Norman: Univ. of Oklahoma Press.

———. 1992b. The story of Santa Cruz, Quiché. In *Harvest of violence: The Maya Indians and the Guatemalan crisis,* ed. Robert M. Carmack, 39–69. 1988. Norman: Univ. of Oklahoma Press.

———. 1994. Politics of human rights in Guatemala. Paper presented at the 93rd Annual Meeting of the American Anthropological Association. Atlanta, Georgia.

———. 1995. *Rebels of highland Guatemala: The Quiché-Mayas of Momstenango.* Norman: Univ. of Oklahoma Press.

Carmack, Robert M., Janine Gasco, and Gary H. Gossen, eds. 1996. *The legacy of Mesoamerica: History and culture of a Native American civilization.* Upper Saddle River, N.J.: Prentice Hall.

Casanova, José. 1994. *Public religions in the modern world.* Chicago: Univ. of Chicago Press.

———. 2001. Religion, the new millenium, and globalization. *Sociology of Religion* 62 (4): 415–41.

CEH [Comisión para el Esclarecimiento Histórico]. 1999. *Guatemala, memoria del silencio / Tz'inil na'tab'al: Conclusiones y recomendaciones del informe de la Comisión para el Esclarecimiento Histórico.* Guatemala City.

———. 2000. *Guatemala: Causas y orígenes de enfrentamiento armado interno.* Guatemala City: F&G Editores.

Chase-Dunn, Christopher, Susanne Jonas, and Nelson Amaro, eds. 2001. *Globalization on the ground: Postbellum Guatemalan democracy and development.* Lanham, Md.: Rowan and Littlefield.

Chea Urruela, José Luis. 1988. *Guatemala: La cruz fragmentada.* San José, Costa Rica: Departamento Ecuménico de Investigaciones.

Chesnut, R. Andrew. 2003. *Competitive spirits: Latin America's new religious economy.* New York: Oxford Univ. Press.

Chiappari, Christopher Louis. 1999. Rethinking religious practice in highland Guatemala: An ethnography of Protestantism, Maya religion, and magic. Ph.D. diss., Univ. of Minnesota.

———. 2002. Toward a Maya theology of liberation: The reformulation of a "traditional" religion in the global context. *Journal for the Scientific Study of Religion* 41 (1): 47–67.

CIEDEG [Conferencia de Iglesias Evangélicas de Guatemala]. N.d. Condiciones nacionales a crear para el impulso del modelo democrático y alternativo de desarrollo. Programa de Formación para el desarollo, Cuaderno no. 6.

Cleary, Edward L. 1985. *Crisis and change: The church in Latin America today.* Maryknoll, N.Y.: Orbis.

———. 1992. Evangelicals and competition in Guatemala. In *Conflict and competition: The Latin American church in a changing environment,* ed. Edward L. Cleary and Hannah W. Stewart-Gambino, 167–95. Boulder: Lynne Rienner Publishers.

———. 1997. Birth of Latin American indigenous theology. In *Crosscurrents in indigenous spirituality: Interface of Maya, Catholic, and Protestant worldviews,* ed. Guillermo Cook, 171–88. Studies in Christian Mission, vol. 18. Leiden: Brill.

———. 2001. From theology of liberation to inculturation: Emergence of indigenous religious centers in Peru and Bolivia. Paper presented at the meeting of the Latin American Studies Association. Washington, D.C., 6–8 September.

———. 2004. New voices in religion and politics in Bolivia and Peru. In *Resurgent voices in Latin America: Indigenous peoples, political mobilization, and religious change,* ed. Edward L. Cleary and Timothy Steigenga, 43–64. New Brunswick, N.J.: Rutgers Univ. Press.

Cleary, Edward L., and Timothy Steigenga. 2004. Resurgent voices: Indians, politics, and religion in Latin America. In *Resurgent voices in Latin America: Indigenous peoples, political mobilization, and religious change,* ed. Edward L. Cleary and Timothy Steigenga, 1–24. New Brunswick, N.J.: Rutgers Univ. Press.

Cleary, Edward L., and Hannah W. Stewart-Gambino, eds. 1997. *Power, politics, and Pentecostals in Latin America.* Boulder: Westview Press.

Clendinnen, Inga. 1987. *Ambivalent conquests: Maya and Spaniard in Yucatan, 1517–1570.* Cambridge: Cambridge Univ. Press.

Cohen, Anthony P. 1985. *The symbolic construction of community.* London: Routledge.

——. 1993. Culture as identity: An anthropologist's view. *New Literary History* 24 (1): 195–209.

——. 1994. *Self consciousness: An alternative anthropology of identity.* London: Routledge.

Cojtí Cuxil, Demetrio. 1991. Los censos nationales de población: Medios de opresión del pueblo indio? *A Saber* (Political De La Lengua) 1:36–50.

——. 1994. *Políticas para la reivindicación de los mayas de hoy.* Guatemala City: Editorial Cholsamaj and Seminario Permanente de Estudios Mayas.

——. 1996. The politics of Maya reivindication. In *Maya cultural activism in Guatemala,* ed. Edward F. Fischer and R. McKenna Brown, 19–50. Austin: Univ. of Texas Press.

——. 1997. *Ri Maya' Moloj pa Iximulew, El movimiento Maya (en Guatemala).* Guatemala City: Editorial Cholsamaj.

Colby, Benjamin N., and Pierre L. van den Berghe. 1969. *Ixil country: A plural society in highland Guatemala.* Berkeley: Univ. of California Press.

Colop, Moisés. 1997. Is Christ being resurrected among the indigenous people? In *Crosscurrents in indigenous spirituality: Interface of Maya, Catholic, and Protestant worldviews,* ed. Guillermo Cook, 199–203. Studies in Christian Mission, vol. 18. Leiden: Brill.

Cook, Guillermo, ed. 1997. *Crosscurrents in indigenous spirituality: Interface of Maya, Catholic, and Protestant worldviews.* Studies in Christian Mission, vol. 18. Leiden: Brill.

Corten, André, and Ruth Marshall-Fratani. 2001. *Between Babel and Pentecost: Transnational Pentecostalism in Africa and Latin America.* Bloomington: Indiana Univ. Press.

Dalquist, Anna Marie. 1995. *Burgess of Guatemala.* 2nd ed. Kingsburg, Calif.: Kings River Publications.

Dary, Claudia. 1997. *El derecho internacional humanitario y el orden jurídico Maya: Una perspective histórico-cultural.* Guatemala City: Facultad Latinoamericana de Ciencias Sociales.

Davis, Shelton. 1992. Introduction: Sowing the seeds of violence. In *Harvest of violence: The Maya Indians and the Guatemalan crisis,* ed. Robert M. Carmack, 3–36. 1988. Norman: Univ. of Oklahoma Press.

Deiros, Pablo A. 1991. Protestant fundamentalism in Latin America. In *Fundamentalisms observed,* ed. Martin E. Marty and R. Scott Appleby, 142–96. The Fundamentalism Project, vol. 1. Chicago: Univ. of Chicago Press.

De las reformas constitucionales a la consulta popular. *Revista Política y Sociedad* no. 37. www.usac.edu.gt/cpol/REFORMASCONSTITUCIONAL37.htm (accessed 18 February 2004).

Delli Sante, Angela. 1996. *Nightmare or reality: Guatemala in the 1980s.* Amsterdam: Thela Publishers.

Diamond, Larry. 1999. *Developing democracy: Toward consolidation.* Baltimore: Johns Hopkins Univ. Press.

Díaz Polanco, Héctor. 1997. *Indigenous peoples in Latin America: The quest for self-determination.* Trans. Lucía Rayas. Latin American Perspectives Series, no. 18. Boulder: Westview Press.

Dirks, Nicholas B., Geoff Eley, and Sherry B. Ortner. 1994. Introduction. In *Culture/power/history: A reader in contemporary social theory,* ed. Nicholas B. Dirks, Geoff Eley, and Sherry B. Ortner, 3–45. Princeton, N.J.: Princeton Univ. Press.

Dow, James W., and Alan R. Sandstrom, eds. 2001. *Holy saints and fiery preachers: The anthropology of Protestantism in Mexico and Central America.* Westport, Conn.: Praeger.

Drogus, Carol Ann. 2000. Religious pluralism and social change: Coming to terms with complexity and convergence. Review essay. *Latin American Research Review* 35 (1): 261–70.

Earle, Duncan M. 1992. Authority, social conflict, and the rise of Protestantism: Religious conversion in a Mayan village. *Social Compass* 39 (3): 377–88.

———. 2000. The metaphor of the day in Quiché, Guatemala: Notes on the nature of everyday life. In *On earth as it is in heaven: Religion in modern Latin America,* ed. Virginia Garrard-Burnett, 71–106. Wilmington, Del.: Scholarly Resources.

Ebel, Roland H. 1972. Political modernization in three Guatemalan Indian communities. In *Community culture and national change,* ed. M. A. L. Harrison and Robert Wauchope, 131–206. New Orleans: Middle American Research Institute, Tulane Univ.

———. 1992. When Indians take power: Conflict and consensus in San Juan Ostuncalco. In *Harvest of violence: The Maya Indians and the Guatemalan crisis,* ed. Robert M. Carmack, 174–91. 1988. Norman: Univ. of Oklahoma Press.

Eck, Diana L. 2001. *A new religious America: How a "Christian country" has now become the world's most religiously diverse nation.* New York: HarperSanFrancisco.

Eckstein, Susan. 2001a. Epilogue. Where have all the movements gone? Latin American social movements at the new millennium. In *Power and popular protest: Latin American social movements,* ed. Susan Eckstein, 351–406. Berkeley: Univ. of California Press.

———. 2001b. Power and popular protest in Latin America. In *Power and popular protest: Latin American social movements,* ed. Susan Eckstein, 1–60. Berkeley: Univ. of California Press.

Elizondo, Virgilio P. 1983. *Galilean journey: The Mexican-American promise.* Maryknoll, N.Y.: Orbis.

———. 1992. *The future is mestizo: Life where cultures meet.* New York: Crossroad.

England, Nora C. 1983. *A grammar of Mam, a Mayan language.* Austin: Univ. of Texas Press.

———. 1995. Linguistics and indigenous American languages: Mayan examples. *Journal of Latin American Anthropology* 1 (1): 122–49.

———. 1996. The role of language standardization in revitalization. In *Maya cultural activism in Guatemala,* ed. Edward F. Fischer and R. McKenna Brown, 178–94. Austin: Univ. of Texas Press.

———. 2003. Mayan language revival and revitalization politics: Linguists and linguistic ideologies. *American Anthropologist* 105:733–43.

Escobar, Arturo, and Sonia E. Alvarez, eds. 1992. *The making of social movements in Latin America: Identity, strategy, and democracy.* Boulder: Westview Press.

Evans, Timothy Edward. 1990. Religious conversion in Quetzaltenango, Guatemala. Ph.D. diss., Univ. of Pittsburgh.

Fabri, Antonella. 1995. Memories of violence, monuments of history. In *The labyrinth of memory: Ethnographic journeys,* ed. Marea C. Teski and Jacob J. Climo, 141–58. Westport, Conn.: Bergin & Garvey.

Fairclough, Norman. 1992. *Discourse and social change.* Cambridge, U.K.: Polity Press.

Falla, Ricardo. 1992. Struggle for survival in the mountains: Hunger and other privations inflicted on internal refugees from the central highlands. In *Harvest of violence: The Maya Indians and the Guatemalan crisis,* ed. Robert M. Carmack, 235–55. 1988. Norman: Univ. of Oklahoma Press.

———. 1993. *Historia de un gran amor* (no publication data).

———. 1994. *Massacres in the jungle: Ixcan, Guatemala, 1975–1982.* Boulder: Westview Press.

——. 1995. *Quiché rebelde: Estudio de un movimiento de conversión religiosa, rebelde a las creencias tradicionales, en San Antonio Ilotenango, Quiché (1948–1970).* Colleción "Realidad Nuestra," vol. 7. Reprint. Guatemala City: Editorial Universitaria.

——. 2001. *Quiché rebelde: Religious conversion, politics, and ethnic identity in Guatemala.* Trans. Phillip Berryman. Austin: Univ. of Texas Press.

FEPAZ [Foro Ecuménico por la Paz y la Reconciliación]. 2005. *Guatemala: El dilema ético de la violencia.* Guatemala City: Litografía Nawal Wuj.

Fernández García, María Cristina. 2004. Lynching in Guatemala: Legacy of war and impunity. Manuscript. Harvard: Weatherhead Center for International Affairs. http://www.wcfia.harvard.edu/fellows/papers/2003-04 fernandez.pdf (accessed 28 April 2006).

Fischer, Edward F. 1996. Induced culture change as a strategy for socioeconomic development: The pan-Maya movement in Guatemala. In *Maya cultural activism in Guatemala,* ed. Edward R. Fischer and R. McKenna Brown, 51–73. Austin: Univ. of Texas Press.

——. 1999. Cultural logic and Maya identity: Rethinking constructivism and essentialism. *Current Anthropology* 40 (4): 473–88.

——. 2001. *Cultural logics and global economics.* Austin: Univ. of Texas Press.

Fischer, Edward F., and R. McKenna Brown. 1996. Introduction: Maya cultural activism in Guatemala. In *Maya cultural activism in Guatemala,* ed. Edward R. Fischer and R. McKenna Brown, 1–18. Austin: Univ. of Texas Press.

Forand, Nancy Anne. 2001. Maya in the age of apocalypse: Folk evangelicals and Catholics in Quintana Roo. Ph.D. diss., Univ. at Albany, State Univ. of New York.

——. 2002. The language ideologies of courtship ritual: Maya Pentecostals and folk Catholics. *Journal of American Folklore* 115:332–77.

Freston, Paul. 1998. Pentecostalism in Latin America: Characteristics and controversies. *Social Compass* 45 (3): 335–58.

——. 2001. *Evangelicals and politics in Asia, Africa, and Latin America.* Cambridge: Cambridge Univ. Press.

——, ed. 2006. *Evangelical Christianity and democracy in Latin America.* New York: Oxford Univ. Press.

Friedlander, Judith. 1975. *Being Indian in Hueyapan: A study of forced identity in contemporary Mexico.* New York: St. Martin's Press.

Gálvez Borrell, Víctor, and Esquit Choy, Alberto. 1997. *The Mayan movement today: Issues of indigenous culture and development in Guatemala.* Trans. Matthew Creelman. Guatemala City: Facultad Latinoamericana de Ciencias Sociales.

García, Eduardo. 2004. Anthropologists digging up the truth. *Latinamerica Press* 36 (7): 11–12.

García Ruiz, Jesús. 1997. *Hacia una nación pluricultural en Guatemala.* Guatemala City: Centro de Documentación e Investigación Maya.

Garma Navarro, Carlos. 1989. Los estudios antropológicos sobre el protestantismo en México. *Cristianismo y sociedad* 27 (3): 89–101.

Garrard, Virginia Carroll. 1986. A history of Protestantism in Guatemala. Ph.D. diss., Tulane Univ.

Garrard-Burnett, Virginia. 1990. Positivismo, liberalismo, e impulso misionero: Misiones protestantes en Guatemala, 1880–1920. *Mesoamérica* 19 (June): 13–31.

——. 1992. Protestantism in Latin America. Review essay. *Latin America Research Review* 27 (1): 219–31.

———. 1996. Resacralization of the profane: Government, religion, and ethnicity in modern Guatemala. In *Questioning the secular state,* ed. David Westerlund, 96–116. London: Hurst.

———. 1998a. *Protestantism in Guatemala: Living in the New Jerusalem.* Austin: Univ. of Texas Press.

———. 1998b. Transnational Protestantism. Review essay. *Journal of Interamerican Studies and World Affairs* 40 (3): 117–25.

———. 2004. "God was already here when Columbus arrived": Inculturation theology and the Mayan movement in Guatemala. In *Resurgent voices in Latin America: Indigenous peoples, political mobilization, and religious change,* ed. Edward L. Cleary and Timothy Steigenga, 125–53. New Brunswick, N.J.: Rutgers Univ. Press.

Garrard-Burnett, Virginia, and David Stoll, eds. 1993. *Rethinking Protestantism in Latin America.* Philadelphia: Temple Univ. Press.

Gauchet, Marcel. 1997. *The disenchantment of the world: A political history of religion.* Trans. Oscar Burge. Princeton, N.J.: Princeton Univ. Press.

Geertz, Clifford. 1973a. The integrative revolution: primordial sentiments and civil politics in the new states. In *The interpretation of cultures,* 255–310. New York: Basic Books.

———. 1973b. Religion as a cultural system. In *The interpretation of cultures.* 87–125. New York: Basic Books.

———. 1973c. Thick description: Toward an interpretation of culture. In *The interpretation of cultures.* 3–30. New York: Basic Books.

Gellner, Ernest. 1983. *Nations and nationalism.* Ithaca, N.Y.: Cornell Univ. Press.

Gill, Anthony James. 1998. *Rendering unto Caesar: The Catholic Church and the state in Latin America.* Chicago: Univ. of Chicago Press.

Gleijeses, Piero. 1991. *Shattered hope: The Guatemalan revolution and the United States, 1944–1954.* Princeton, N.J.: Princeton Univ. Press.

Goldín, Liliana R. 1999. Identities in the (maquila) making: Guatemalan Maya in the world economy. In *Identities on the move: Transnational processes in North America and the Caribbean Basin,* ed. Liliana R. Goldín, 151–68. Albany, N.Y.: Institute for Mesoamerican Studies.

———. 2001. Maquila age Maya: Changing households and communities of the central highlands of Guatemala. *Journal of Latin American Anthropology* 6 (1): 30–57.

Goldín, Liliana R., and Brent Metz. 1991. An expression of cultural change: Invisible converts to Protestantism among highland Guatemala Maya. *Ethnology* 30 (4): 325–38.

Gooren, Henri. 2001. Reconsidering Protestant growth in Guatemala, 1900–1995. In *Holy saints and fiery preachers: The anthropology of Protestantism in Mexico and Central America,* ed. James W. Dow and Alan R. Sandstrom, 169–203. Westport, Conn.: Praeger.

Gossen, Gary H. 1986. Mesoamerican ideas as a foundation for regional synthesis. In *Symbol and meaning beyond the closed corporate community: Essays in Mesoamerican ideas,* ed. Gary H. Gossen, 1–8. Studies on Culture and Society, vol. 1. Albany: Institute for Mesoamerican Studies, Univ. at Albany, State Univ. of New York.

———. 1999. Life, death, and apotheosis of a Chamula Protestant leader: Biography as social history. In *Telling Maya tales: Tzotzil identities in modern Mexico,* by Gary H. Gossen, 209–24. New York: Routledge.

Gossen, Gary H., with Miguel León-Portillo, eds. 1993. *South and Meso-American native spirituality.* Vol. 4 of *World spirituality: An encyclopedic history of the religious quest.* New York: Crossroad.

Gossen, Gary H., and Richard Leventhal. 1999. The topography of ancient Maya religious pluralism: A dialogue with the present. In *Telling Maya tales: Tzotzil identities in modern Mexico,* by Gary H. Gossen, 159–87. New York: Routledge.

Greenberg, Linda Joan. 1984. Illness and curing among Mam Indians in highland Guatemala: Cosmological balance and cultural transformation. Ph.D. diss., Univ. of Chicago.

Grenfell, James. 1995. The participation of Protestants in politics in Guatemala. Master's thesis, Oxford Univ.

Gros, Christian. 1999. Evangelical Protestantism and indigenous populations. *Bulletin of Latin American Research* 18 (2): 175–97.

Gros, David. 1992. *The past in ruins: Tradition and the critique of modernity.* Amherst: Univ. of Massachusetts Press.

Gross, Toomas. 2003. Protestantism and modernity: The implications of religious change in contemporary rural Oaxaca. *Sociology of Religion* 64 (4): 479–98.

Grossman, Roger. 2002. Interpreting the development of the evangelical church in Guatemala, 2002. D.Min. diss., Southeastern Baptist Theological Seminary.

Gudmundson, Lowell, and Héctor Lindo-Fuentes. 1995. *Central America, 1821–1871: Liberalism before liberal reform.* Tuscaloosa: Univ. of Alabama Press.

Gutiérrez, Benjamín F., ed. 1995. *En la fuerza del espíritu.* Mexico City and Guatemala City: AIPRAL and CELEP (with Skipjack Press).

Gutiérrez, Edgar. 1994. Rural upheaval and the survival of the Maya. *NACLA Report on the Americas* 28 (3): 34–36.

Hale, Charles. 1994. Between Che Guevara and the Pachamama: Mestizos, Indians, and identity politics in the anti-quincentenary campaign. *Critique of Anthropology* 14 (1): 9–39.

———. 1997. Consciousness, violence, and the politics of memory in Guatemala. *Cultural Anthropology* 38 (5): 817–24.

———. 1999. Travel warning: Elite appropriations of hybridity, mestizaje, antiracism, equality, and other progressive-sounding discourses in highland Guatemala. *Journal of American Folklore* 112:297–315.

Hallum, Anne Motley. 1996. *Beyond missionaries: Toward an understanding of the Protestant movement in Central America.* Lanham, Md.: Rowan and Littlefield.

Hamilton, Sarah, and Edward F. Fischer. 2003. Non-traditional agricultural exports in highland Guatemala: Understandings of risk and perceptions of change. *Latin America Research Review* 38 (3): 82–110.

Handy, Jim. 1984. *Gift of the Devil: A history of Guatemala.* Boston: South End Press.

———. 1994. *Revolution in the countryside: Rural conflict and agrarian reform in Guatemala, 1944–1954.* Chapel Hill: Univ. of North Carolina Press.

Hanks, William F. 1996. *Language and communicative practices.* Boulder: Westview Press.

Harding, Susan. 1992. The gospel of giving: The narrative construction of a sacrificial economy. In *Vocabularies of public life,* ed. Robert Wuthnow, 39–56. London: Routledge.

———. 1994a. The born-again telescandals. In *Culture/power/history: A reader in contemporary social theory,* ed. Nicholas B. Dirks, Geoff Eley, and Sherry B. Ortner, 539–56. Princeton, N.J.: Princeton Univ. Press.

———. 1994b. Imagining the last days: The politics of apocalyptic language. In *Accounting for fundamentalisms: The dynamic character of movements,* ed. Martin E. Marty and

R. Scott Appleby, 57–78. The Fundamentalism Project, vol. 4. Chicago: Univ. of Chicago Press.

Harkin, Michael E., ed. 2004. *Reassessing revitalization movements: Perspectives from North America and the Pacific Islands.* Lincoln: Univ. of Nebraska Press.

Hartch, Todd. 2006. *Missionaries of the state: The Summer Institute of Linguistics, state formation, and indigenous Mexico, 1935–1985.* Tuscaloosa: Univ. of Alabama Press.

Hawkins, John. 1984. *Inverse images: The meaning of culture, ethnicity, and family in postcolonial Guatemala.* Albuquerque: Univ. of New Mexico Press.

Heelas, Paul, and Anna Marie Haglund-Heelas. 1988. The inadequacy of "deprivation" as a theory of conversion. In *Vernacular Christianity,* ed. Wendy James and Douglas H. Johnson, 112–19. New York: Lilian Barber Press.

Hefner, Robert W., ed. 1993. *Conversion to Christianity.* Berkeley: Univ. of California Press.

Helweg-Larsen, Simon. 2004. Ríos Montt under house arrest. *Latinamerica Press* 36 (6): 4–5.

Hendrickson, Carol. 1995. *Weaving identities: Construction of dress and self in a highland Guatemala town.* Austin: Univ. of Texas Press.

———. 1996. Women, weaving, and education in Maya revitalization. In *Maya cultural activism in Guatemala,* ed. Edward F. Fischer and R. McKenna Brown, 156–64. Austin: Univ. of Texas Press.

Hernández Castillo, R. Aída. 2001. *Histories and stories from Chiapas: Border identities in southern Mexico.* Austin: Univ. of Texas Press.

Hill, Jane H., and Kenneth C. Hill. 1986. *Speaking Mexicano: Dynamics of syncretic language in central Mexico.* Tucson: Univ. of Arizona Press.

Hill, Robert M., II. 1992. *Colonial Cakchiquels: Highland Maya adaptation to Spanish rule, 1600–1700.* Fort Worth, Tex.: Harcourt, Brace, Jovanovich.

Hill, Robert M., II, and Edward F. Fischer. 1999. States of heart: An ethnohistorical approach to Kaqchikel Maya ethnopsychology. *Ancient Mesoamerica* 10 (2): 317–32.

Hoeben, Allan, and Robert Hefner. 1991. The integrative revolution revisited. *World Development* 19 (1): 17–30.

Holland, Dorothy, and Jean Lave. 2001. History in person: An introduction. In *History in person: Enduring struggles, contentious practice, intimate identities,* ed. Dorothy Holland and Jean Lave, 3–33. Santa Fe and Oxford: School for American Research Press and James Currey Ltd.

Horst, Oscar H. 1967. The specter of death in a Guatemalan highland community. *Geographical Review* 57 (2): 151–67.

Hostnig, Rainer, with Luis Vásquez. 1991. *Monografía del municipio de Ostuncalco.* Quetzaltenango, Guatemala: Centro de Capacitación e Investigación Campesina.

IENPG [Iglesia Evangélica Nacional Presbiteriana de Guatemala]. 1982. *Apuntes para la historia.* Guatemala City.

INE [Instituto Nacional de Estadística]. 1996a. *Chimaltenango: X censo de población y V de habitación.* Guatemala City.

———. 1996b. *Quetzaltenango: X censo de población y V de habitación.* Guatemala City.

———. 2003. *Censos 2002: XI de población y VI de habitación.* Guatemala City.

Jeffrey, Paul. 1998. *Recovering memory: Guatemalan churches and the challenge of peacemaking.* Uppsala, Sweden: Life & Peace Institute.

Jenkins, Philip. 2002. *The next Christendom: The coming of global Christianity.* New York: Oxford Univ. Press.

Jonas, Susanne. 2000. *Of centaurs and doves: Guatemala's peace process.* Boulder: Westview Press.

Jones, Christopher Newell. 1996. "Constructing a future for our past": Pan-Mayanism and nation-building in contemporary Guatemala. Manuscript.

Jones, Grant D. 1989. *Maya resistance to Spanish rule: Time and history on a colonial frontier.* Albuquerque: Univ. of New Mexico Press.

Kaplan, Steven, ed. 1995. *Indigenous responses to Western Christianity.* New York: New York Univ. Press.

Kehoe, Alice Beck. 2006. *The Ghost Dance: Ethnohistory and revitalization.* 2nd ed. Long Grove, Ill.: Waveland Press.

Knauft, Bruce M. 1996. *Genealogies for the present in cultural anthropology.* New York: Routledge.

Koll, Karla Ann. 2004. Struggling for solidarity: Changing mission relations between the Presbyterian Church (USA) and Christian organizations in Central America during the 1980s. Ph.D. diss., Princeton Theological Seminary.

Kovic, Christine. 2005. *Mayan voices for human rights: Displaced Catholics in highland Chiapas.* Austin: Univ. of Texas Press.

Kray, Christine Anne. 1997. Worship in body and spirit: Practice, self, and religious sensibility in Yucatán. Ph.D. diss., Univ. of Pennsylvania.

Krech, Shepard, III. 1991. The state of ethnohistory. *Annual Review of Anthropology* 20:345–75.

La Farge, Oliver. 1994. *La costumbre en Santa Eulalia, Huehuetenango en 1932.* Trans. Fernando Peñalosa. Rancho Palos Verdes, Calif., and Guatemala City: Yax Te' Press and Editorial Cholsamaj.

LaFeber, Walter. 1993. *Inevitable revolutions.* 2nd ed. New York: Norton.

Lalive d'Epinay, Christian. 1969. *Haven of the masses: A study of the Pentecostal movement in Chile.* London: Lutterworth Press.

LeBaron, Alan. 1993. The creation of the modern Maya. In *The rising tide of cultural pluralism: The nation-state at bay?* ed. Crawford Young, 265–84. Madison: Univ. of Wisconsin Press.

Le Bot, Yvon. 1995. *La guerra en tierras Mayas.* Mexico City: Fondo de Cultura Económica.

———. 1999. Churches, sects and communities: Social cohesion recovered? *Bulletin of Latin American Research* 18 (2): 165–74.

Levine, Daniel H. 2000. The news about religion in Latin America. In *Religion on the international news agenda,* ed. Mark Silk, 120–42. Hartford, Conn.: Trinity College (The Pew Program on Religion and the News Media, The Leonard E. Greenberg Center for the Study of Religion in Public Life).

Levine, Daniel H., and Scott Mainwaring. 2001. Religion and popular protest in Latin America: Contrasting experiences. In *Power and popular protest: Latin American social movements,* ed. Susan Eckstein, 203–40. Berkeley: Univ. of California Press.

Lincoln, Bruce, ed. 1985. *Religion, rebellion, revolution.* London: MacMillan Press Limited.

———. 2003. *Holy terrors: Thinking about religion after September 11.* Chicago: Univ. of Chicago Press.

Loucky, James, and Robert Carlsen. 1991. Massacre in Santiago Atitlán: A turning point in the Maya struggle? *Cultural Survival* 15 (3): 65–70.

Lovell, George W., and Christopher H. Lutz. 1996. "A dark obverse": Maya survival in Guatemala, 1520–1994. *Geographical Review* 86 (3): 398–407.

———. 2001. Pedro de Alvarado and the conquest of Guatemala, 1522–1524. In *The past and present Maya: Essays in honor of Robert M. Carmack,* ed. John M. Week, 47–61. Lancaster, Calif.: Labrinthos.

Manly, Jim. 1997. *The wounds of Manuel Saquic: Biblical reflections from Guatemala.* Etobicoke, Ont.: United Church Publishing House.

Manz, Beatriz. 1988. *Refugees of a hidden war: The aftermath of counterinsurgency in Guatemala.* Albany: State Univ. of New York Press.

———. 2004. *Paradise in ashes: A Guatemalan journey of courage, terror, and hope.* Berkeley: Univ. of California Press.

Marroquín, Enrique. 1994. Un signo apocalíptico del milenio: Presecución a los protestantes indígenas de Oaxaca. In *Religiosidad y resistencia: Indígenas hacia el fin del milenio,* ed. Alicia Barabas, 217–35. Quito, Ecuador: Ediciones Abya-Yala.

Marsden, George. 1991. *Understanding fundamentalism and evangelicalism.* Grand Rapids, Mich.: Eerdmans.

Martin, David. 1990. *Tongues of fire: The explosion of Protestantism in Latin America.* Oxford: Basil Blackwell.

Maurer, Eugenio. 1996. Tseltal Christianity. In *The Indian face of God in Latin America,* by Manuel M. Marzal, Eugenio Maurer, Xavier Albó, and Baromeu Meliá, trans. Penelope R. Hall, 23–66. Maryknoll, N.Y.: Orbis.

Maxwell, Judith. 1996. Prescriptive grammar and Kaqchikel revitalization. In *Maya cultural activism in Guatemala,* ed. Edward F. Fischer and R. McKenna Brown, 195–207. Austin: Univ. of Texas Press.

Maybury-Lewis, David. 1997. *Indigenous peoples, ethnic groups, and the state.* Boston: Allyn and Bacon.

———, ed. 2002. *The politics of ethnicity: Indigenous peoples in Latin American states.* Cambridge: DRCLAS/Harvard Univ.

McArthur, Harry S., and Ebel, Roland H. 1969. *Cambio político en tres comunidades indígenas de Guatemala.* Seminario de Integración Social Guatemalteca, no. 21. Guatemala City: Editorial José de Pineda Ibarra, Ministerio de Educación.

McCreery, David. 1994. *Rural Guatemala, 1760–1940.* Stanford, Calif.: Stanford Univ. Press.

Menchú, Rigoberta. 1984. *I, Rigoberta Menchú: An Indian woman in Guatemala.* Ed. Elisabeth Burgos-Debray. Trans. Ann Wright. London: Verso.

Metz, Allan. 1994. Protestantism in Mexico: Contemporary contextual developments. *Journal of Church and State* 36 (1): 57–78.

Míguez Bonino, José. 1997. *Faces of Latin American Protestantism: 1993 Carnahan lectures.* Trans. Eugene L. Stockwell. Grand Rapids, Mich.: Eerdmans.

Miller, Daniel R., ed. 1994. *Coming of age: Protestantism in contemporary Latin America.* Lanham, Md.: Univ. Press of America.

MINUGUA [Misión de las Naciones Unidas de Verificación de los Derechos Humanos en Guatemala]. 1995. *Tercer informe del director de la Misión de las Naciones Unidas de Verificación de los Derechos Humanos y del Cumplimiento de los Compromisos del Acuerdo Global sobre Derechos Humanos en Guatemala.* Guatemala City.

———. 2003. Informe de MINUGUA sobre los disturbios del 24 al 25 de julio de 2003 en la Ciudad de Guatemala (Comunicado de prensa) 6 de agosto. http://www.minugua.guate.net/CENTRO%20DE%20PRENSA/PRESSCENTER.htm(accessed 18 November 2003).

Monaghan, John D. 2000. Theology and history in the study of Mesoamerican religions. In *Ethnology,* ed. John D. Monaghan (with Barbara W. Edmonson), 24–49.

Supplement to the handbook of Middle American Indians, vol. 6. Victoria Reifler Bricker, general ed. Austin: Univ. of Texas Press.

Montejo, Victor. 1987. *Testimony: Death of a Guatemalan village.* Trans. Victor Perera. Willimantic, Conn.: Curbstone Press.

———. 1993. Tying up the bundle and the *katuns* of dishonor: Maya worldview and politics. *American Indian Culture and Research Journal* 17 (1): 103–14.

———. 1999. *Voices from exile: Violence and survival in modern Maya history.* Norman: Univ. of Oklahoma Press.

———. 2002. The multiplicity of Mayan voices: Mayan leadership and the politics of self-representation. In *Indigenous movements, self-representation, and the state in Latin America,* ed. Kay B. Warren and Jean E. Jackson, 123–48. Austin: Univ. of Texas Press.

———. 2004. Angering the ancestors: Transnationalism and economic transformation of Maya communities in western Guatemala. In *Pluralizing ethnography: Comparison and representation in Maya cultures, histories, and identities,* ed. John M. Wantanabe and Edward F. Fischer, 231–55. Santa Fe: School of American Research Press.

———. 2005. *Maya intellectual renaissance: Identity, representation, and leadership.* Austin: Univ. of Texas Press.

Moran-Taylor, Michelle. 2003. International migration and culture change in Guatemala's Maya *Occidente* and Ladino *Oriente.* Ph.D. diss., Arizona State Univ.

Morkovsky, Mary Christine. 1993. Guerrilleros, political saints, and the theology of liberation. In *South and Meso-American native spirituality: From the cult of the feathered serpent to the theology of liberation,* ed. Gary H. Gossen (with Miguel León-Portilla), 526–47. New York: Crossroad.

Morris, Brian. 1987. *Anthropological studies of religion.* New York: Cambridge Univ. Press.

———. 2006. *Religion and anthropology: A critical introduction.* New York: Cambridge Univ. Press.

Mulholland, Kenneth B. 1997. Review of *Trailblazers for translators: The Chichicastenango Twelve* by Anna Marie Dahlquist. *International Bulletin of Missionary Research* 21 (1): 41–42.

Myerhoff, Barbara G. 1974. *Peyote hunt: The sacred journey of the Huichol Indians.* Ithaca, N.Y.: Cornell Univ. Press.

Nagel, Joane. 1996. *American Indian ethnic renewal: Red power and the resurgence of identity and culture.* New York: Oxford Univ. Press.

———. 1998. Constructing ethnicity: Creating and recreating ethnic identity and culture. In *New tribalisms: The resurgence of race and ethnicity,* ed. Michael W. Hughey, 237–72. Washington Square, N.Y.: New York Univ. Press.

Nash, June. 1963. Protestantism in an Indian village in the western highlands of Guatemala. *Southwestern Journal of Anthropology* 19:131–48.

———. 2001. *Mayan visions: The quest for autonomy in an age of globalization.* New York: Routledge.

———. 2004. Beyond resistance and protest: The Maya quest for autonomy. In *Pluralizing ethnography: Comparison and representation in Maya cultures, histories, and identities,* ed. John M. Wantanabe and Edward F. Fischer, 163–98. Santa Fe: School of American Research Press.

Oakes, Maude. 1951. *The two crosses of Todos Santos: Survivals of Mayan religious ritual.* Princeton, N.J.: Princeton Univ. Press.

OAS [Organization of American States, Inter-American Commission on Human Rights]. 1993. *Fourth report on the situation of human rights in Guatemala.* Washington D.C.: General Secretariat Organization of American States.

ODHAG [Human Rights Office of the Archdiocese of Guatemala]. 1999. *Guatemala: Never again!* (Recovery of Historical Memory Project of the Human Rights Office of the Archdiocese of Guatemala [REMHI]). Maryknoll, N.Y.: Orbis.

Ordóñez Cifuentes, José Emilio Rolando. 1997. *Justicia y pueblos indígenas: Crítica desde la antropología jurídica.* Colección debates, no. 2. Guatemala City: Consejo de Investigaciones para el Desarrollo de Centroamérica.

Ortner, Sherry B. 1973. On key symbols. *American Anthropologist* 75:1338–46.

———. 1989. *High religion: A cultural and political history of Sherpa Buddhism.* Princeton, N.J.: Princeton Univ. Press.

———. 1994. Theory in anthropology since the sixties. In *Culture/power/history: A reader in contemporary social theory,* ed. Nicholas B. Dirks, Geoff Eley, and Sherry B. Ortner, 372–411. Princeton, N.J.: Princeton Univ. Press.

———. 1995. Resistance and ethnographic refusal. *Comparative Studies in Society and History* 37 (1): 173–93.

Otzoy, Antonio. 1996. The struggle for Maya unity. *Report on the Americas* 29 (5): 33–35.

———. 1997. Traditional values and Christian ethics: A Maya Protestant spirituality. In *Crosscurrents in indigenous spirituality: Interface of Maya, Catholic, and Protestant worldviews,* ed. Guillermo Cook, 261–69. Studies in Christian Mission, vol. 18. Leiden: Brill.

———. n.d. La espiritualidad y la vida cotidiana: Pistas para una experiencia transformadora. Manuscript.

Palka, Joel W. 2002. Left/right symbolism and the body in ancient Maya iconography and culture. *Latin American Antiquity* 13 (4): 419–43.

Palmer, Steven Paul. 1990. A liberal discipline: Inventing nations in Guatemala and Costa Rica, 1870–1900. Ph.D. diss., Columbia Univ.

Peck, Horace Dudley. 1970. Practice and training of Guatemalan Mam shamans. Ph.D. diss., Hartford Seminary Foundation.

Perera, Victor. 1993. *Unfinished conquest: The Guatemalan tragedy.* Berkeley: Univ. of California Press.

Perez-Brignoli. 1989. *A brief history of Central America.* Trans. Ricardo B. Sawrey A. and Susana Stettri de Sawrey. Berkeley: Univ. of California Press.

Peterson, Anna L. 1997. *Martyrdom and the politics of religion: Progressive Catholicism in El Salvador's civil war.* Albany: State Univ. of New York Press.

Peterson, Anna L., Manuel Vásquez, and Philip J. Williams. 2001. The global and the local. In *Christianity, social change, and globalization,* ed. Anna Peterson, Manuel Vásquez, and Philip J. Williams, 210–28. New Brunswick, N.J.: Rutgers Univ. Press.

¿Qué es un martir? 1998. *FAMDEGUA* (Asociación Familiares de Detenidos-Desaparecidos de Guatemala) 26:5–6.

Recinos, Adrián, Delia Goetz, and Sylvanus Griswold Morley. 1950. *Popol Vuh: The sacred book of the ancient Quiché Maya.* Norman: Univ. of Oklahoma Press.

Reck, Gregory. 1983. Narrative anthropology. *Anthropology and Humanism Quarterly* 8 (1): 1–12.

———. 1986. *In the shadow of Tlaloc.* Prospect Heights, Ill.: Waveland Press.

Recopilación de los acuerdos de paz. n.d. Guatemala City.

Reep, Edwin Charles. 1997. Revolution through evolution: The dynamics of evangelical Christian belief systems in Senahu, Alta Verapaz, Guatemala. Ph.D. diss., Univ. of Georgia.

Reina, Ruben E., and Norman B. Schwartz. 1974. The structural context of religious conversion in Peten, Guatemala: Status, community, and multicommunity. *American Ethnologist* 1 (1): 157–91.

Resolution of the Inter-American Court of Human Rights Strengthens Kakchiquel Presbytery's Call for Justice. 1996 (20 May). The Center for Human Rights Legal Action. www-personal.engin.umich.edu/~pavr/harbury/archive/guatemala/052196. html (accessed 3 November 2002).

Restall, Matthew. 2004. Maya ethnogenesis, 1500–1859. *Journal of the Society for Latin American Anthropology* 9 (1): 64–89.

Richardson, Miles. 1994. Unamuno and the flesh-and-blood, celebratory critique of the postmodern play of signification. *Journal of the Steward Anthropological Society* 22 (2): 177–94.

———. 1996. Humanistic anthropology. In *Encyclopedia of cultural anthropology,* vol. 2, ed. David Levinson and Melvin Ember, 613–18. New York: Henry Holt.

Richardson, Miles, and Robert Dunton. 1989. Culture in its places: A humanistic presentation. In *The relevance of culture,* ed. Morris Freilich, 75–89. New York: Bergin and Garvey.

Roberts, Bryan. 1967. *El Protestantismo en dos barrios marginales de Guatemala.* Estudios Centroamericanos, no. 2. Guatemala City: Ministerio de Educación.

Rodríguez, Luisa. 2002. Lideres religiosos se unen por la paz. *Presa Libre-edición electrónica* (24 January 2002). http://www.prensalibre.com/pls/prensa/detnoticia.jsp?p_cnoticia=19018&p_fedicion=24-01-02 (accessed 24 March 2004).

Rolando Cabrera, Mario, and Arlena D. Cifuentes. 1997. *El proceso de negociaciones de paz en Guatemala.* Guatemala City: Ediciones Nueva Era.

Roof, Wade Clark, ed. 1991. *World order and religion.* Albany: State Univ. of New York Press.

Roosens, Eugene E. 1989. *Creating ethnicity: The process of ethnogenesis.* Frontiers of Anthropology, vol. 5. Newbury Park, Calif.: Sage.

Rudolf, Susanne Hoeber. 1997. Introduction: Religion, states, and transnational civil society. In *Transnational religion and fading states,* ed. Susanne Hoeber Rudolf and James Piscatori, 1–24. Boulder: Westview Press.

Sahlins, Marshall. 1999. Two or three things that I know about culture. *Journal of the Royal Anthropological Institute* (ns) 5:399–421.

Samson, C. Mathews. 1994. Who is my hermano? The Word of God and Protestant communal identity in the Mexican Huasteca Potosina. Master's thesis, Louisiana State Univ.

———. 1999. Interpretando la identidad religiosa: La cultura Maya y la religión evangélica bajo una perspectiva etnográfica. En *Ukab' Umolib' Chikixol Ajnao'j puwi' Pop Wuj/Memorias del segundo congreso internacional sobre el Pop Wuj.* Quetzaltenango, Guatemala: TIMACH.

———. 2003. The martyrdom of Manuel Saquic: Constructing Maya Protestantism in the face of war in contemporary Guatemala. *Le Fait Missionnaire, Social Science and Missions* 13:41–74.

———. 2007. From war to reconciliation: Guatemalan evangelicals and the transition to democracy, 1982–2001. In *Evangelicals and democracy in Latin America,* ed. Paul Freston. Oxford: Oxford Univ. Press.

Sanchíz Ochoa, Pilar. 1998. *Evangelismo y poder: Guatemala ante el nuevo milenio.* Sevilla: Universidad de Sevilla.

Sandstrom, Alan R. 1991. *Corn is our blood: Culture and ethnic identity in a contemporary Aztec Indian village.* Norman: Univ. of Oklahoma Press.

———. 1992. Ethnic identity and the persistence of traditional religion in a contemporary Nahua village. *Journal of Latin American Lore* 18:37–52.

———. 2001. Conclusion: Anthropological perspectives on Protestant conversion in Mesoamerica. In *Holy saints and fiery preachers: The anthropology of Protestantism in Mexico and Central America,* ed. James W. Dow and Alan R. Sandstrom, 263–89. Westport, Conn.: Praeger.

Sanford, Victoria. 2003. *Buried secrets: Truth and human rights in Guatemala.* New York: Pelgrave MacMillan.

Schäfer, Heinrich. 1992. *Protestantismo y crisis social en América Central.* San José, Costa Rica: Departmento Ecuménico de Investigaciones.

———. 2002. *Entre dos fuegos: Una historia socio-política de la Iglesia Presbiteriana de Guatemala.* Trans. Violaine de Santa Ana. Guatemala City: CEDEPCA y SEP.

Schwartz, Norman B. 1983. The second heritage of conquest: Some observations. In *Heritage of conquest: Thirty years later,* ed. Carl Kendall, John Hawkins, and Laurel Bossen, 339–62. Albuquerque: Univ. of New Mexico Press.

Schlesinger, Stephen, and Stephen Kinzer. 1999. *Bitter fruit: The story of the American coup in Guatemala.* Expanded edition. Cambridge: Harvard Univ. David Rockefeller Center Series on Latin American Studies.

Scotchmer, David G. 1985. Called for life: The literary contribution of Edward M. Haymaker to an ethnohistory of Protestant mission ideology, Guatemala, 1877–1947. In *Missionaries, anthropologists, and cultural change,* ed. Darrell L. Whiteman, 323–68. Studies in Third World Societies, vol. 25. Williamsburg, Va.: College of William and Mary.

———. 1986. Convergence of the gods: Comparing traditional Maya and Christian Maya cosmologies. In *Symbol and meaning beyond the closed community: Essays in Mesoamerican ideas,* ed. Gary Gossen, 197–226. Albany, N.Y.: Institute for Mesoamerican Studies.

———. 1989. Symbols of salvation: A local Mayan Protestant theology. *Missiology* 17: 293–310.

———. 1991. Symbols of salvation: Interpreting highland Maya Protestantism in context. Ph.D. diss., Univ. at Albany, State Univ. of New York.

———. 1993. Life of the heart: A Maya Protestant spirituality. In *South and Meso-American native spirituality: From the cult of the feathered serpent to the theology of liberation,* ed. Gary H. Gossen (with Miguel León-Portilla), 496–525. New York: Crossroad.

———. 1994. Blood or water? Mayan images of church and mission from the underside. Paper presented at the American Society of Missiology Meetings, Techny, Illinois, 18 June.

———. 1996. Symbols become us: Toward missional encounter with our culture through symbolic analysis. In *The church between gospel and culture: The emerging mission in North America,* ed. George R. Hunsberger and Craig Van Gelder, 158–72. Grand Rapids, Mich.: Eerdmans.

———. 2001. Pastors, preachers, or prophets? Cultural conflict and continuity in Maya Protestant leadership. In *Holy saints and fiery preachers: The anthropology of Protestantism in Mexico and Central America,* ed. James W. Dow and Alan R. Sandstrom, 235–62. Westport, Conn.: Praeger.

Sexton, James D. 1978. Protestantism and modernization in two Guatemalan towns. *American Ethnologist* 5 (2): 280–302.

Shaull, Richard. 1992. Latin America: Three responses to a new historical situation. *Interpretation: A Journal of Bible and Theology* 46 (3): 261–70.

Sieder, Rachel, ed. 1998. *Guatemala after the peace accords.* London: Institute of Latin American Studies, Univ. of London.

Similox Salazar, Vitalino. 1992. *La expresion y metodologia del pensamiento maya contemporaneo en Guatemala.* Licentiate thesis, Universidad Mariano Gálvez. Guatemala City: Editorial Cholsamaj.

———. 1997. The invasion of Christianity into the world of the Mayas. In *Crosscurrents in indigenous spirituality: Interface of Maya, Catholic, and Protestant worldviews,* ed. Guillermo Cook, 35–48. Studies in Christian Mission, vol. 18. Leiden: Brill.

Similox V., Ronaldo O. n.d. La manifestación de dios en el presbiterio Kaqchikel. Manuscript.

Sinclair, Minor. 1995. Faith, community, and resistance in the Guatemalan highlands. In *The new politics of survival: Grassroots movements in Central America,* ed. Minor Sinclair, 75–106. New York: EPICA/Monthly Review Press.

Smith, Alexa. 1999 (19 August). Guatemalan church leaders face fear, paranoia. PCUSA News. https://pcusa.org/pcnews/oldnews/1999/99268.htm (accessed 11 September 2006).

Smith, Brian H. 1998. *Religious politics in Latin America: Pentecostal vs. Catholic.* Notre Dame, Ind.: Univ. of Notre Dame Press.

Smith, Carol A. 1990. Origins of the national question in Guatemala. In *Guatemalan Indians and the state: 1540–1988,* ed. Carol A. Smith (with Marilyn M. Moors), 72–95. Austin: Univ. of Texas Press.

———. 1991. Maya nationalism. *Report on the Americas* 25 (3): 29–33.

Smith, Dennis A. 1991. Coming of age: A reflection on Pentecostals, politics, and popular religion in Guatemala. *Pneuma* 13 (2): 65–81.

Smith, Dennis A., and James Grenfell. 1999. Los evangélicos y la vida pública en Guatemala: Historia, mitos, y pautas para el futuro. *Voces del Tiempo* 31:25–34.

Smith, Waldemar. 1977. *The fiesta system and economic change.* New York: Columbia Univ. Press.

Son Turnil, José David. 1997. *Aportes a la construcción de la paz.* Guatemala City: Conferencia de Iglesias Evangélicas de Guatemala.

Sosa, John R. 1997. Maya of the Yucatán: The sacred in everyday life. In *Portraits of culture: Ethnographic originals,* vol. 2, ed. Melvin Ember, Carol R. Ember, and David Levinson, 257–82. Englewood Cliffs, N.J.: Prentice Hall.

Stavenhagen, Rodolfo. 1994. Challenging the nation-state in Latin America. In *Race and ethnicity in Latin America,* ed. Jorge I. Domínguez, 329–48. Essays on Mexico, Central and South America, vol. 7, Jorge I. Domínguez, series ed. New York: Garland.

Steigenga, Timothy J. 1999. Guatemala. In *Religious freedom and evangelization in Latin America: The challenge of religious pluralism,* ed. P. E. Sigmund, 150–74. Maryknoll, N.Y.: Orbis.

———. 2001. *The politics of the spirit: The political implications of Pentecostalized religion in Costa Rica and Guatemala.* Lanham, Md.: Lexington Books.

———. 2004. Conclusion: Listening to insurgent voices. In *Resurgent voices in Latin America: Indigenous peoples, political mobilization, and religious change,* ed. Edward L. Cleary and Timothy Steigenga, 231–53. New Brunswick, N.J.: Rutgers Univ. Press.

Steinberg, M. K., and M. J. Taylor. 2003. Public memory and political power in Guatemala's post-conflict landscape. *Geographical Review* 93 (4): 449–68.

Stephen, Lynn, and James Dow, eds. 1990. *Class, politics, and popular religion in Mexico and Central America.* Society for Latin American Anthropology Publication Series, vol. 10. Washington, D.C.: Society for Latin American Anthropology and American Anthropological Association.

Still no justice in Manuel Saquic case. 1996. *Reunion* 3 (2): 1.

Stoll, David. 1982. *Fishers of men or founders of empire? The Wycliffe Bible translators in Latin America.* London and Cambridge, Mass.: Zed Press and Cultural Survival.

———. 1990. *Is Latin America turning Protestant?* Berkeley: Univ. of California Press.

———. 1992. Evangelicals, guerrillas, and the army: The Ixil Triangle under Ríos Montt. In *Harvest of violence: The Maya Indians and the Guatemalan crisis,* ed. Robert M. Carmack, 90–116. 1988. Norman: Univ. of Oklahoma Press.

———. 1993. *Between two armies in the Ixil towns of Guatemala.* New York: Columbia Univ. Press.

Sullivan-González, Douglass. 1998. *Power, piety, and politics: Religion and nation formation in Guatemala, 1821–1871.* Pittsburgh: Univ. of Pittsburgh Press.

Swatos, William H., Jr., and Kevin J. Christiano. 1999. Secularization theory: The course of a concept. *Sociology of Religion* 60 (3): 209–28.

Tambiah, S. J. 1990. *Magic, science, religion, and the scope of rationality.* The Henry Lewis Morgan Lectures, 1981. Cambridge: Cambridge Univ. Press.

Tarn, Nathaniel (with Martin Prechtel). 1997. *Scandals in the house of birds: Shamans and priests on Lake Atitlán.* New York: Marsilio Publishers.

Taylor, Lawrence J. 1995. *Occasions of faith: An anthropology of Irish Catholics.* Philadelphia: Univ. of Pennsylvania Press.

Taylor, Mark Kline. 1990. *Remembering Esperanza: A cultural-political theology for North American praxis.* Maryknoll, N.Y.: Orbis.

———. 1998. Toward a revolution of the sun: Protestant Mayan resistance in Guatemala. In *Revolution of spirit: Ecumenical theology in global context,* ed. Nantawan Boon Prasat, 246–69. Grand Rapids, Mich.: Eerdmans.

Tedlock, Barbara. 1983. A phenomenological approach to religious change in highland Guatemala. In *Heritage of conquest thirty years later,* ed. Carl Kendall, John Hawkins, and Laurel Bossen, 235–46. Albuquerque: Univ. of New Mexico Press.

———. 1991. From participant observation to the observation of participation: The emergence of narrative ethnology. *Journal of Anthropological Research* 47 (1): 69–94.

———. 1992. *Time and the highland Maya.* Rev. ed. Albuquerque: Univ. of New Mexico Press.

Tedlock, Dennis. 1983. *The spoken word and the work of interpretation.* Philadelphia: Univ. of Pennsylvania Press.

———, trans. 1996. *Popol Vuh: The definitive edition of the Mayan book of the dawn of life and the glories of gods and kings.* Rev. ed. New York: Touchstone.

Teski, C. Marea, and Jacob J. Climo. 1995. Introduction. In *The labyrinth of memory:*

Ethnographic journeys, ed. Marea C. Teski and Jacob J. Climo, 1–10. Westport, Conn.: Bergin and Garvey.

Thompson, Charles D., Jr. 2001. *Maya identities and the violence of place: Borders bleed.* Aldershot, U.K.: Ashgate.

Tillich, Paul. 1957. *The Protestant era.* Trans. James Luther Adams. Abridged ed. Chicago: Univ. of Chicago Press.

Tinker, George E. 1993. *Missionary conquest: The gospel and Native American cultural genocide.* Minneapolis: Fortress Press.

Turner, Bryan S. 1996. *For Weber: Essays on the sociology of fate.* 2nd ed. Thousand Oaks, Calif.: Sage.

Twicken, Lawrence. 1994. Protestants and democracy in the United States, Mexico, and Guatemala. Ph.D. diss., Claremont Univ. Center.

Tzian, Leopoldo. 1994. *Mayas y Ladinos en cifras: El caso de Guatemala.* Guatemala City: Cholsamaj.

UN Economic and Social Council. 2003. Fifty-ninth Session. *Report of the special rapporteur on the situation of human rights and fundamental freedoms of indigenous people, Rodolfo Stavenhagen (Addendum: Mission to Guatemala).* E/CN.4/2003/90/Add.2, 24 February.

UN General Assembly. 1995. Forty-ninth Session. *Report of the director of the United Nations mission for the verification of human rights and of compliance with the commitments of the comprehensive agreement on human rights in Guatemala.* A/49/856, 1 March.

Urban, Greg, and Joel Sherzer, eds. 1991. *Nation-states and Indians in Latin America.* Austin: Univ. of Texas Press.

URNG-Government dialogue: Indians excluded once again. 1995. *Abya Yala News* 9 (1): 33.

Vásquez, Manuel A. 1999. Toward a new agenda for the study of religion in the Americas. *Journal of Interamerican Studies and World Affairs* 41 (4): 1–20.

Vásquez, Manuel A., and Marie Friedmann Marquardt. 2003. *Globalizing the sacred: Religion across the Americas.* New Brunswick, N.J.: Rutgers Univ. Press.

Vásquez, Manuel A., and Philip J. Williams. 2005. Introduction: The power of religious identities in the Americas. *Latin American Perspectives* 32 (1): 5–26.

Wallace, Anthony F. C. 1956. Revitalization movements. *American Anthropologist* 58: 264–81.

———. 1966. *Religion: An anthropological view.* New York: Random House.

Warren, Kay B. 1989. *Symbols of subordination: Indian identity in a Guatemalan town.* Austin: Univ. of Texas Press.

———. 1993. Interpreting la violencia in Guatemala: Shapes of Kaqchikel resistance in the 1970s and 1980s. In *The violence within: Cultural and political opposition in divided nations,* ed. Kay B. Warren, 25–56. Boulder: Westview Press.

———. 1998. *Indigenous movements and their critics: Pan-Maya activism in Guatemala.* Princeton, N.J.: Princeton Univ. Press.

———. 2001. Indigenous activism across generations: An intimate social history of antiracism organizing in Guatemala. In *History in person: Enduring struggles, contentious practice, intimate identities,* ed. Dorothy Holland and Jean Lave, 63–91. Santa Fe and Oxford: School for American Research Press and James Currey Ltd.

———. 2002. Voting against indigenous rights in Guatemala: Lessons from the 1999 referendum. In *Indigenous movements, self-representation, and the state in Latin America.* ed. Kay B. Warren and Jean E. Jackson, 149–80. Austin: Univ. of Texas Press.

Warren, Kay B., and Jean E Jackson. 2002. Introduction: Studying indigenous activism in Latin America. In *Indigenous movements, self-representation, and the state in Latin America,* ed. Kay B. Warren and Jean E. Jackson, 1–46. Austin: Univ. of Texas Press.

Watanabe, John. 1990. From saints to shibboleths: Image, structure, and identity in Maya religious syncretism. *American Ethnologist* 17 (1): 129–48.

———. 1992. *Maya saints and souls in a changing world.* Austin: Univ. of Texas Press.

———. 1995. Mam. In *Middle America and the Caribbean: Encyclopedia of world cultures,* vol. 8, ed. James W. Dow and Robert Van Kemper, 157–60. Boston: G. K. Hall.

———. 1996. Conversion, commitment, and identity: Religious change in twentieth-century Mesoamerica. Paper presented at the 14th Northeast Mesoamerican Conference. Univ. at Albany, New York, 2–3 November.

———. 1999. Getting over hegemony and resistance: reinstating culture in the study of power relations across difference. *European Review of Latin American and Caribbean Studies* 66 (June): 117–26.

———. 2000. Maya and anthropologists in the highlands of Guatemala since the 1960's. In *Ethnology,* ed. John D. Monaghan with Barbara W. Edmonson, 224–46. *Supplement to the handbook of Middle American Indians,* vol. 6. Victoria Reifler Bricker, general ed. Austin: Univ. of Texas Press.

Watanabe, John M., and Edward F. Fischer. 2004. Introduction: Emergent anthropologies and pluricultural Ethnography in two postcolonial Nations. In *Pluralizing ethnography: Comparison and representation in Maya cultures, histories and identities,* ed. John M. Wantanabe and Edward F. Fischer, 3–33. Santa Fe: School of American Research Press.

Weber, Max. 1964. *The sociology of religion.* Trans. Epraim Fischoff. Boston: Beacon Press.

Wellmeier, Nancy J. 1998. *Ritual, identity, and the Mayan diaspora.* New York: Garland.

Willems, Emilio. 1967. *Followers of the new faith: Culture change and the rise of Protestantism in Brazil and Chile.* Nashville: Vanderbilt Univ. Press.

Williams, Philip J., and Timothy J. Steigenga. 2005. Religion, transnationalism, and collective action among Guatemalan and Mexican immigrants in two Florida communities. Paper presented at the annual meeting of the American Political Science Association, September 1–4. Washington, D.C.

Wilmsen, Edwin N., and Patrick McAllister, eds. 1996. *The politics of difference: Ethnic premises in a world of power.* Chicago: University of Chicago Press.

Wilson, Everett. 1997. Guatemalan Pentecostals: Something of their own. In *Power, politics, and Pentecostals in Latin America,* ed. E. L. Cleary and H. W. Stewart-Gambino, 139–62. Boulder: Westview Press.

Wilson, Richard. 1991. Machine guns and mountain spirits: The cultural effects of state repression among the Q'eqchi' of Guatemala. *Critique of Anthropology* 11 (1): 33–61.

———. 1995. *Maya resurgence in Guatemala: Q'eqchi' experiences.* Norman: Univ. of Oklahoma Press.

———. 1998. The politics of remembering and forgetting in Guatemala. In *Guatemala after the peace accords,* ed. Rachel Sieder, 181–95. London: Institute of Latin American Studies, Univ. of London.

Woodward, Ralph Lee, Jr. 1999. *Central America: A nation divided.* 3rd ed. New York: Oxford Univ. Press.

Worsely, Peter. 1968. *The trumpet shall sound: A study of "cargo" cults in Melanesia.* 2nd ed. New York: Schocken Books.

Wuqub' Iq'. 1997. Understanding Mayan spirituality: A proposed methodology for dialogue with Christians. In *Crosscurrents in indigenous spirituality: Interface of Maya, Catholic, and Protestant worldviews,* ed. Guillermo Cook, 241–60. Studies in Christian Mission, vol. 18. Leiden: Brill.

Wuthnow, Robert. 1992a. Introduction: New directions in the empirical study of cultural codes. In *Vocabularies of public life,* ed. Robert Wuthnow, 1–16. London: Routledge.

———. 1992b. *Rediscovering the sacred: Perspectives on religion in contemporary society.* Grand Rapids, Mich.: Eerdmans.

———. 1994. *Public expression of religion in America.* Grand Rapids, Mich.: Eerdmans.

Yashar, Deborah J. 1997. The quetzal is red: Military states, popular movements, and political violence in Guatemala. In *The new politics of inequality in Latin America: Rethinking participation and representation,* ed. Douglas A. Chalmers, Carlos M. Vilas, Katherine Hite, Scott B. Martin, Kerianne Piester, and Monique Segarra, 239–60. New York: Oxford Univ. Press.

Young, Crawford, ed. 1993. *The rising tide of cultural pluralism: The nation-state at bay?* Madison: Univ. of Wisconsin Press.

Zapata Arceyuz, Virgilio. 1982. *Historia de la iglesia evangélica en Guatemala.* Guatemala City: Génesis Publicidad.

Zapeta, Estuardo. 1994. Guatemala peace talks: Are Maya rights negotiable? *Abya Yala News* 8 (4): 26.

Index